POPULATION, POVERTY AND ENVIRONMENT IN NORTH-EAST INDIA

About the Editors

Dr. B. Datta Ray is a veteran freedom fighter, a *tamrapatra* holder and a social scientist. He is the founder Secretary of North East India Council for Social Science Research since 1974.

Mr. H.K. Mazhari belongs to Indian Administrative Service and a specialist in urban and town planning studies. He is Commissioner and Secretary, Urban Affairs, Government of Meghalaya.

Dr. P.M. Passah is a Professor of Economics, North Eastern Hill University, Shillong and an eminent tribal scholar of North East India.

Dr. M.C. Pandey is a Professor of North Eastern Hill University. He is a serious scholar in Population Studies and Continuing and Adult Education in North East India.

POPULATION, POVERTY AND ENVIRONMENT IN NORTH-EAST INDIA

Edited by

B. DATTA RAY
H.K. MAZHARI
P.M. PASSAH
M.C. PANDEY

CONCEPT PUBLISHING COMPANY, NEW DELHI-110059

ISBN 81-7022-770-4

First Published 2000

Published and Printed by

Ashok Kumar Mittal
Concept Publishing Company
A/15-16, Commercial Block, Mohan Garden,
New Delhi-110059 (India)
Phones : 5648039, 5649024
Fax : 091-11-5648053

INTRODUCTION

The papers included in this volume were presented in the seminar held in 1996 organised by North East India Council for Social Science Research, Shillong, the premier Social Science Research institution in North East India since 1974. The papers in the volume deal with the population dynamics, poverty and environment of the region, which are very much interlinked. All processes of Social and Economical Development Planning must take into account, the demographic dimension, levels of poverty and the physical and social environment in which the people live. The right size of population and its quality are important factors for Social and Economic development. But the population growth in a stagnant economy leads to the decline of capital formation and increase the unemployment and poverty. In such a situation as in North East India, it has led to an adverse situation on land-man ratio. As a result of immobility of the people of North East India, both in respect of space and occupation, the economy is over burdened, particularly agriculture is over crowded. As a result, poverty is wide spread and nutritional level is low. Though the growth of urbanization between 1981-91 has not been spectacular compared to 1971-81 decade, when the rate of growth was 46 per cent for the decade, during 1981-91, the growth has been only 36 per cent, the poor infrastructure, growing population and the housing shortage have been making the living condition in the urban areas of the country pitiable. The major investment in urban infrastructure have gone, by and large, to the major metros. Though the overall level of urbanization in North East India has been low, hardly 18 per cent, as compared 27 per cent for all India average, the pace of urbanization has been rapid at least in Mizoram, currently 46 per cent, and Manipur, 28 per cent. But the civic infrastructure, like roads, sewage, water supply and municipal services are deplorable. The rural scenario is no better. The environmental hygiene is appalling both in rural and urban areas in North East India. The quality of life in terms of infrastructure like sewages, roads, potable water supply, primary education and health services is determined by the assured and required income level. The degrading urban-rural scape in the region needs immediate attention of the leadership. Even in the North East Tribal areas, the inbuilt environmental defence mechanism is fast breaking down due to wide spread poverty in North East India. It is important to analyse and suggest counter remedies for the degrading social situation. The papers included in the volume is an attempt to study the issues.

The minimum needs of the people are, primary health services, primary education, supply of potable water, basic sanitation and shelter. In North East India, of the total 31,547,314 people at least 52 to 63 per cent of the population in the rural areas and 33 to 37 per cent in urban areas live below the poverty line as determined by nutritional level. The consumption needs like minimum clothing should also be considered in estimating poverty line. At least 40 per cent of the people, particularly women of the region are illiterate. In urban areas, potable water supply is most inadequate of the total population of 31,547,314 (1991) the Scheduled Castes and Scheduled Tribes forming 6.85 per cent and 25.81 per cent of the total population are mostly victims of poverty. The rapid growth of population and environmental degradation are ultimately traceable to the appalling poverty of the people of the region which is one of the poorest areas of the country.

This grim situation is the result of rising poverty level created by an unequal socio-economic and political forces. The land relations in North East India is chaotic. Except in Assam, land reform legal measures are non-existant, particularly in the tribal areas. In Assam, land reform measures remain hidden in papers. In the tribal areas, the community ownership of land is, by and large fictional. The 'Benami' transfers, in favour of rich owners are rampant. In Manipur and elsewhere tribal chief own major tracts of land and forests. There is growing army of landless agricultural workers even in a tiny state of Meghalaya. The urban areas in tribal states offer a misleading picture. The towns are fortresses of wealth surrounded by hungry people, the victims of poverty due to unequal production relations. The poverty is due to low land-man ratio, dependence of the poor on wage income and their inability to find wage employment throughout the year in the villages. They migrate to the towns in search of employment. The towns are unable to offer them, gainful employment, most of them being illiterate and unskilled labour, there is no worthwhile employment to sustain urban growth in a stagnant economy.

B. DATTA RAY

ACKNOWLEDGEMENTS

In the preparation of this volume we have incurred obligation to a number of organisations and scholars. The Department of Urban Affairs, particularly Meghalaya Pollution Control Board, Meghalaya Urban Development Agency, Centre of Eco Development and Centre of Population Education, North Eastern Hill University have most generously helped us. The list of scholars helping us is too long to be mentioned. We thank them all.

We record our gratitude for the help and advice received from Mr. Ashok Kumar Mittal of Concept Publishing Company of New Delhi. We deeply acknowledge the kind technical help rendered by Mr. Mittal in publishing the volume expeditiously.

NEICSSR
Shillong

B. Datta Ray
H.K. Mazhari
P.M. Passah
M.C. Pandey

CONTENTS

LIST OF CONTRIBUTORS

Adak, Dipak Kumar

Anthropological Survey of India, Shillong.

Agnihotri, S.K.

Indian Administrative Service, Shillong.

Athparia, R.P.

Anthropological Survey of India, Shillong.

Banerjee, M.

Anthropological Survey of India, Shillong.

Barman, Tapash Kumar

Department of Chemistry, Cotton College, Guwahati.

Bhattacharyya, N.N.

Department of Geography, Gauhati University, Guwahati.

Bhattacharyya, S.P.

Former Director, Department of Health, Government of Meghalaya, Shillong.

Borah, A.K.

Department of Sociology, Dibrugarh University, Dibrugarh.

Butola, B.S.

Department of Geography, North Eastern Hill University, Shillong.

Choudhury, Rabindra Kumar

Department of Economics, Gauhati University, Guwahati.

Das, Susmita

Research Scholar, Department of Geography, North Eastern Hill

University, Shillong.

Datta, Sutapa

Department of Geography, St. Mary's College, Shillong.

Devi, Premalata

State Resource Centre, North Eastern Hill University, Shillong.

Dey, B.P.

Department of Botany, St. Anthony's College, Shillong.

Dutta, Rangan

Indian Administrative Service, Shillong.

Dwivedi, K.K.

Department of Chemistry, North Eastern Hill University, Shillong.

Goswami, H.

Department of Economics, Dibrugarh University, Dibrugarh.

Goswami, Pranay Jyoti

Department of Economics, Guru Charan College, Silchar, Assam.

Katiyar, S.C.

Meghalaya Pollution Control Board, Shillong.

Lahiri, Benay

Scholar, Shillong.

Mahapatra, A.C.

Department of Geography, North Eastern Hill University, Shillong.

Marbaniang, Nazarene V.

Research Scholar, NEHU, Shillong.

Mazhari, H.K.

Indian Administrative Service, Shillong.

Misra, P.K.

Department of Anthropology, North Eastern Hill University, Shillong.

Mitra, A.

Department of Economics, Arunachal University, Itanagar.

Mohapatra, A.C.

Department of Geography, NEHU, Shillong.

Mukherjee, S.

Anthropological Survey of India, Shillong.

Nandi, S.D.

Formerly of Lady Keane Girls College, Shillong.

Nayak, Debendra Kumar

Department of Geography, NEHU, Shillong.

Neog, A.K.

Indian Economic Service, New Delhi.

Panda, B.K.

Department of Economics, Govt. College, TEZU, Arunachal Pradesh.

Pandey, D.N.

Anthropological Survey of India, Shillong.

Pandey, M.C.

Department of Adult and Continuing Education, North Eastern Hill University, Shillong.

Passah, Philomath

Department of Economics, North Eastern Hill University, Shillong.

Pulloppillil, Thomas

Orient Theological College, Shillong.

Purkayastha, Subrata

Department of Geography, St. Mary's College, Shillong.

Ray, B. Datta

North East India Council for Social Science Research, Shillong.

Sachan, A.K.

Indian Administrative Service, Guwahati.

Sarin, Geeta

Research Scholar, Department of Geography, North Eastern Hill University, Shillong.

Sengupta, Keya

Department of Economics, Assam University, Silchar, Assam.

Sinha, Neelam

National Open School, New Delhi.

Thakurta, S.N. Guha

Formerly Department of Economics, North Eastern Hill University, Shillong.

Tyagi, D.

Anthropological Survey of India, Calcutta.

Varte, R.Th.

Anthropological Survey of India, Shillong.

LIST OF FIGURES

LIST OF TABLES

1

GROWTH TREND OF POPULATION AND ITS CHARACTERISTIC FEATURES IN NORTH EASTERN REGION

RABINDRA KUMAR CHOUDHURY

The economy of north-eastern region exhibits many characteristics of backwardness, the most important of which are large scale disguised unemployment in farm sector, poor capacity of non-farm sector to absorb surplus labour and less than subsistence level of food grains production. The region shelters 3.7 per cent of India's population, but can hardly produce 2.8 per cent of the country's total food grains. The extent of backwardness in a predominantly agricultural society of the kind of north-eastern region can be easily understood from this deficiency character vis-a-vis its demographic pressure.

Growth Trend of Population

There has been a tremendous rise in population of the North-Eastern Region in the second half of twentieth century. From 102.6 lakh in the year 1951, the population of the region has registered an increase of more than three times by 1991 as against 2.3 times in the country as a whole.

During these four decades, the highest rise in population among north-eastern states is recorded by Nagaland at 471 per cent, followed by Tripura with 330 per cent, Mizoram with 250 per cent and Manipur with 216 per cent. Those states with less than three times of population growth during the period, 1951-91 are Meghalaya and Assam which accounted for an increase by 191 per cent and 178 per cent respectively as against 134 per cent in the country as a whole (Table 1.1). Leaving aside the inter-state growth differentials in population all the north-eastern states grew at a faster rate than the all states average rate in the country.

TABLE 1.1: **Growth Trend of Population (1951-91) in NE Region**

(in lakhs)

States	1951	1961	1971	1981	1991	Growth times over 1951-91
1	2	3	4	5	6	7
Arunachal Pradesh	—	3.37	4.68	6.32	8.58	NA
Assam	80.29	108.37	146.25	198.97	222.95	2.78
Manipur	5.78	7.80	10.73	14.21	18.27	3.16
Meghalaya	6.06	7.69	10.12	13.36	17.61	2.91
Mizoram	1.96	2.66	3.32	4.94	6.86	3.50
Nagaland	2.13	3.69	5.16	7.75	12.16	5.71
Tripura	6.39	11.42	15.56	20.53	27.45	4.30
N.E. India	102.61	145.00	195.82	266.08	314.12	3.06
All India	3611.00	4392.00	4582.00	6852.00	8443.00	2.34

Source: Basic Statistics of North Eastern Region, 1992, Page 1.

Characteristics of Growth Trend

Decadal Variation

In so far as decadal growth variation in population of the north-eastern region is concerned, the states do not exhibit any uniform pattern. Different decades appear to characterise largest growth variation for different states. Thus, Tripura records the highest growth of population in 1951-61 decade at 78.7 per cent. Whereas the highest growth period in Nagaland occurs in

1981-91 decade at 56.8 per cent, it is the period of 1971-81 decade for Mizoram at 48.5 per cent, 1961-71 decade for Manipur at 37.5 per cent and both the two decades between 1951 and 1971 for Assam at 34.9 per cent as against the all India decadal growth rate varying between 21 per cent and 25 per cent. Arunachal Pradesh recorded its highest growth in the decade 1961-71 at 38.9 per cent whereas Meghalaya did it during 1971 and 1981 at 32 per cent.

An important point to note here is that the recorded figures for growth variation in the decades of Assam are a bit confusing. The 1961 and 1971 census figures show that the decadal growth of population of Assam works out to 34.9 per cent in each of the two periods of 1951-61 and 1961-71. In the absence of 1981 census, the projected population put the decadal growth at 36 per cent for 1971-81. However, the census figures for 1991 shows the 10 year growth rate of population in Assam at 23.4 per cent for 1971-81 and at 23.6 per cent for 1981-91 period. What could be observed shortly from in-migration figures and net reproduction rate would be unable to explain the phenomenon of how decadal growth variation in population of Assam could so abruptly come down from 35 per cent in the decades ending in 1961 and in 1971 to as low a level as 23.4 per cent and then 23.6 per cent respectively in the decades, 1971-81 and 1981-91.

The decadal growth of rural population during the past four decades of the second half of present century has always been at higher than all India rate, except for Nagaland and Meghalaya in the decades 1951-61 at 6.9 per cent and 19.1 per cent respectively. Mizoram during 1961-71 at 17 per cent, Manipur during 1971-81 at 12.3 per cent and Assam as well as Mizoram in the decade, 1981-91 at 11.1 per cent and (–) 0.7 per cent respectively. The highest rate of growth in rural population was recorded by Tripura in both the decades, 1951-61 and 1961-71 at 74.2 per cent and 34.2 per cent respectively as against 20.5 per cent and 21.9 per cent in the country as a whole, while Nagaland claimed the highest growth in the other two decades at 40.8 per cent and 53.6 per cent respectively as against the corresponding all states of Indian average of 19.7 per cent and 19.3 per cent respectively. Here also one fails to understand how the decadal growth rate of rural population in Assam could come down to so low a level as 11 per cent in 1980's from the rate ranging between 31 per cent and 34 per cent in the earlier three decades between 1951-61 and 1971-81. Another peculiarity of the kind could be noticed in case of Nagaland and Mizoram. In Nagaland, rural population is recorded to have registered a growth of less than 7 per cent in the decade 1951-61, though the rate ranges between 33 per cent and 53.6 per cent in the subsequent decades. One explanation that may be given for the reason is that the urban growth of population was highest at 364.4 per cent in the period 1951-61 in the state and it is possible that there was large-scale in-migration from rural to urban areas in this decade. However, this is still a bit unusual. In the case of Mizoram, again, the decade 1981-91 shows a large scale reduction in the rural population registering a negative growth of around one per cent though the decadal growth rate varied between 17 per cent and 33 per cent in the previous three decades (Table 1.2). The migration of people from rural to urban areas is also not that spectacular as compared to earlier decadal trend.

Density and Sex Ratio

The population of North-Eastern Region forms 3.7 per cent of the country's total population. More than 71 per cent of the region's population lives in Assam which accounts for 2.64 per cent of the country's total and the all India proportion of population in all the other states of north-east is negligible. The density of population per sq. km. in Assam was 102 in 1951 as against 177 in the country as a whole. However, in the period of forty years that followed, its density increased by almost 180 per cent at 284 in 1991 and surpassed the all India figure of 267. The next important densely populated state of the region is Tripura where the density during four decades has increased by more than four times from just 61 per sq. km. in 1951 to 262 in 1991 as against the all India density rising from 117 to 267 in the same period. However, from the growth rate point of view, the increase is highest in Nagaland which accounts for a rise of more than 5.5 times in density of population per sq. km. in the period between 1951 and 1991 (Table 1.3).

In regard to sex ratio in the region during these four

TABLE 1.2: **Decadal Variation of Population Growth in NE Region**

(Percentage)

Year	Assam	Manipur	Meghalaya	Mizoram	Nagaland	Tripura	Arunachal Pradesh	All India
1	2	3	4	5	6	7	8	9
1951-61								
Total	34.9	35.0	27.0	35.6	14.1	78.7	—	21.5
Rural	30.8	23.9	19.1	33.0	6.9	74.2	—	20.5
Urban	127.6	2226.0	100.8	105.1	364.4	141.8	—	26.4
1961-71								
Total	34.9	37.5	31.5	24.9	39.9	36.3	38.9	24.8
Rural	32.6	30.7	32.6	17.0	32.9	34.2	33.7	21.9
Urban	65.0	108.9	25.3	164.8	168.3	57.6	—	38.2
1971-81								
Total	23.4	32.5	32.0	48.5	50.0	31.9	35.1	25.0
Rural	33.8	12.3	26.6	26.2	40.8	31.1	31.1	19.7
Urban	58.8	165.4	64.0	222.6	133.9	38.9	139.7	46.4

(Contd.)

TABLE 1.2 (*Contd.*)

1	2	3	4	5	6	7	8	9
1981-91								
Total	23.6	28.6	31.8	39.0	56.8	33.7	35.8	23.2
Rural	11.1	26.3	30.8	(–) 0.7	53.6	27.6	27.6	19.3
Urban	20.7	34.7	170.0	160.4	74.7	85.8	153.0	36.0

Source: *Basic Statistics of NE Region*, 1992, p. 4.

TABLE 1.3: **Distribution of Population, Density and Sex Ratio**

States	Proportion to India's population (per cent) (1991)	Density per square km.			Sex ratio: No. of females per 1000 males		
		1951	1981	1991	1951	1981	1991
1	2	3	4	5	6	7	8
Arunachal Pradesh	0.10	4	8	10	—	862	861
Assam	2.64	102	230	284	908	910	925
Manipur	0.22	26	64	82	1036	971	961
Meghalaya	0.08	9	23	33	1041	919	924
Nagaland	0.14	13	47	73	999	863	890
Tripura	0.32	61	196	262	904	940	946
Total N.E.	3.72	NA	104	123	NA	900	927
All India	100.00	171	216	267	946	934	939

Source: 1. *Basic Statistics of North-Eastern Region,* 1992.
2. Census of India, 191-Series 4.

Note: In 1981, NE population was 3/9 per cent of all India total.

decades, four distinct trends may be noticed, viz.

(i) a continuous increase throughout the period in Assam and Tripura,

(ii) a continuous decline throughout the period in Manipur as in the case of all India average picture,

(iii) fall in the Sex ratio during the period from 1951 to 1981 and then rise in it in Mizoram and Nagaland, and

(iv) rise in the Sex ratio during the period from 1951 to 1981 and then fall in it in case of Meghalaya.

The fall in Sex ratio may be caused by the following factors:

(a) High rate of infant mortality, the ratio being higher for female babies than male babies.

(b) High death rate of women in to the pre-pregnancy and

post-pregnancy periods.

(c) The illegal practice of female infanticide.

(d) Illegal pre-pregnancy test and abortion of female foetus.

(e) Immigration of male workers.

(f) High death rate of female children due to less care for them in food, hygiene and health

On the other hand, the rise in Sex ratio may be caused chiefly by the following factors:

(1) Due to improved health measures and medical facilities, infant mortality rate has fallen and since female infant mortality ratio should have been reversed after improved health measures in favour of rise in the Sex ratio.

(2) Due to the same above reason, death rate of women in both pre-pregnancy and post-pregnancy periods has fallen.

(3) Because of strong legal measures and spread of education, the practice of female infanticide has been reduced.

(4) In some north-eastern states, there has been a large flow of immigrant labour having higher Sex ratio.

(5) The incidence of high death rate of female children due to comparatively less care for them in regard to food, hygiene and health has always been less in the north-eastern states, particularly the hill states where women have a better social status.

From the above-noted relationship between causes and effects, while increase in the growth rate of Sex ratio in case of Assam and Tripura for the whole period and in Nagaland and Mizoram for the decade, 1981-91 is accounted for, the fall in the Sex ratio in case of Manipur throughout the whole period, in Meghalaya for the period, 1981-91 and also in Nagaland and Mizoram during the period from 1951 to 1981 can not be properly explained by this general cause-effect relationship. Further research is necessary to reveal the actual circumstances which have led to such a peculiar situation in the trend of sex ratio in tribal states.

Urbanisation

According to 1991 census, the urban population of Assam accounts for 24.7 lakhs which constitutes only 11.8 per cent of the State's total population. The percentage of urban population in Assam was 10 per cent in 1981. In the forty-year period from 1951 to 1991, the urban population of Assam increased by 567 per cent. This high growth rate in the backdrop of poor percentage of urban population is due to a very low base figure of only 3.7 lakhs people living in urban areas of the State in 1951.

TABLE 1.4: **Urbanisation in N.E. Region**

State	Percentage of urban population to total 1991		Annual average growth rate			
			1961-71 (%)		1981-91 (%)	
	Urban (%)	Rural (%)	Urban	Rural	Urban	Rural
Arunachal Pradesh	12.21	87.79	—	3.3	9.3	2.4
Assam	11.00	88.92	5.0	2.8	3.3	2.0
Manipur	27.69	72.31	7.4	2.7	3.0	2.3
Meghalaya	18.69	81.31	2.2	2.8	2.7	2.8
Mizoram	46.20	53.80	9.7	1.5	9.6	(-) 0.1
Nagaland	17.28	82.72	9.9	2.8	5.6	4.3
Tripura	15.26	84.74	4.5	2.9	6.2	2.4
All India	25.72	74.28	3.2	2.0	3.1	1.8

Source: Basic Statistics of NE Region, 1992, pp. 6 and 21.

The growth rate of urban population, among other states of the north-eastern region, is much higher than that of Assam. The highest growth during the decade 1981-91 is registered by Mizoram at 46.2 per cent, followed by Manipur at 27.7 per cent and the rates are larger that all India average of 25.7 per cent. Urban population in Arunachal Pradesh is also very low at 12.2 per cent only. In other states of the region also, the growth of urban population is found to be at lower levels than the all India rate, viz., 18.7 per cent in Meghalaya, 17.3 per cent in

Nagaland and 15.3 per cent in Tripura (Table 1.4).

If we take into account the growth rate of urbanisation for the 30 year period between 1961 and 1991, we find that except for Meghalaya and Tripura, the growth trend is declining. The largest fall is accounted for in Nagaland where the annual average growth rate of urban population has declined from 9.9 per cent in the decade 1961-71 to 5.6 per cent during 1981-91 period. In case of Manipur, the corresponding fall in the rate is from 7.4 per cent to 3.0 per cent. The figures for reduction in annual average growth rate of urban population during this 30 year period in case of other states are from 5 per cent to 3.3 per cent in Assam and from 9.7 per cent to 9.6 per cent in Mizoram. The States registering increase in the annual average growth rate of urban population during the period from 1961-71 to 1981-91 are Meghalaya from 2.2 per cent to 2.7 per cent and Tripura from 4.5 per cent to 6.2 per cent. It may be noted here that the all India annual average growth rate of urban population has also shown a slightly declining trend from 3.2 per cent in the decade 1961-71 to 3.1 per cent in the decade 1981-91. Whereas in 1961-71 period, only one state, viz., Meghalaya had its urban growth rate below all India level, now two states, viz., Meghalaya and Manipur appear to have registered their annual average growth rate below the corresponding all India figure.

Migration Quantum

The data for migrant population is available in 1971 census after which whatever figures can be had are not reliable. In 1971-72, the total number of migrant population in the north-eastern region was 64.60 lakhs which forms 33.56 per cent of the total population of the region or 1.2 per cent of the country's population. The following figures will give us different type of migration in the north-eastern states (Table 1.5).

There are two principal types of migrants, viz., migrants from other states and migrants from outside India. The proportion of migrants from other states to total population is the highest in Arunachal Pradesh at 8.5 per cent, followed by Nagaland at 6.9 per cent and Meghalaya at 6.1 per cent as against 3.4 per cent in each of the cases of total North

TABLE 1.5: **Types of Migration in North Eastern Region (1971 census)**

States	Migrants from other States		Migrants from outside India		No. of migrants from outside India in 1991 (lakhs)
	Absolute No. (lakhs)	% to total population	Absolute No. (lakhs)	% to total population	
1	2	3	4	5	6
Assam	4.72	3.23	8.19	5.60	12.49
Manipur	0.20	1.82	0.12	1.08	0.20
Meghalaya	0.62	6.09	0.41	4.09	0.72
Nagaland	0.36	6.90	0.10	1.85	0.22
Tripura	0.29	1.84	4.22	27.09	7.44
Arunachal Pradesh	0.40	8.54	0.17	3.66	0.31
Total N.E.	6.59	3.42	13.21	6.86	21.55
All India	188.57	3.44	75.10	1.37	115.67

Sources: (1) 1971 Census and 1991 Census (for population only)

(2) S.C. Srivastava, *Demographic Profile of North-East India,* 1986 (for migration figures of 1971 census).

Note: Column (6) is calculated on the basis of same percentage figures of column (5).

Eastern Region and India as a whole. Such proportions are 3.2 per cent in Assam and 1.8 per cent in each of Manipur and Tripura. In so far as migration from outside India is concerned, its proportion to total population is highest in Tripura at more than 27 per cent, followed by Assam, Meghalaya and Arunachal Pradesh at 5.6 per cent, 4.1 per cent and 3.7 per cent respectively as against 1.9 per cent in Nagaland, 1.1 per cent in Manipur and 6.9 per cent in the North Eastern as a whole. In the absence of reliable data, if we assume validity of the same percentages for 1991 also, we shall find that the number of migrants from outside India will amount to 12.5 lakhs in Assam followed by 7.4 lakhs in Tripura, the total number of such migrants in the whole of region being 21.6 lakhs (Table 1.5).

Conclusion

Following are the findings of the study:

(1) During the four decades between 1951 and 1991, there has been tremendous growth of population in the north-eastern region. The highest growth rate is recorded by Nagaland, followed by Tripura, Mizoram, Manipur, Meghalaya and Assam in descending order. Though there has been inter-state growth differential in rates, the population of all the north-eastern states grew at a faster rate than the all India average.

(2) The census figures for the growth of Assam's population are confusing. The decadal growth rate in 1961 and 1971 works out to 34.9 per cent in each case. In the absence of 1981 census, the projected population of the state was put at 36 per cent for 1971-81, but census figures for 1991 show the decadal growth rate of Assam's population at 23.4 per cent and 23.6 per cent for 1971-81 and 1981-91 periods respectively. With the recorded figures for flow of migration of people both from other States of India and from outside India, as well as the birth and death rates, it is difficult to reconcile with the abruptly reduced growth rate figures shown for Assam. This requires further investigation.

(3) The density of population has enormously increased in the region during the 40-year period from 1951 to 1991. Assam has far exceeded the all India average. This has reduced the share of the per capita land and efficiency of large scale land productivity. This points to the urgent need of more intensive cultivation with improved technology on the one hand and serious efforts for development of small scale industries, on the other. The housing problem is also more acute than Indian average.

(4) The fall in Sex ratio in Manipur throughout the whole period of four decades, in Meghalaya for the period 1981-91 and in Mizoram during three decades from 1951 to 1981 can not be explained by the general cause-effect relationship. Further, research is necessary to reveal the

actual circumstances which led to such a peculiar situation in the trend of Sex ratio in these States.

(5) Except Meghalaya and Manipur, the annual growth rate of urban population during the decade 1981-91 is found to be higher than the all India rate in all other States. This is in the midst of very poor urbanisation in terms of percentage of total population in the region. Except Mizoram and Manipur, urban population as proportion to total population is lower than the all India figure of 25.7 per cent. The higher annual growth rate may be explained by the fact of very low figure of urbanisation in the base year 1951. Urban population of Assam forms the lowest percentage to total population at 11.08 among all the States of the region.

(6) As per 1971 census beyond which reliable figures are not available, migrant people from across international borders were as high as 27.1 per cent of total population in Tripura followed by Assam with 5.6 per cent, Meghalaya with 4.1 per cent and Arunachal Pradesh with 3.7 per cent as against 6.9 per cent in the total N.E. Region and 1.4 per cent in the country as a whole. In regard to the stream of migrants from other States of India, the highest percentage is recorded by Arunachal Pradesh at 8.5 per cent of its total population, followed by Nagaland and Meghalaya at 6.9 and 6.1 per cent respectively as against 3.4 per cent in the region as well as in the country as a whole. If we assume that the percentage of migrant population from outside India into this region still remains the same as in 1971, the number of immigrant population particularly from Bangladesh and Nepal will come to 12.5 lakhs in Assam and 7.4 lakhs in Tripura in 1991.

(7) There is an urgent necessity of reducing the pressure of population in the region both by taking more intensive population control measures and by containing flow of migration into the region from outside India.

REFERENCES

Basic Statistics of North Eastern Region, 1992, Shillong.

Centre for Monitoring Indian Economy, October 1992, Bombay.

Census of India, 1971 and 1991.

Choudhury, R.K., "Human Resources in North East India—Its Use and Development Strategy", Chap. 17 of the book , (ed.) *The Pattern and Problems of Population in North East India*, B. Datta Ray, Uppal Publishing House, New Delhi, 1986.

Draft Eighth Five-Year Plan of Assam, Planning and Development, Government of Assam, Dispur, Guwahati.

Srivastava, S.C., "Demographic Profile of North East India", *Ibid.*, 1986, Chap. 2.

Statistical Hand Book of Assam, 1988, Dispur, Guwahati.

2

DEMOGRAPHIC DYNAMICS OF THE NORTH EASTERN REGION

A.K. NEOG

Introduction

Population is a very important factor in the whole process of socio-economic development. The other important factors are natural resources, capital and technology. Population plays a dual role in development process as producers and consumers. Hence its size, growth, composition and quality are important aspects. There is, however, no clear-cut yardstick regarding the optimum size and rate of growth of population. The size of available resources and the level of technology are the appropriate yardsticks to determine the desirable size and growth of population. A large population undergoing hyper growth in a poor economy with limited resources and traditional technology can be a liability. When population is productively employed, it can be an asset and a resource. If population growth is subject to increasing return while the supply of basic needs is subject to law of decreasing return then population growth can be an economic threat.

North Eastern Scenario

According to 1991 census the size of India's population is about 8463.03 lakh. The final population figure of the seven N.E. states is around 315.47 lakh i.e. 3.73 per cent of the all

India figure. Its geographical area accounts for 7.7 per cent of the country's size and its output is about 3.27 per cent of the national product.

The geographical space being given, the size and growth of population has serious implications for development. Density of population is an indicator of both level of living and of the prospects for future development. Density in the hill states of the region is very low, ranging from 10 to 82 persons per sq. km. But it is high in Assam: 286 persons (higher than the all-India average), Tripura and in Manipur's valley area. This indicates population pressure. Assam's population accounts for 71 per cent and its geographical area is only 30.75 per cent in the region. Table 2.1 presents population and density of the region alongwith Sex ratio: (females per thousand males).

TABLE 2.1: **Size, Density and Sex Ratio of 1991 Population**

State	Population (lakhs)	Density (persons)	Sex ratio (Numbers)
Arunachal Pradesh	8.65	10	859
Assam	224.14	286	923
Manipur	18.37	82	958
Meghalaya	17.75	79	955
Mizoram	6.90	33	921
Nagaland	12.10	73	886
Tripura	27.57	263	945
India	8463.03	274	927

Source: Economic Survey (1992-93), Government of India Publication.

Trend of Population Growth

We now examine the population trend since the beginning of this century by using the data published by the North Eastern Council (NEC) (Basic Statistics of North Eastern Region). It may be noted that census data for Arunachal Pradesh are available only from 1961. There was no census for 1981 in Assam. The population of Assam for 1971-81 is estimated at

180.41 lakhs.

The growth rates of population are calculated with the help of continuous version of the exponential growth formula. Thus if g is the percentage annual exponential growth rate of population between two census years, then

$$g = \text{Log}\,(Pt/Po)\ 100/t$$

where Log denotes natural logarithm to the base *e*, *Pt* and *Po* are populations of the later and previous censuses respectively, and *t* is the number of years (ten) between the two censuses. The right hand side of the formula is multiplied by 100 for percentage. The calculated growth rates are given in Table 2.2.

The following observations are evident from Table 2.2.

(i) Throughout the period 1901-91 population growth of the N.E. states are much higher than the national average, except for Assam during 1971-81.

(ii) Intra-regionally, for most parts of tl. period population growth is higher in the states/areas than in Assam.

(iii) Prior to 1941 the growth rate was fluctuating in all the states of the region.

(iv) Even though the all-India population growth rate was negative during 1911-21, it was positive in the region, though it declined significantly from the previous decade except for Assam.

(v) Growth was particularly high during 1951-71 in all the states.

(vi) Population growth tends to decline during 1971-81 in Arunachal Pradesh, Assam, Manipur and Tripura but tends to rise after 1981 in Arunachal Pradesh, Assam, Meghalaya and Nagaland. In fact, Nagaland retains the record of highest population growth rate in the country.

Demographers have characterized the population growth of the North East Region as accelerating. The simplest way to examine this is by fitting a parabola to the population figures over time. Since Assam accounts for the largest share of the region's population so we test it for Assam only *vis-a-vis* India

TABLE 2.2: **Exponential Annual Growth Rate (per cent) of Population, 1901-1991**

Period	Assam	Arunachal	Manipur	Meghalaya	Mizoram	Nagaland	Tripura	India
1901-11	1.57	—	1.97	1.44	1.04	3.79	2.85	0.56
1911-21	1.86	—	1.04	0.69	0.74	0.65	2.79	(–)0.03
1921-31	1.82	—	1.50	1.31	2.35	1.18	2.28	1.04
1931-41	1.86	—	1.38	1.45	2.10	0.60	2.95	1.33
1941-51	1.82	—	1.21	0.86	2.48	1.14	2.20	1.25
1951-61	3.00	—	3.00	2.38	3.05	5.50	5.81	1.96
1961-71	3.00	3.28	3.19	2.75	2.22	3.35	3.09	2.22
1971-81	2.10	3.00	2.81	2.78	3.97	4.07	2.77	2.24
1981-91	2.17	3.14	2.57	2.84	3.34	4.45	2.24	2.14

Source: *Basic Statistics of North Eastern Region.*

for the period from 1901 till 1991. The estimated equations are:

Assam : $P = 44 - 8.92t + 2.68t$
India : $P = 29.74 - 9.91t + 1.025t$

where P is the population and t is the census years. The second term in the right hand side of the equations has a negative coefficient indicating that population tends to decline overtime, but the quadratic term (t) has a positive coefficient indicating a reversal after a point of time in the direction of the initial relationship between population and time. The rate of acceleration in the growth of population is extremely high for Assam. It is 168 per cent i.e. (2.68 – 1) × 100. For India's population it is only 2.5 per cent during the period 1901 to 1991. The slope of the population curve is increasing at positive rates for both Assam and Tripura, but it is much steeper for Assam. Since the population growth is much higher in the rest of the region so, *ipso facto*, their rates of acceleration are far higher than that of Assam.

Rural-Urban Composition

Population growth is contributed by rural-urban composition and their growth rates. As most of the states in the region are created after 1971, so we consider 1971 and subsequent censuses. Table 2.3 presents the percentage of rural and urban population in 1991 alongwith annual exponential growth in them during 1971-81 and 1981-91 decades.

From Table 2.3, it is seen that rural population percentage in the region is much higher than the national average of 74.3 per cent except in Manipur and Mizoram. Barring these two states, the proportion of urban population also is much lower than the national average of 25.7 per cent. Assam is the least urbanised while Mizoram is the most urbanized state in the North East. The growth of urban population is much higher than that of rural population in the last two decades, even though its momentum has declined in Manipur, Meghalaya, Mizoram and Nagaland. During the last decadel (1981-91), growth of rural population has declined in Arunachal Pradesh

TABLE 2.3: **Percentage of Rural-Urban Population in 1991 and their Annual Growth Rates in 1971-81 and 1981-91**

State	Population (%) 1991		Annual Growth Rate (%) (1971-81)		(1981-91)	
	R	U	R	U	R	U
Arunachal Pradesh	87.2	12.8	2.76	8.74	2.44	9.82
Assam	88.9	11.1	—	—	2.01	3.29
Manipur	72.5	27.5	1.16	9.76	2.42	2.98
Meghalaya	81.4	18.6	2.36	4.95	2.78	3.13
Mizoram	53.9	46.1	2.33	11.71	(-Ve)	9.59
Nagaland	82.8	17.2	3.42	8.50	4.25	5.49
Tripura	84.7	15.3	2.71	3.29	2.45	6.26
India	74.3	25.7	1.80	3.81	1.79	3.09

Note : R = Rural, U = Urban, (-Ve) = Negative
NB : For Assam, growth rate is for 1971-91.

and Tripura while it is negative in Mizoram.

Urbanization is one of the characteristics of development. Lower birth rate is correlated with urbanization. However, the level of urbanization is very low in the region except Mizoram and Manipur. Higher proportion of rural population in the region may suggest that rural development activities introduced by the government are having some positive impact in confining the people to rural areas. Alternatively, it may suggest that urban life has failed to attract the people due to congestion, conflicts, lack of basic amenities, etc. In the words of Prof. M. Taher, what is happening in the name of urbanization in the North East, is in fact ruralisation of urban settlements. The rural-urban dichotomy is not sharp.

Ethnic Composition

We may now investigate which population group is accelerating in growth ratio. For this, we classify the population into three broad groups viz. Scheduled Castes (SC), Scheduled Tribes (ST) and the others. The "others" group include the rest. Table 2.4

TABLE 2.4: **Percentage of Population of SC, ST and Others, and their Growth Rates during 1971 and 1991**

State	Groups	Percentage of Population			Annual Growth (%)	
		1971	1981	1991	1971-81	1981-91
1	2	3	4	5	6	7
Arunachal Pradesh	SC	0.07	0.46	0.47	21.53	3.28
	ST	79.02	69.82	63.66	1.78	2.21
	Others	20.91	29.72	35.87	6.53	5.02
Assam	SC	6.24	—	7.40	—	2.99
	ST	10.99	—	12.82	—	2.91
	Others	82.77	—	79.77	—	1.95
Meghalaya	SC	0.38	0.41	0.51	3.46	5.02
	ST	80.48	80.58	85.53	2.79	3.44
	Others	19.13	19.01	13.96	2.72	(-)0.25
Manipur	SC	1.53	1.25	2.02	0.81	7.37
	ST	31.18	27.30	34.41	1.48	4.88
	Others	67.29	71.45	63.57	3.41	1.40
Mizoram	SC	0.02	0.03	0.10	4.99	16.33
	ST	94.26	93.55	94.75	3.88	3.47
	Others	5.72	6.42	5.15	5.12	1.13
Nagaland	ST	88.61	83.99	87.70	3.52	4.88
	Others	11.39	16.01	12.30	7.46	1.81
Tripura	SC	12.39	15.12	16.36	4.76	3.74
	ST	28.95	28.44	30.95	2.59	3.79
	Others	58.66	56.44	52.69	2.38	2.26
India	SC	14.60	15.29	16.33	2.70	2.77
	ST	6.94	7.53	8.01	3.06	2.72
	Others	78.46	77.18	75.66	2.07	1.91

NB: In Nagaland SCs are not counted.

Source: Census of India Reports 1971, 1981 and 1991.

presents the percentage share of each group in the total population in the respective states in 1971, 1981 and 1991 alongwith their growth rates.

Though the scheduled castes accounts for over 16 per cent of the country's population it is negligible in the North East. In fact, in Nagaland no scheduled caste was found and recorded in any census. Only in Tripura, the scheduled castes population percentage i.e. 16.36 is higher than the national average, while in Assam it is 7.4 per cent. Though the scheduled tribes population in the country is only 8 per cent, it is extremely high in the North Eastern hills. In Assam it is 12.82 per cent of the state's population. Arunachal Pradesh, Meghalaya, Mizoram, Nagaland, the hill areas of Assam and Manipur are predominantly tribal. The tribal society of those states is, however, not homogeneous. The number of tribes including sub-tribes stands at 110 in Arunachal, 60 in Assam, 49 in Manipur, 54 in Meghalaya, 61 in Mizoram, 39 in Nagaland and 35 in Tripura. While some of the tribes are sizeable in number the others are marginal and some are commonly found in more than one state.

From Table 2.4, it is seen that though the SC population is insignificant their share and growth has been rising fast since 1971.

Contrary to the decreasing national growth rate of ST population, the growth of ST population in the region is rising except in Mizoram where it is falling. This shows that both the SCs and STs are not benefited from the family welfare measures introduced to check the population growth. As a result, the N.E. region not trapped in the initial phase of demographic transition and is unable to graduate to the declining phase. In Manipur the percentage of ST population and also that of the SCs are fluctuating mainly due to ethnic assertions among some tribes and castes to enlist them in the census by their ethnic names. Since such names do not figure in the census list so they may have been recorded in "others" group. In Meghalaya, the percentage of ST population is rising. It may be noted that the communities viz. Boro, Kachari, Koch and Rabha are included in the tribal list of the state from 1987.

The percentage of "others" group of population is declining in the country as a whole. In the North East region also it is declining except in Arunachal Pradesh. In fact, the growth of this group in Meghalaya is negative i.e. (-) 0.25

during 1981-91. During 1971-81 the growth of "others" population has been phenomenal in Arunachal Pradesh, Nagaland and Mizoram, and remains high in Arunachal Pradesh in the last decade. Since this cannot be explained in terms of natural rate of growth so migration must have been the reason.

Trend of Birth and Death Rates

The growth of population may be due to both natural growth and migration. The difference between birth rate (BR) and death rate (DR) gives the estimate of natural growth rate (NGR). These rates are measured per thousand population. Table 2.5 presents such data available for rural (R) and urban (U) sectors at three points of time viz. 1971, 1981 and 1989.

It is seen from the table 2.5 that both birth and death rates are gradually declining. In the rural areas birth rate is considerably higher than in the urban areas. On the other hand, in 1989 both the rural births and death rates in Arunachal Pradesh and Meghalaya are higher than national average. In Assam the rural birth and death rates in the same year are 30.0 and 10.6, yielding a natural growth rate of 19.4 per thousand or 1.94 per cent. For the urban areas those rates are 21.7 and 7.6 yielding 1.41 per cent natural growth rate. These rates are lower than the all-India rates, and also much lower than the actual growth rate of population in the state. The difference may be explained by the high migration rate, the burden of which being borne by the state and the region as a whole.

It may be noted that the fertility and gross reproduction rates in respect of Assam for which data are available, are lower than the all-India average. As for instance, the latest data for 1988 reveal the total fertility rate of 3.9 for rural Assam as against the national average of 4.3 and for urban sector the rates are 2.5 and 3.1 respectively. In the same year, the gross reproduction rates for rural and urban were 1.9 and 1.2 in Assam against 2.0 and 1.5 respectively for the country as a whole. The N.E. region is yet to respond to family planning measures. It is also evident from the percentages of couples effectively protected through all the methods of family

TABLE 2.5: **Sector-wise Birth Rate, Death Rate and Natural Growth Rate for the Given Years**

State	Sector	Year 1971			Year 1981			Year 1989		
		BR	DR	NGR	BR	DR	NGR	BR	DR	NGR
Arunachal	R	36.8	19.8	17.0	32.1	12.1	20.0	36.3	15.1	21.2
Pradesh	U	—	—	—	—	—	—	29.1	4.7	24.4
Assam	R	39.3	18.7	20.6	38.8	13.0	25.8	30.0	10.6	19.4
	U	31.0	9.5	21.5	23.2	8.0	15.2	21.7	7.6	14.1
Manipur	R	34.0	7.1	26.9	26.8	6.8	20.0	24.8	7.0	17.8
	U	26.4	5.5	20.9	24.4	4.5	19.9	16.5	6.1	10.4
Meghalaya	R	—	—	—	35.0	8.9	26.1	33.6	12.6	21.0
	U	—	—	—	18.5	4.3	14.2	19.0	4.7	14.3
Nagaland	R	—	—	—	21.4	5.3	16.1	20.8	4.7	16.1
	U	—	—	—	—	—	—	14.9	1.3	13.6
Tripura	R	37.2	16.1	21.1	27.6	8.2	19.4	26.6	7.9	18.7
	U	23.1	7.6	15.5	14.8	5.4	9.4	16.8	5.7	11.1

(Contd.)

TABLE 2.5 *(Contd.)*

India	R	38.9	16.4	22.5	35.6	13.7	21.9	32.2	11.1	21.1
	U	30.1	9.7	20.4	27.0	7.8	19.2	25.2	7.2	18.0

NB: BR = Birth Rate, DR = Death Rate, NGR = Natural Growth Rate.
R = Rural, U = Urban

Source : (i) *Basic Statistics of North Eastern Region*, 1990: North Eastern Council Secretariat, Shillong.
(ii) Govt. of India *Pocket Book on Family Welfare Information* (1990).

planning. As on 31st March, 1990 this percentage was 43.3 for the country as a whole while it was 37.7 per cent in Mizoram, 26.7 in Manipur, 25.2 in Assam, 17.9 in Tripura, 9.9 in Arunachal Pradesh, 5.3 in Meghalaya and only 4.8 per cent in Nagaland.

Effects of Population Growth

In backward areas rapid population growth tends to effect the benefits of development. It results in family frustration, dependency burden, unemployment and social tensions leading to a breakdown of an ordered society. Unchecked population growth jeopardizes environment as more people consume more and their net impact on the environment is more, thereby threatening the survival of the future generations. Hence the crux of the problem is the correlation between sustainable development and population explosion.

Views on Population Control

Rapid population growth is a global problem, particularly of the South. There are three views on the measures to control population growth. According to Prof. Amartya Sen, the Malthusian scare is uncalled for as food production has kept pace with the population boom in two major growth areas of South Asia and China. The population issue does not present any immediate problem although it is necessary to take long-term measures to solve it through social and economic planning, welfare and education. Prof. Sen expressed this view in 1994 on the eve of UN-sponsored Cairo conference on population development. To him the real problems of population are consumption patterns and their effect on environment. In other words, if average consumption of the rich comes down then more people can be supported. However, it may not be feasible as there may be consumption rigidly downwards.

The second view is of Gary Becker, the 1992 Nobel laurate in Economics who argues that free market would "defuse the population bomb". The question, however, arises: Is there such a thing as a genuine free market?

The third view (which of course was earlier than the above two) is of the world population conference held at Bucharest in 1974, which coined the slogan "development is the best contraceptive" to check population growth. It is a stylized fact that people in lower income groups have more children than those in higher income groups. This view holds that large demographic shifts would have to be preceded by substantial progress in developing areas.

There is a positive correlation between education and population growth. The better-off and the more educated people (particularly women) are, the fewer babies they would prefer to produce as they are more conscious of the quality of life for themselves and for the future generations than their illiterate counterparts.

Concluding Remarks

In India the burden of the population problem among its different states is flat. The seven most populous states viz. Bihar, Madhya Pradesh, Rajasthan, Uttar Pradesh (BIMARU states), West Bengal, Maharashtra and Andhra Pradesh account for 60 per cent of India's population. The total fertility rates in these states (barring the last two) are higher than the national average and are mainly responsible for a higher national growth rate in population. These are also the states where figures of 'unmet needs' for birth control are high. If the population growth in these states is controlled then more than half of the problem can be solved. This will also meet the problem of unplanned migration of the surplus population elsewhere. However, it does not mean that other regions like the North East can afford to avoid population control. For sustainable development and in the interest of inter-generational equity, all the states will have to control population growth. Further, its reduction is also necessary to attain the national goal of net reproduction rate of one corresponding to 1.2 per cent annual population growth rate by 2010 AD, i.e. prior to the time when Indian population is expected to stabilise. Hence, population control is a *sine-qua-non*. However, a check on the domestic population growth will be meaningless if trans-border migration into India persists without check.

REFERENCES

Basic Statistics of North Eastern Region: Publication of North Eastern Council, Secretariat, Shillong.

Census of India Reports, 1971, 1981 and 1991.

Economic Survey, 1992-93: Government of India Publication.

Government of India, *Pocket Book on Family Welfare Information*, 1990.

3

DECLINING FERTILITY IN THE NORTH-EAST STATES

An Analysis of Roles Played by Social, Economic and Demographic Factors

H. GOSWAMI

The theory of Multiphases Response[1] states that a sustained natural increase in population resulting from continued declines in mortality levels in the context of socio-economic developments, provides a multiphasic demographic response involving postponement of marriage, increased celibacy, resort to abortion, use of contraceptives and out-migration which eventually decreases fertility rates.

If a population, due to various reasons, fails to respond in time to the stimulus of declining mortality generated by socio-economic developments by way of resorting to family control measures, the resulting chaos would retard the process of development. The high birth rates will be handicapping people in their efforts to take advantages of the new opportunities provided by the emerging economy.[2] The family will be enlarged with more siblings with whom to share whatever is available; fragmentation of patrimony; heavy task of rearing and educating them even at conventional standard; savings, hence capital formation which is necessary to seize opportunities in the growing economy will be retarded because of increasing dependence; accentuation of rate at which the store of exhaustible and non-exhaustible natural resources are used up; diminution in the rate of growth of capital equipments of labour force.[3]

Alongwith the entire nation, fertility has been declining in all the states of the NE region. Table 3.1 shows the percentage decline in fertility in the NE states during 1971-91. It shows that Manipur and Tripura have the highest percentage decline in fertility over the years. Very low decline is observed in Meghalaya and Arunachal Pradesh while Assam and Nagaland have achieved moderate decline in fertility.

TABLE 3.1: **Levels and Differentials of Fertility Decline in the N.E. States 1971-91**

State	1971	1981	1991	Percentage decline 1971-91
Arunachal Pradesh	36.8	32.1	30.9	16.03
Assam	38.5	33.0	30.4	21.04
Manipur	33.3	26.6	20.1	39.64
Meghalaya	37.2	32.6	32.4	12.90
Mizoram	N.A.	N.A.	20.8	NA
Nagaland	24.0	21.4	18.5	22.92
Tripura	35.8	26.4	23.1	35.47
India	36.9	33.9	29.7	19.51

NA : Not available.
Source: Census of India, 1971, pp. 81 and 91.

Table 3.2 also explains the same phenomenon but in a different manner. If there has been no change in fertility for last three or four decades the Total Fertility Rate (TFR) and the Completed Cohort Fertility Rate (CCFR) would be nearly identical. If fertility has declined, TFR will be lesser than the CCFR, with larger difference generally indicating more rapid decline. For example, the gap between TFR (3.39) and the CCFR (5.11) indicates that a substantial fertility decline has taken place in India during last 35 to 40 years. Among the NE States, relatively large decline in fertility is observed in Tripura with 3.04, Assam 2.42, Manipur 2.26 and Mizoram 2.15 children lower than average number of children ever born.

TABLE 3.2: **Cohort Fertility and Total Fertility Rates by Residence, NE States, 1992-93**

State	Cohort Fertility Rate			Total Fertility Rate		
	R	U	T	R	U	T
Arunachal Pradesh	5.19	N.A.	5.00	4.38	3.23	4.25
Assam	6.25	4.32	5.95	3.68	2.53	3.53
Manipur	5.29	4.44	4.99	3.00	2.17	2.73
Meghalaya	5.13	4.70	5.03	3.81	3.42	3.74
Mizoram	4.46	3.36	4.41	2.28	2.24	2.26
Nagaland	4.08	3.39	3.93	3.55	2.03	3.22
Tripura	6.07	N.A.	5.72	2.91	1.78	2.63
India	5.35	4.46	5.11	3.67	2.70	3.39

Source: *National Family Health Survey*, 1992-93; pp. 94-96.

This decline in fertility over the years has been brought about by a complex mix of social, economic and demographic factors. Socio-Economic developments create an atmosphere wherein the high fertility culture of the pre-development stage cannot thrive. This results into declining fertility in a population. It has been observed that the fertility decline resulting from socio-economic changes differ very widely among the NE states. For example, while Manipur and Tripura have achieved a very large percentage fall in fertility over the years, Meghalaya and Arunachal Pradesh have experienced a very slow decline in fertility.

The purpose of this chapter is to identify the reasons for such inter-state variations in fertility decline and to assess the relative roles of social, economic and demographic determinants of fertility decline in the NE States.

Methodology

Various social, economic and demographic variables correlate

TABLE 3.3: **Correlation Coefficients Between Some Major Social, Economic and Demographic Variables on the One Hand and Fertility Decline on the other, Among the N.E. States**

	Variable	Category of variable	Value of r	r^2 (%)
1.	Urbanization	Social	.688	47.31
2.	Singulate mean age of marriage	Social	.6596	43.5
3.	Ignorance about reproduction	Social	.537	28.8
4.	Social infrastructure	Social	.51	26.0
5.	Female literacy level	Social	.488	24.0
6.	Use of contraceptives	Demographic	.57	32.0
7.	Crude Death Rate	Demographic	.436	19.0
8.	Knowledge of family planning	Demographic	.3992	16.0
9.	Infant mortality rate	Demographic	.0127	—
10.	Per capita state domestic product	Economic	.360	13.0

Source: *National Family Health Survey*, 1992-93.

differently with fertility decline of a population. Therefore, with a view to knowing the relative influence of each of such variables on fertility decline, a set of correlation coefficients of various social, economic and demographic variables on the one hand and the levels of fertility decline of the NE Units on the other has been worked out. Thereafter, the behaviour of those variables which are found to have high correlation with fertility decline has been analyzed in such State of the region, to determine their relative significance in fertility decline in each state.

Findings

1. The correlation coefficients (Table 3.3) shows that the social factors like level of unbanization and mean age at marriage have the highest influence in reducing fertility in the NE States. Other social factors like level of

TABLE 3.4: **Social Variables and Decline in Fertility**

State	Urban pop. as % of total pop.	Singulate Mean age at marriage of female	Percentage of married women ignorant of reproduction	Social infrastructure indices India=100	Female literacy rate	Percentage of married women who use contraceptive	Crude DR	% of married women having knowledge of family planning	Infant mortality	Per-capita SDP indices India=100
1	2	3	4	5	6	7	8	9	10	11
Arunachal Pradesh	12.80	20.0	5.4	112.50	29.37	23.6	13.5	77.7	40.0	105.0
Assam	11.11	21.6	1.0	94.90	43.70	42.8	11.5	97.5	88.7	70.4
Manipur	27.52	25.0	1.5	85.70	48.64	34.9	5.4	93.6	42.4	83.0
Meghalaya	18.60	21.2	4.6	107.00	44.78	20.7	8.8	78.0	64.2	84.1
Mizoram	46.10	22.9	2.2	129.30	78.09	53.8	N.A.	98.1	14.6	87.5
Nagaland	17.21	22.7	6.4	92.80	55.72	13.0	3.3	44.4	17.2	96.2
Tripura	15.30	21.2	1.1	122.80	50.01	56.1	7.6	99.7	75.8	76.1
India	26.13	20.0	3.7	100.00	39.42	40.6	9.8	95.8	78.5	100.0

Source : Columns 2, 6 and 8 = Census of India 1991.

Columns 3, 4, 7, 9 & 10 = *National Family Health Survey*, IIPS, 1992-93, pp. 78, 185, 143, 132, 221 respectively.

Columns 5 and 11 = Ananta, T C.A.; Krishna, K.L. and Roy Choudhury, U., *Measuring Inter-state Differentials in Infrastructure*, 1994.

ignorance of women about reproduction, social infrastructure, female literacy rate have moderate influence in fertility decline. The demographic variables like level of use of contraceptives, crude death rate, knowledge of family planning have moderate influence on fertility decline in the NE States. It is surprising that the declining infant mortality rates have little influence on fertility decline among the NE States. Another peculiar findings is that economic developments, like rise in per capita income, have failed to make any impact on fertility decline in the NE States.

2. Since social factors have the highest influence in reducing fertility in the NE region it follows that in those states of the region where social variables have made better progress over the years, the decline of fertility would be faster.

The reasons for relatively slow decline in fertility in Arunachal Pradesh and Meghalaya were the slow progress of social variables in these two years. The relatively higher economic development in these two states have failed to make any impact on fertility decline, because economic variables, as stated earlier, have little impact on fertility decline in the NE region. On the other hand, in Manipur and Tripura social variables have made relatively good progress over the years, which has brought down the fertility levels sharply in these two states.

NOTES

1. Davis, Kingsley, The Theory of Change and Response in Modern Demographic History, *Population Index* 26, pp. 345-365.
2. Namboodiri, N.K., "Societal Development and Population Change—A Reappraisal of Selected Theory", in *Fertility and Mortality* (ed.) K. Mahadevan, Sage, New Delhi-1986, pp. 37-54.
3. Spengler, J.J., *Population Theory: Selected Readings*, The Free Press of Glence, NY 1956.

REFERENCES

Ananta, T.C.A., K.L. Krishna & U. Roy Choudhury, *Measuring Inter-State Differentials in Infrastructure*, 1994.

Census of India, 1971 & 1991.

National Family Health Survey, IIPS, 1992-93.

4

POPULATION AND POPULATION PRESSURES ON FOREST RESOURCES IN THE NORTH EASTERN REGION

M.C. PANDEY

There is a growing concern in the North Eastern Region about the increased degradation of the environment. Seventy per cent of the area being hilly it is felt that much of the deterioration is due to indiscriminate falling of trees, shifting cultivation and minning. Thus the environmental challenges that the region is facing to-day are greater than at any other time in the history of the North Eastern Region. Due to increased human activities towards massive utilisation of National resources, the climate and ecology has been affected.

Geographically the North Eastern Region is a compact unit covering an area 2.55 lakh square kilometre constituting approximately 7 per cent of the total land area. The number of people living in the region are increasing at an alarming rate. It has increased from 13.3 million in 1961 to 31.38 million in 1991, which is 2.5 folds increase since 1961. In size (area) the region has remained constant. If the population continues to grow at the present rate, there will be more than 35 million men, women and children by 2000 AD occupying the same space and sharing the same natural resources. The region is already showing signs of severe strains on the problem of land degradation, water stress, food shortages, and depletion of natural resources particularly forest resource. Massive degradation of the environment due to population pressures have started showing. The daily struggle of the rural poor to obtain the basic necessities of life are taking a severe toll on the natural resources particularly forest upon which depends their very survival.

Economy

The economy of the North Eastern Region is dominated by tea, oil and timber. Industries do not have significant impact on the economy of the region. There is no denying of the fact that sufficient financial allocation have been allocated to the region but, the pace of development has not been achieved. Moreover, resource and development have not fallen in line. It is interesting to note that education has outstriped economic development resulting in unemployment leading to resentment in the unemployed youth. Added to this is the pressure of population, which has nullified economic developments. Thus the major cause of economic inbalances are due to increasing demand for fuelwood, timber, raw material for paper industries. These demands are causing disaster to the forests. In Meghalaya, increased excavation of coal is becoming a major cause for soil degradation and air pollution. Tables 4.1 and 4.2 give the area under forest in the North Eastern Region.

TABLE 4.1: **Forest Statistic of North East 1984-85**

(area in sq.km.)

1.	Total Geographical Area (Reported)	2,55,050	
2.	Reserved forest	46649.0	(34.10)
3.	Protected forests	9283.0	(6.7)
4.	Unclassed forest	80672.0	(58.9)
5.	Other forest	253.0	(0.2)
	Total Forest Area	136857	(53.6)
	Per cent Area		

Source: *Basic Statistic of North Eastern Region*, 1995.

The consumption of forest product for timber and fuel-wood is summarised in Table 4.2.

TABLE 4.2: **Consumption of Timber (1976-77)**

(in 000 cubic metres)

States	Timber	Fuelwood	Total
Arunachal Pradesh	172	36	208
Assam	457	895	1352
Manipur	45	144	189
Meghalaya	43	1	44
Mizoram	6	57	63
Nagaland	48	27	75
Tripura	30	286	310
Total	801	1440	2241
India	8500	12456	20956

Source: *Basic Statistic of North Eastern Region*, 1982.

Shifting Cultivation

Shifting cultivation, which originated during the neolithic period, is still practised in the tribal dominated areas of the North Eastern Region. About four lakhs families practise shifting cultivation in the region, accounting for less than 6 per cent of the area (NEC). Annually about 1.5 per cent of the area is under shifting cultivation. It has been reported that during the nine year period (1975-84) the area under shifting cultivation has been reduced by 10556 sq. kilometres. Thus the efforts to discourage shifting cultivation during the seventies and eightees have achieved positive results. Table 4.3 summarises the increase and decrease of area under shifting cultivation during 1975 to 1984.

Alpine Pasture in the North Eastern Region

Alpines are those regions which are above coniferous forests and below line of permanent snow. In the North Eastern Region 12,335 sq. km. is under alpine pasture. The entire

TABLE 4.3: **Shifting Cultivation in the North Eastern Region**

State	Geographical area (sq. km.)	Extent of forest affected by shifting cultivation (sq. km.)		% change in 1984 as compared to 1975
		1975	1984	
Arunachal Pradesh	83590	7940	8521	(+) 7.3
Assam	78520	4160	7276	(+) 74.0
Manipur	22360	17770	13846	(-) 22.1
Meghalaya	22480	10240	6812	(-) 33.5
Mizoram	21090	16110	12442	(-) 22.8
Nagaland	16520	10970	10641	(-) 3.0
Tripura	10490	6220	3315	(-) 46.7
Total	255050	73410	62854	(-) 14.4
%	100.0	28.8	24.6	—

Source: Forest Survey Report, 1989.

area is in Arunachal Pradesh, constituting 7.1 per cent of the total area in the country and 14.75 of the total geographical area of Arunachal Pradesh.

Area Under Forest

The 1989 and 1991 Forest Survey Report have shown that the percentage of actual forest cover to geographical area in the North Eastern Region is 65.1 per cent against 53.6 per cent reported in official documents. Actual forest area cover to official records vary by 2.95 million hectares. In terms of percentage the actual forest cover is 11.60 per cent higher than officially reported figures. This is true for all the hilly states of the North Eastern Region. In Assam and Tripura the officially reported forest cover is higher than the actual forest cover. The reasons for actual forest cover being higher than the officially reported forest is that in the hilly regions of the North Eastern

Region which are mostly inhabited by different tribal communities forest are privately owned by individuals, owned by religious groups, village communities or by Forest department. A substantial proportion of the forest not owned by state government has not been included in the official documents. Table 4.4 below gives the details of the forest cover in the region and Table 4.5 gives the per cent of forest in the North Eastern Region since 1961-62 to 1987-88 (Recorded).

TABLE 4.4: **Forest Cover Assessment Cover 1991**

(Area in sq. km.)

	Geographical Area	Forest Cover 1991 Assessment		Total	Per cent Forest Cover to Total Area
		Dense	Open		
Arunachal Pradesh	83743	54542 (61.5)	14215 (16.9)	69757	82.1
Assam	78438	15842 (20.1)	8909 (11.35)	24751	31.5
Manipur	22327	5309 (23.7)	12376 (55.4)	17685	79.2
Meghalaya	24429	3305 (13.5)	12570 (51.4)	15875	70.8
Mizoram	21081	4279 (20.2)	14574 (69.1)	18853	89.4
Nagaland	16579	3531 (21.29)	10790 (65.0)	14321	86.38
Tripura	10486	1825 (17.40)	3710 (35.3)	5535	60.0
North East	257083	88633 (34.47)	77144 (30.0)	165777	64.47

Source: State of Forest Report 1991, GOI (Ministry of Environment & Forest).
Note: Figures in brackets indicate percentage.

TABLE 4.5: **Per cent Area under Forest in the North Eastern Region (Reported)**

S.No.	State	1961-62	1975-76	1980-81	1987-88
1.	Arunachal Pradesh	—	61.6	61.8	61.6
2.	Assam	36.6	36.4	39.2	39.1
3.	Manipur	27.3	67.7	67.8	67.7
4.	Meghalaya	a	38.0	38.0	37.8
5.	Mizoram	a	60.5	75.5	75.5
6.	Nagaland	a	17.4	17.3	52.2
7.	Tripura	59.6	59.9	56.4	59.9
8.	North East	—	49.3	51.2	53.5

Sources: *Basic Statistics of North Eastern Region*, 1980-1990.
Fertilizer Statistics 1990-91.
Forest Survey Report 1989 and 1991.

Population Density and Forest

There is a positive co-relation between population density and forest cover in the different states of the North Eastern Region. Increase in population is directly corelated with per capita decrease in forest area. Increase in population has shown significant decline in per capita availability of forest in all the states in the region particularly in Arunachal Pradesh, Manipur, Mizoram and Nagaland. Table 4.6 summarises per capita availability of forest in relation to population pressures during eightees (from 1981 to 1991).

Dense and Open Forest Cover

As per the latest report on "the State of Forests 1991", the forest cover in the country stands at 19.00 per cent and for the North Eastern Region is 53.5 per cent (recorded). Both are short by the minimum standard recommended by the National Forests Policy. The National Forests Policy 1988 has recommended a minimum of 60 per cent for the hilly areas and

TABLE 4.6: **Recorded and Actual Forest Cover, Population and Per Capita Forest Area**

State	Population (in Lakhs)		Forest Cover (in sq. km.)		Per Capita* Forest Area (in ha)	
	1981	1991	Recorded	Actual	1981	1991
Arunachal Pradesh	6.31	8.58	51540	68763	8.15	6.00
Assam	198.96	222.94	30708	26058	0.15	0.13
Manipur	14.20	18.26	15155	17885	1.07	0.82
Meghalaya	13.35	17.60	8514	15690	0.64	0.48
Mizoram	4.93	6.86	15935	18178	3.20	2.32
Nagaland	7.74	12.15	8625	14356	1.11	0.70
Tripura	20.53	27.44	6280	5325	0.31	0.22
North-East	266.07	313.86	136657	166255	0.51	0.43

*Per Capita based on Recorded forest area.

Source: State of Forest Report, 1989.

33 per cent for the country as a whole. As per the forest survey report the forest area in the North Eastern Region has increased marginally. When individual states are taken into consideration, there is an marginal decline in the forest cover in Arunachal Pradesh, Assam and Manipur. While in Nagaland, Mizoram, Tripura, the forest area has marginally increased. The decline in forest cover is significant in Meghalaya. An interesting feature of the forest survey report is a distinct difference between Recorded area and Actual area under forest. The difference between recorded forest area and actual forest area is highly significant. As indicated the difference between actual and recorded cover is that a substantial portion of forest cover in the hilly states of the North Eastern Region is owned by private individuals, religious groups, village communities and other agencies other than forest department. Thus only forest owned by the forest department have been shown as forest in recorded records.

When forest area is classified on the basis of actual forest the entire forest area has been taken into consideration (Table 4.7).

Discussion

Conservation of environment has been regarded important for development. Environment is a store house of resources. One of the most important resources are the forests. Forests provide the basic amenities of life, food, fiber, fodder firewood etc. Exploitation of the natural resources particularly forest may be detrimental to all living organism. It has been revealed that the environmental resources are shrinking, particularly forest. Going by the current figures approximately 1 to 1.5 per cent of the forest cover is lost every year in the North Eastern Region due to deforestation. With the increase in population pressures the need for firewood is expected to increase which means cutting down trees faster than they can grow. Since 1972 the area under dense forest and open forest cover has declined. As per the 1989 forest survey report only 34.47 per cent of forest area is under dense forest cover (Table 4.4), ranging from 13.5 per cent in Meghalaya to 65 per cent in Arunachal Pradesh. Open forest cover means, higher degree of soil erosion leading to silting in Barak and Brahmaputra, the two important rivers in the North East, indicating the effects of deforestation. The catchment area of the Brahmaputra, Barak and their tributaries have also shown sign of erosion. Rainfall in the North Eastern has been below the average during 1990, 1991 and 1992. Average temperature is continuously on the rise and there is scarcity of water. Associated with this is the problem of dirty water, soil degradation, global warming, sewage problem, polluted air, endangered species etc. leading to poverty. Increase in population has further aggravated the problem.

In the hilly regions of the North Eastern trees are the most important natural resources but it is being squandered ruthlessly. There is a greater need now to protect them as much of the economy is based on forest wealth. In the North Eastern Region wood is the prime source of energy especially for cooking and this demand has to be met. The demand for

TABLE 4.7: **Forest Cover in the North Eastern Region 1972 to 1989**

	Geographical area in sq. km.	Percentage of population to the country's	Density of population per sq. km. (national average)	Percentage of dense forest cover to area	Dense Primary Forest (Cover 40 per cent density) in sq. km			Open forest cover (35 per cent density in sq. km.)		
					1972-75	1980-82	1987-89	1972-75	1980-82	1985-87
Arunachal Pradesh	83,580	.09	10	61	50,460	49,486	54,272	978	2,618	14,491
Assam	78,520	2.64	284	18	18,691	15,590	15,688	2,364	4,206	9,370
Manipur	22,360	.22	82	20	13,678	NA	5,060	1,412	N.A.	12,825
Mizoram	21,090	.08	33	19	13,206	11,155	3,883	654	816	4,295
Meghalaya	22,490	.21	78	13	10,083	7,448	3,427	4,307	5,010	12,263
Nagaland	16,530	.14	73	28	7,067	4,921	4,632	1,087	3,174	9,724
Tripura	10,480	.32	262	16	5,972	4,554	1,214	350	629	4,111
North East	2,55,050	3.7	123	46.7	1,19,157	1,02,523	88,176	11,052	—	67,079
India	32,87,797	100.0	267	21.9	3,78,470	—	—	—	—	—

Source: Forest Survey Report, 1989.

Density Figures: Census of India 1991.

forest product in the form of timber, plywood and industrial needs will have to be curtailed otherwise there will be forests with scattered trees. Temperature will rise continuously and rainfall levels will drop. The very survival of the living beings will be threatened.

REFERENCES

Basis Statistics of North Eastern Region, 1990, NEC Publication.

Census of India 1991, Part-2 of 1991.

Dattagupta Rupak, 1991, "Consciousness of Environment", *Indian Express*, May 2, 1991.

Gengal, S.C., 1992, An Eco-Emergency, *The Hindustan Times*, May 25, 1992.

Status of Forests in India, 1989, Forest Survey of India, Ministry of Environment and Forest SIP.

The State of Forest Report 1991, Government of India, Ministry of Environment and Forest, Dehradun.

Statistical Abstract, 1985.

5

SPATIAL DISTRIBUTION OF TRIBAL POPULATION AND INTER-TRIBAL DIFFERENCES IN GROWTH

A Study in Tribal Demography of the North East

DEBENDRA KUMAR NAYAK and SUSMITA DAS

Generalities

A very significant proportion of India's population has been scheduled as tribes. This segment which accounts for around 8.08 per cent of India's total population is not a homogeneous category either socially or economically. They belong to different ethnolingual groups, profess diverse faiths and are at disparate levels of socio-economic development. "Spread along the entire spectrum-ranging from stone age hunters and gatherers of forest produced to the urbanised, industrial wage earners—the tribal communities constitute an important segment of the Indian population" (Raza *et al.* 1977 : 1).

An interesting aspect of their geographical distribution is the striking tendency of this segment to cluster and concentrate in a few pockets of diverse degrees of isolation within an environmental setting which is by and large averses to intensive settled cultivation. It is this fact which have contributed in the past to the lack of adequate interaction between the tribal and non-tribal components of the population. Governed by a complex process of peopling, ecological habitats of their later settlement, varied degrees of their interactions with their neighbouring tribal or peasant groups—this component of India's population represents an interesting profile of country's social diversity. "Constrained by a vigorous environment which has fostered physical and social isolation for ages, the tribal communities have been by and large brought under exogenetic forces only marginally. Thus, over time, the tribal communities seem to have developd a mode of living generically linked to the ecological conditions in the enclaves which have provided them with a resource base and have favoured the survival of their way of life with marginal modifications." (Raza *et al.* 1977 :2). It is not surprising, therefore, that the areas of tribal concentration and the so called backward regions are by and large coterminous.

No studies on tribal geography and tribal demography is complete without a reference to the north-eastern part of this country which supports not only an extremely high proportion of tribes in its total population, but also a region of tribal communities belonging to diverse ethnic, linguistic and religious categories. In more than one sense the North-Eastern region represents a microcosm of the entire sub-continent. The partially closed character of the region has fostered an isolation of the communities living in this part of the country— a situation which has been broken in the past but not too frequently. The replica is not only in terms of physiography, but also in the cultural frame which remains intact for far too long. The ethnic diversity of this region is indeed closely entwined to inter-tribal differences in the modes of living and ways of living practised by these little communities.

"Nestled within the complex of the sub-Himalayan ranges, the Indo-Burmese hills of Nagaland, Manipur and Mizoram and the eroded surfaces of the Meghalaya plateau, the tribes of the north-east India have a world of their own. Having lived in the marchland between India and China and in the triangle where the Indian and the Chinese worlds meet, they have picked up the impression that they belong to none." (Ahmed 1983: 24-28) An interesting feature of tribal population in the north-east refers to their incredibly small size with a high degree of concentration as against the low degree of concentration of their counterparts in the mid-India. Conversely, the level of agglomeration is low in the former compared to the latter. It is this particular feature of the geographical distribution of the north-eastern tribes which makes it a distinct category wherein most tribes have developed knife-edged boundaries between and among themselves with a core of their concentration often without a periphery or a transition over space where the presence of one tribe gives rise to the dominance of another. It is this geographical patterning of the tribes which create a neatly defined tribal habitats exclusive to each other renders any treatment of tribes as a whole meaningless and incongruous to existing tribal reality. The typical distributional pattern demands studies to be conducted for different tribes separately as the habitat, resource base, cultural patterns vary over space as one moves from one tribal group to enter another.

An important dimension of the tribal situation in the north-east refers to the dynamics of demographic changes taking place among these communities of varying sizes and located in diverse ecological milieux. The present study, however, limits its scope to study the dynamics of demographic growth among the North-East tribes. It is a pity that the general population growth has attracted a serious attention from social scientists interested in the demographic situation of the region, but the question of tribal population has been either glibly grossed over or has been addressed to through a meek disaggregation of the data according to general and scheduled tribe population. This is in spite of the fact that the demographic processes appear to have diverse manifestations in relation to different tribal groups living in this region. An attempt is made in this chapter to examine and analyse inter-tribal differences in population growth which is expected to plug this serious gap in research concerning tribal demography as well as to unravel the true nature of the demographic processes operating among the tribes. Needless to say that the demographic processes operate differently for each community depending upon a host of factors: ecological, economic, social and cultural.

The Region

The region presents the complexities of the sub-Himalayan ranges, Indo-Burmese hills of Nagaland, Manipur and

Mizoram and the eroded surface of the Meghalayan Plateau—all encircling the Brahmaputra valley. The hills are sharply marked from the plains physically as well as culturally through so linked locationally that to some extent they must be treated together (Spate and Learmonth: 1972).

The complex physiographic conditions have provided an excellent habitat for the tribes to continue with their primitive modes of economy and has fostered isolation to varying degrees to the numerous tribal groups who have curved out their little world unmindful of the turbulence in the mainland often described as the microcosm of the Indian sub-continent. The North-East is represented by all the three physiographic division of the country though on a much smaller scale—the northern mountains, the central valley and the southern plateau.

The northern mountains and the hill ranges of the indo-Burmese Border are in fact an extension of the Himalayas with modifications introduced in the erosional features by much heavier rainfall. These ranges take a sharp turn towards the south and the south-west and much of these hills are covered under heavy forest ranging from tropical evergreen in the wetter south to rough grass of the highest ridges. The Indo-Burmese hills are much less imposing as a relief feature and the ranges are aligned in north-south axis with intervening parallel ridges. The altitude of the Manipur and Naga hills varies between 900 and 2100 metres. Parts of Tripura and Imphal Valley represents areas of low relief.

Assam valley is almost a flat plain with little variation in relief. The valley consists of alluvium deposited by the mighty Brahmaputra and its numerous tributaries and provides ideal environment for the settlement of agricultural communities. The tribal population, however, finds suitable sites in isolated hill features forested portions and marshy lands within the valley. The islands within the valley for example continue their predominantly tribal character. The level of isolation for these tribes located within the valley has been less intense, they have been forced to develop some contacts with their non-tribal neighbours in close spatial proximity. Recent contacts with the non-tribal societies and the tea plantations in the hill slopes of Assam have provided new incentives under which the tribals have migrated out of their traditional homelands and have been absorbed as labour in the tea plantations. (Raza and Ahmad 1990: 39).

The southern plateau is designated as Meghalaya—the abode of clouds and is indeed a fragment of the peninsular block. Most of the plateau is highly dissected and is studded with several hill features, the most prominent of them being Garo, Khasi and Jaintia. The summit level in these hills rise upto 1300-1800 metres. While the northern face of the plateau rising from the Brahmaputra valley is more gradual, the southern face descends precipitously towards the Surma valley. In a climate characterised by congenial temperature, high humidity and excessive rainfall, forest growth is luxuriant providing suitable habitats for the tribes who practise shifting cultivation as their chief mode of economy.

Spatial Distribution

In spite of the fact that the North-Eastern region as a whole supports a very high proportion of tribal population, their spatial distribution reveals striking variation both at state and district level. The share of tribal population is the lowest in Assam where they constitutes a little over 10 per cent of the total population. On the other hand, the tribes constitutes an overwhelming majority of the population living in the states located in the Eastern Himalayas namely Arunachal Pradesh, Nagaland and Mizoram where they account for over 80 per cent of the total population. Meghalaya, located south of Brahmaputra valley and characterised by hill features associated with the plateau surface too is included in this category. The tribal population in Manipur and Tripura is substantially low—a little over a quarter—as compared to Mizoram, Nagaland, Arunachal Pradesh and Meghalaya. This indicates the generally open character of the former which has permitted a higher degree of infiltration of non-tribal groups. (Raza and Ahmad : 1990: 28).

District level patterns (Table 5.1) reveal a further accentuation in the degree of spatial variation in the distribution of tribal population. According to 1991 census counts, as many as 12 districts, mostly located in the

TABLE 5.1: **Percentage of Tribal Population**

Percentage of tribal population	1981			1991		
	T	R	U	T	R	U
Nil	—	—	5	—	—	7
< 5	3	3	5	8	8	22
5 - 10	—	—	2	4	4	2
10 - 20	—	—	1	9	9	6
20 - 30	2	2	2	3	1	3
30 - 50	4	4	4	6	7	5
50 - 70	5	3	5	4	3	2
70 - 90	9	8	10	11	11	9
> 90	12	15	1	15	17	4

Brahmaputra and Barak Valley in Assam as well as in the Imphal Valley in Manipur, have a tribal population as low as 10 per cent and less. In most of the remaining districts in the Brahmaputra Valley, the tribes account for 10 to 20 per cent of the population. The tribes constitute a significant 20 to 50 per cent in whole of Tripura and Lakhimpur, Kokrajhar and Dhemaji districts of Assam and Dibang Valley, Lohit and Changlang districts of Arunachal Pradesh. In the remaining districts, most of which are hilly in character and are located in higher altitudes, the tribes constitute a clear majority. For example the Karbi and North Cachar hills in Assam support as high as 50 to 70 per cent tribal population, a situation similar to Siang district in Arunachal Pradesh. Remaining districts, all of which are located in hilly terrain contain more than 70 per cent tribes in their total population.

It is clear that the tribal population is far more concentrated in the hilly and forested areas. The river valleys as well as the Manipur basin supports much smaller proportion of tribal population. Within Brahmaputra valley the isolated hills and the marshy areas as well as the islands still retain their predominantly tribal character. Areas favourable to intensive agriculture generally support fewer tribal population.

The Brahmaputra valley represents the lowest concentration of tribal population and acts as a transition between high concentration areas lying on the north and the south. Presence of some important tribal groups in the valley makes a sharp distinction between the 'hill' and 'plain' tribes.

It is important to note that the hilly tracts of the region generally represent a very high concentration of tribal population but with a low level of agglomeration and low densities. This is primarily due to the low resource base and primitive modes of economy organised on the basis of simple technology.

Spatial Variation in Population Growth

There is a great deal of variation in the rate of growth of the tribal population when viewed in terms of spatial dimension. Even at the state level, the difference in the rate of growth of the tribal population is remarkable. During the 1981-91 decade, the tribal population in Assam registered less than 25 per cent growth. On the other hand the tribes living in the states in Indo-Burmese hills and the plateau recorded over 25 per cent growth rate. The tribal population grew at a phenomenal rate of over 40 per cent in Nagaland, closely followed by Arunachal Pradesh and Mizoram where the tribe registered a growth rate ranging between 35 to 40 per cent. The tribes in Meghalaya and Tripura experienced a growth rate of 30 to 35 per cent. The lowest growth rate of tribal population in the Indo-Burmese Border was experienced in Manipur, where the tribes recorded a growth of 25 to 30 per cent during 1981-91 decade.

Differential growth of tribal population becomes far more evident when the data are examined at a lower spatial scale i.e., the districts (Table 5.2). At the district level, a very large number of districts experienced a growth rate ranging between 20 to 40 per cent. As many as three districts in Arunachal Pradesh and two in Assam registered marginal increase to the total tribal population which was less than 20 per cent. The growth rate ranges between 20 to 40 per cent in large number of districts including two each in Manipur, Meghalaya and Tripura; six in Arunachal Pradesh and three in Assam. In the 40 to 60 per cent range are included two districts from Manipur, the remaining districts of Meghalaya, two districts

TABLE 5.2: **Growth Rate of Tribal Population (1981-91)**

Growth Rate (in %)	Number of Districts		
	Total	Rural	Urban
< (-20)	—	—	1
0 - (-20)	—	1	—
0 - 20	5	7	—
20 - 40	16	17	3
40 - 60	14	9	1
60 - 80	4	5	7
80 - 100	2	1	8
100 - 150	1	1	2
150 - 200	1	2	2
200 - 300	—	—	7
> 300	—	—	4
Nil			8

from Mizoram, four districts of Nagaland and three more districts of Assam.

It is interesting to note that only three districts experienced tribal growth rate ranging between 60 to 80 per cent. These districts are, however, highly dispersed in Manipur, Nagaland and Tripura.

Area of high tribal growth rate is confined to three districts of Manipur and one district of Nagaland. It is noteworthy that the growth rate of tribal population shows a sharp contrast in Manipur between the valley and the plateau.

Significantly the tribal population is growing at an exceedingly high rate in the urban areas indicating a process of rural to urban migration of the tribal population. However, it is also not surprising considering a greater proliferation of towns in the tribal dominated areas, wherein many hitherto large rural settlements have been designated as 'urban' by the 1991 census (Nayak *et al.* 1995).

It is evident that the tribal population is growing at a much faster rate in the hilly portion of the region compared to the plains. However, within the hilly region too, the variation in the growth rate is extremely large with some pockets experiencing high growth.

Inter-Tribal Differences in Population Growth

Spatial variation in the rate of growth of tribal population, important as it may be, conceals the specificities of growth patterns experienced by individual tribes. Complex forces are at work in determining the trends of population growth in each tribal community ranging from demographic processes of fertility, mortality and migration to socio-economic factors like their stage of development and institutional frame within which the demographic processes operate. It is not possible to go into an explanation of the inter-tribal differences in the rate of growth. The main aim of this section is to get an insight into the manner in which the tribal communities experience demographic change with regard to their size over time. The analysis, it is expected, should throw up pertinent questions pertaining to the differential demographic experiences of the tribal communities living in this region.

Before analysing the growth patterns among different tribes of the north-east, it is worth mentioning that the policy of scheduling is not based on any scientific definition of a 'tribe'. For example, the 1981 census records as many as six tribe consisting of one member in each—a situation posing philosophical difficulty in accepting the concept of one man tribe. A second problem confronted by this research refers to the gaps in data particularly in the year 1981 when no census was taken in Assam. This posed serious problem of comparability. The third problem refers to the varying number of scheduled tribes in different census periods. In order to overcome these problems, only those tribal communities have been considered who were found to be common in all the three censuses held in 1961, 1971 and 1981, and for those tribe for whom the data was readily available. As many as 111 scheduled tribes could be considered as against 162 listed in 1981, due to the difficulties mentioned above. The only limitation which could not be avoided pertains to those tribes who are far more numerous in Assam but also have a presence elsewhere in the North-East as no census was held in 1981 in Assam. The growth rate of these tribes was certainly negatively affected as the few of them present in Assam could not be included. In spite of the limitation, the analysis is undertaken as the impact of these limitations have been restricted by excluding many groups in the analysis who are likely to be affected more.

It may be safely stated, however, that the tribal communities are experiencing strikingly different rates of growth in diverse areas of the region. A study of the size of the tribal communities in the North-East reveals that a very large proportion of such groups are extremely small in terms of their population size. (Table 5.3) It is interesting that over one third of all the tribal groups considered for the study have a population size of less than 1,000 persons each. Interestingly, this proportion remains constant over time which is a sufficient indication of the stagnation of their size or even a decline in their population size over time. That the number of tribes with a population size of over 10,000 persons each shows an increase in successive periods of census counts is indicative of

TABLE 5.3: **Number of Common Tribes According to Size-Classes**

Population Size	1961	1971	1981
Above 300,000	2	3	5
100,000 - 300,000	6	5	—
50,000 - 100,000	2	4	6
20,000 - 50,000	11	16	13
10,000 - 20,000	11	11	8
5,000 - 10,000	12	11	17
1,000 - 5,000	31	27	24
500 - 1,000	14	13	13
200 - 500	8	5	4
50 - 200	8	9	10
10 - 50	.1	4	7
2 - 10	4	2	4
1 member	1	1	—
Total	111	111	111

the fact that the tribes having greater numerical strength are the ones experiencing fast increase to their population size.

This conclusion is further reinforced by a reference to the relative rank of the 111 tribes in relation to their numerical strength. There is little change in the relative rank of the tribes with a population size of over three lakhs, namely the Khasi-Jaintias, the Nagas, the Mizos, the Garos or the Riangs, the Nissis, the Mao and the Chakmas having a population size of 50,000 to 100,000 persons each. It is also interesting that many numerically small tribes, with a few exceptions witness dramatic improvements in their ranks indicating faster growth. The study of the relative ranks of tribes according to their population size reveals faster increases on both extremes—the larger as well as extremely small tribes.

A perusal of data in Appendix-I shows that as many as 13 tribes mostly belonging to the numerically small sizes recorded a net and continuous decline in their population over 1961-81 period. Notable among them are Dimasas, Ashing, Dafla, Khambas, Kongbos, Longsang, Miniyongs and Morang—most of whom are found in Arunachal Himalayas and the foothills. On the other hand, 48 more tribes have been registering a continuous rise in their population over the period of the study. Most of these tribes are numerically large enough and are the dominant tribes in each state of the north-east. However, interestingly enough, some of the numerically small tribes too have significantly added to their population. Some of these tribes are: Pawi, Aimol, Anal, Chiru, Kom, Mariang, Moyon, Paite, Simte, Munda, Orang, Santal, Khowa, Bokars etc.

In large number of tribes numbering 50, the trends of population growth, however, is highly fluctuating. As many as 30 tribes show an increase upto 1971 and then declined in the following decade. Notable among them are the Chothe, Kabui, Paite, Abor, Synteng, Hill Miris, Nishang etc. On the other hand, as many as 20 tribes showed a decline in their population in the earlier decade, but picked up a momentum of growth during 1971-81 decade. These include the tribal communities of Hajong, Bhutia, Longris, Pangis, Boris etc.

Some of these changes in population size may be administrative in nature and may flow from their identification as a tribe during census counts. But, much of the change may be occurring due to dynamics of demographic processes involving differential birth and death rates as well as migration. These are some of the issues needing urgent attention. Moreover, demographic processes do not operate in a vaccum; they need to be viewed in the context of spatial, ecological, economic and other socio-cultural institutional frames. Such information would be extremely beneficial in truely capturing the dynamics of tribal demographic scene as is unfolding itself in the north-east in modern times arising out of greater contacts with the outside world and renewed aspirations of the tribal people in the changed socio-economic order to which the tribal segment in North-East is increasingly subjected to.

Some of the findings are only preliminary in nature and further research is necessary at this stage. Most of the questions arising out of these findings can only be answered through intensive field based investigations to be conducted among selected tribes in order to get deeper insights into the ecological, economic, demographic and socio-cultural factors contributing to differential growth patterns.

REFERENCES

Ahmad, A. (1983), "Education of the Scheduled Tribe: Some Aspect of Inequality", *Workshop on Indicators of Equity in Education*, Oct. 24-28, NIEPA, New Delhi.

Barkataki, S. (1969), *Tribes in Assam*, National Book Trust, New Delhi.

Bose, N.K. (1971), *Tribal Life in India*, National Book Trust, New Delhi.

Census of India (1961), *General Population Tables*, Vol. XXII, Manipur, Part II-A.

Census of India (1961), *Cultural and Migration Tables*, Vol. XXII, Nagaland, Part II-A.

Census of India (1961), *General Population Tables and NEFA Special Tables*, Vol. XXIV, NEFA, Part II-A.

Census of India (1961), *District Census Handbook*, Vol. XXVI, Tripura, Section I.

Census of India (1961), *Special Tables for SC and ST*, Vol. XXII, Manipur, Part V.

Census of India (1961), *Special Tables for SC and ST*, Vol. III, Assam, Part V-A.

Census of India (1961), *Special Tables on SC and ST*, Vol. XXIV, NEFA, Part V-A.

Census of India (1961), *Special Tables for SC and ST*, Vol. XXVI, Tripura, Part V-A.

Census of India (1961), *Special Tables for ST*, Vol. I, India, Part V-A (ii).

Census of India (1971), *General Population Tables*, Series-3, Assam, Part II-A.

Census of India (1971), *General Population Tables*, Meghalaya, Series 13, Part II-A.

Census of India (1971), *General Report*, Arunachal Pradesh, Series 24, Part I-A.

Census of India (1971), *Primary Census Abstract*, Mizoram, General Population Tables, Part B.

Census of India (1971), *General Population Tables*, Nagaland, Series 15, Part II-B.

Census of India (1971), *General Population Tables*, Tripura, Series 20, Part II-A.

Census of India (1971), *Special Tables on Scheduled Tribes*, Nagaland, Series 15, Part V-A.

Census of India (1971), *Special Tables for SC and ST*, Tripura, Series 20, Part V-A.

Census of India (1971), *Special Tables for SC and ST*, Arunachal Pradesh, Series 24, Part V-A.

Census of India (1971), *Town and Village Directory and Primary Census Abstract*, Manipur, Series 12, Part X A & B.

Census of India (1981), *General Population Tables and Primary Census Abstract*, Meghalaya, Series 14, Part II-A & B.

Census of India (1981), *General Population Tables and Primary Census Abstract*, Arunachal Pradesh, Series 25, Part II-A & B.

Census of India (1981), *General Population Tables*, Nagaland, Series 15, Part II-A.

Census of India (1981), *Primary Census Abstract*, India Series 1, Part II-B (iii).

Census of India (1981), *Primary Census Abstract*, India Series 1, Part II-B (iii)

Census of India (1981), *Primary Census Abstract*, Mizoram Series 31, Part II-B.

Deptt. of Economics & Statistics (1969), *Statistical Hand Book of Assam*, Shillong.

Dir. of Economics & Statistics (1989), *Statistical Abstract of Manipur*, Govt. of Manipur, Imphal.

Ministry of Home Affairs, GOI (1978), 'Areas of Tribal Concentration in India', *Background Papers on Tribal Sub-Plan*, No. 2, New Delhi.

Nayak, D.K. (1990), "Social Perspectives on Hill Area Development" in R.K. Rai *et al.* (ed.) *Hill Area Development*, GSNEHR, Shillong.

Nayak, D.K. *et al.* (1995), "Pattern of Urbanisation in the North East" in J.B. Ganguly (ed.) *Urbanisation and Development in North East India*.

Raza, Moonis *et al.* (1977), *Tribal Population of India: Spatial Pattern of Clusturing and Concentration*, Occational Paper No. 5, CSRD, JNU, New Delhi.

Raza, Moonis and A. Ahmed (1978), *General Geography of India*, NCERT New Delhi.

Raza, Moonis and A. Ahmed (1990), *An Atlas of Tribal India*, Concept Publishing Company, New Delhi.

Roy Burman, B.K. (1966), 'Structure of Bridge and Buffer Communities in the Border Areas', *Man in India*, Vol. XLVI (2).

Roy Burman, B.K. (1970), *Demographic and Socio-Economic Profile of the Hill Areas of North East India*, Census of India 1961 New Delhi.

Roy Burman, B.K. (1972), "Distribution of the Scheduled Tribe of India: An Explanatory Geo-Cultural Apprisal" in A Chandra Shekhar (ed.) *Economic and Socio-Cultural Dimensions of Regionalisation*, Census Centenary Monograph, No. 7, New Delhi.

Roy Burman, B.K. (1972), 'Tribal Demography—A Preliminary Appraisal" in K.S. Singh (ed.), *Tribal Situation in India*, Simla, Indian Institute of Advanced Study.

Singh, K.S. (1972) (ed.), *Tribal Situation in India*, Simla, Indian Institute of Advanced Study.

Spate, O.H.K. and A.T.A. Learmonth (1972), *India and Pakistan*, BI Publication, New Delhi.

Subbarao, B. (1958), *The Personality of India*, Baroda Univ. of Baroda, 2nd edition.

Vidyarthi, L.P. (1974), "Tribal Development in Independent India and its Future", *Man in India* LIV (1).

Waddel, L.A. (1975), *Tribes of the Brahmaputra Valley: A Contribution on Their Physical Types and Affinities*, Delhi: Sanskaran Prakashan.

APPENDIX-I

GROWTH RATE OF COMMON TRIBES

Sl.No.	Name of the tribes	Growth Rate		
		1961-71	1971-81	1961-81
(i)	(ii)	(iii)	(iv)	(v)
1.	Chakma	23.33	45.36	79.27
2.	Deori	85.67	-69.76	-43.86
3.	Dimasa	-43.49	-96.59	-98.07
4.	Garo	26.87	21.89	56.85
5.	Hajong	-11.95	22.39	7.76
6.	Hmar	52.41	4.71	59.60
7.	Kachari	14.34	96.45	-96.96
8.	Khasi-Jaintia	30.09	35.57	76.37
9.	Any Kuki tribe	34.30	4.53	40.38
10.	Lakher	46.41	30.10	90.48
11.	Man	281.03	-30.71	164.03
12.	Mikir	51.45	-95.02	-92.46
13.	Miri	56.10	-98.42	-97.54
14.	Any Mizo tribe	16.47	41.86	65.22
15.	Any Naga tribe	31.34	43.05	101.02
16.	Pawi	350.60	11.54	402.59
17.	Aimol	674.07	122.73	1624.07
18.	Anal	37.02	40.13	92.01
19.	Angami	-88.92	710.00	-10.28
20.	Chiru	14.09	34.40	53.34
21.	Chothe	84.06	-11.50	62.90

(Contd.)

Appendix-I (*Contd.*)

(i)	(ii)	(iii)	(iv)	(v)
22.	Gangte	29.88	26.26	63.98
23.	Kabui	37.78	-35.40	-10.99
24.	Kacha Naga	33.82	-2.09	31.03
25.	Kairao	299.01	-584.17	126.35
26.	Kom	19.59	50.06	79.46
27.	Lamgang	40.51	31.69	85.05
28.	Mao	15.86	51.93	76.03
29.	Maram	-7.89	137.39	26.54
30.	Mariang	26.86	21.21	53.76
31.	Monsang	-30.70	22.47	-15.13
32.	Moyon	110.20	20.37	153.01
33.	Paite	45.37	96.12	81.81
34.	Ralte	92.50	29.87	35.00
35.	Simte	48.23	20.52	78.64
36.	Tangkhul	31.65	36.78	80.07
37.	Thadou	24.92	-5.81	17.66
38.	Vaiphut	50.30	25.26	88.27
39.	Zou	48.79	25.01	86.01
40.	Sema	-25.00	733.33	525.00
41.	Bhil	144.93	395.86	1114.49
42.	Bhutia	-66.67	633.33	144.44
43.	Halam	17.05	51.87	77.75
44.	Jamatia	40.37	30.15	82.69
45.	Lepcha	100.00	657.14	1414.29
46.	Mag	26.12	37.35	73.22
47.	Munda	21.27	49.49	81.29
48.	Noatia	35.68	-30.25	-55.14
49.	Orang	19.23	52.19	81.46
50.	Riang	14.36	29.78	48.42
51.	Santal	42.25	22.68	74.52
52.	Tripuri	32.01	32.06	74.33

Appendix-I (*Contd.*)

(i)	(ii)	(iii)	(iv)	(v)
53.	Uchai	38.51	23.09	70.50
54.	Abor	11225.00	-98.23	2000.00
55.	Aka	4.55	25.71	31.43
56.	Gallong	29.48	-6.00	21.71
57.	Khowa	70200.00	-11.10	62400.00
58.	Momba	1.76	7.76	9.66
59.	Synteng	1332.61	-95.60	-36.96
60.	Apatanis	19.41	28.64	53.61
61.	Ashing	-17.33	-93.12	-94.31
62.	Bangris	50.76	42.92	115.47
63.	Bangros	-34.52	-9.31	-40.62
64.	Bogum	-58.40	-92.39	-96.83
65.	Bokar	13.75	24.04	41.10
66.	Boris	-95.75	2314.10	2.62
67.	But Monpa	19.10	-37.30	-25.32
68.	Dafla	-62.20	-98.94	-99.60
69.	Dirang Monpa	-70.18	109.73	-37.45
70.	Havis Tangsa	20.10	-45.06	-34.02
71.	Hill Miris	234.73	-15.15	184.03
72.	Idu Mishmi	15.19	5.30	21.29
73.	Karkas	37.09	-99.91	-99.87
74.	Kemsing Tangsa	42.18	-67.01	-53.10
75.	Khambas	-23.60	-59.67	-69.19
76.	Khamiyang	-65.06	2700.00	878.31
77.	Khampti	59.86	51.54	142.26
78.	Kroding Bangris	-99.77	2100.00	-94.91
79.	Komkars	-58.99	1416.44	521.91
80.	Kongbos	-43.69	-98.67	-99.25
81.	Lish Monpa	17.66	49.81	76.27
82.	Longchang T.	-96.56	3980.95	40.26
83.	Longphis T.	-16.13	10.90	-6.99

Appendix-I (*Contd.*)

(i)	(ii)	(iii)	(iv)	(v)
84.	Longris T.	-65.72	16.54	-60.05
85.	Longsang	-62.04	-92.00	-96.96
86.	Miju/Ramam	8.17	-99.96	-99.96
87.	Milang	6.88	-71.98	-70.06
88.	Miniyong	-1.93	-81.33	-81.69
89.	Moglum Tangsa	-47.93	29.00	-32.83
90.	Monpas	331.19	-7.29	299.76
91.	Morang	-86.47	-25.20	-89.88
92.	Mossang	0.08	6.68	6.76
93.	Nishang	260.34	-43.78	102.56
94.	Nissis	126.23	65.98	275.49
95.	Noctes	20.11	-15.37	1.65
96.	Padams	41.16	-32.00	-4.01
97.	Pailibos	65.28	-55.04	-25.69
98.	Pangis	-89.16	122.09	-75.93
99.	Pasis	5.65	-66.67	-141.90
100.	Ramos	-3.11	24.89	21.01
101.	Rongrang T.	79.93	-51.49	-12.71
102.	Sherdukpen	43.27	27.94	83.30
103.	Singphos	63.74	50.10	145.77
104.	Sulung	180.34	-0.54	178.83
105.	Tagens	-15.29	33.10	12.75
106.	Tanggams	-66.93	-83.33	-94.49
107.	Tangsa	5988.60	42.57	8580.70
108.	Wanchos	22.53	13.23	38.74
109.	Yobins	18.95	-99.46	99.36
110.	Yongkuks	-59.72	103.45	-18.06
111.	Koireng	-13.75	106.77	78.34

Note : Initial 'T' stands for 'Tangsa'.

6

TRENDS OF POPULATION GROWTH IN NORTH EAST REGION OF INDIA

N.N. BHATTACHARYYA

The North East Region of India, stretching between 22°N and 29°5'N latitudes and between 89°70'E and 97°30'E longitudes covers a total geographical area of 225,083 square kilometres. The region supports 31.38 million according to 1991 census. Thus the Region accounts for 7.7 per cent of the total land surface of India and contains about 4 per cent of the total population. The North-Eastern region is landlocked and sandwiched between foreign countries of China, Myanmar, Bangladesh and Bhutan. The region is connected with the mainland by a narrow corridor of foothill. The corridor is subjected to occasional disruptions due to heavy rain and floods. Thus the geographical location of the region has been responsible for its isolation.

But in spite of its geographical isolation, early men of different ethnic stocks having diverse socio-cultural backgrounds entered into the region from different directions at different stages and made the region as their permanent abode. The Austro-Asiatic linguistic groups are believed to be the earliest settlers of North East India. They were followed by the Mongoloids who linguistically belonged to the Tibeto-Burman group. While the migration of the Mongoloids to this region was a continuous process, there came also the Caucasoids or Aryans from the western route along the valleys of the Ganga and the Brahmaputra. Another group of migrants belonging to the Siamese-Chinese branch came to this region from the Shan

Plateau in the thirteenth century. During the pre-Independence and the post-Independence periods, a large number of people belonging to various ethno-linguistic and religious groups have come to this region from other parts of India, Bangladesh and Nepal. The immigrants of the post-Independence period have created many socio-economic problems besides disturbing the original ethnic structure and socio-cultural scenario of the region.

Since Independence, the political map of the North East Region has undergone many changes and its present seven states, namely Arunachal Pradesh, Assam, Manipur, Meghalaya, Mizoram, Nagaland and Tripura have been formed from the erstwhile composite of Assam, princely states of Manipur and Tripura. The population data of the last 90 years of all these states are not available. The population from 1901 to 1991 of the region and the states is shown in Table 6.1.

It may be seen from the table that the population figures for Arunachal Pradesh are available only from 1961 onwards. Since 1901 onwards, the population of the North Eastern states increased gradually (1901-41). But from 1951 onwards the rate of increase was higher. The high rate of increase is primarily due to the influx of the immigrants from inside and outside of India. The increase of population during the last four decades is tremendous and this rise in population figure in the region is attributed to both natural increase and immigration. It is observed that during each decade approximately 5 million people have been added to the population of the region.

The most important aspect of the population trend of the region is the marked differences in spatial growth. For instance the population of Assam has increased by 7 times from 3.3. million in 1901 to 22.4 million in 1991. During the same period the population of Manipur grew by 6 times from 3 lakhs to 18 lakhs. The growth rate of Tripura was 13 times followed by Nagaland (12 times) and Mizoram (7 times) during 1901-91. Districtwise the highest growth rate was recorded during the last decade (1981-91) by Dhemaji district, Assam (104.62 %), followed by North Cachar Hills (96.39 %), Karbi Anglong (72.79 %), Tuensang, Nagaland (69.9 %), Kohima (65.1 %), Kokrajhar (75.94 %) and Kamrup (64.69 %). The only district where the growth rate during the same period is below the

TABLE 6.1: **Population of North Eastern Region (1901-91)**

Census Year	Arunachal Pradesh	Assam	Manipur	Meghalaya	Mizoram	Nagaland	Tripura	North East Region
1901	—	3290	284	341	82	102	173	4272
1911	—	3849	346	394	91	149	230	5059
1921	—	4637	384	422	98	159	304	6004
1931	—	5560	446	481	123	179	382	7172
1941	—	6695	512	556	153	190	513	8619
1951	—	8029	578	606	198	213	639	10281
1961	337	10837	780	769	266	369	1142	14500
1971	468	14625	1073	1012	332	516	1556	19582
1981	632	19897	1421	1336	494	775	2053	26608
1991	865	22414	1837	1775	690	1209	2757	31547

Source: Census of India 1991: Final Population Total: Brief Analysis of Primary Census Abstract, Paper 2 of 1992.

national average was East Kameng (17.55 %).

There has been a declining trend in the general growth of population in the region particularly in Assam. The decadal growth of population in Assam during 1951-61 was 34.98 per cent which declined to 34.95 per cent in the next decade (1961-71). The growth of population in Assam in the following two decades i.e. 1971-91 was registered as 53.26 per cent accounting for 26.63 per cent per decade. This showed a further decline in the growth of population in Assam. Thus the annual growth rate of population in Assam was 2.17 per cent as against India's 2.14 which was higher by .03 per cent only. Though the rate of growth of population of Assam is higher than that of National growth rate, it is the lowest among the states of North East India. The highest decadal growth rate of population was recorded for Nagaland i.e. 56.08 per cent, followed by Mizoram (39.70%), Arunachal Pradesh (36.83%), Tripura (34.40%), Meghalaya (32.86%) and Manipur (29.29%).

It is to be noted that both birth and death rates are also declining in the region. For example rural birth and death rates of Arunachal Pradesh were 3.68 per cent and 1.98 per cent respectively for the year 1971 and the same declined to 3.63 per cent and 1.51 per cent in 1989. Similarly, the rural birth and death rates for Assam were 3.93 per cent and 1.87 per cent in 1971 and 3.0 per cent and 1.06 per cent in 1989. These rates were lower than the all India rates which were 3.89 per cent and 1.64 per cent in 1971 and 3.22 per cent and 1.11 per cent in 1989. Since the natural growth rate of population is lower than that of all India rates, the overall growth of population in the region must be mainly attributed to immigration. The immigrants and their descendands who are the main cause of the rapid increase of population in the region may be grouped into 6 categories: East Bengal Muslim Agricultural Immigrants, East Bengal Hindu Refugees, Tea Garden Labourers, Nepalis, Rajasthani Traders and North Indian Wage Labour Immigrants.

The East Bengal Muslim Agricultural Immigrants are mostly illiterate, landless poor peasants and they are seen to have occupied mainly the uncultivated *charlands* of the Brahmaputra valley. After the partition in 1947, owing to discrimination against the religious minorities by the Muslim rulers in the then East Pakistan, there resulted in a large scale migration of Bengalee Hindus from that country mostly to the North East Region. This group of immigrants mostly settle in urban and semi-urban areas of the region. They are engaged in retail trade and unskilled jobs.

The tea garden and ex-tea garden labourers which form another sizeable category of the immigrants are descendants of the aboriginal tribes who came to this region from Bihar, Orissa and Madhya Pradesh.

The Nepali Hindus came to this region during the British period of Indian history as soldiers, policemen, sentries, graziers, farmers and wood cutters.

Almost all the Rajasthani settlers of the region are form the business and trading community of Rajasthan. The entire business in wholesale trades in food stuff and consumer goods including construction materials are handled by this immigrant group.

The North Indian wage labourer immigrants are mainly engaged in laundering, scavenging, cobblering, construction works etc. and they are mostly settled in urban and semi-urban areas of the region.

During the war of liberation of Bangladesh in 1971 a total of 10,00,000 refugees took shelter in Assam alone. While many of them returned to their native places following the liberation of Bangladesh, about 100,000 of them are believed to have stayed back in Assam. This has now been a never-ending process and its effects have led to the change of demographic and settlement pattern of the whole region. Thus the trans-border migration into the region remains unchecked and the population control has, therefore, become meaningless.

The rapid growth of population due to natural increase and migration has affected the socio-economic and political life of the people of the region. It has adversely affected demographic as well as socio-economic character of the whole region. The high dependency ratio and growing imbalance in sex ratio in all the states are the result of population growth. Fresh immigrants have created many socio-economic problems besides disturbing the original ethnic structure. They not only encroach upon the *charlands*, forest lands, railway colonies, government lands, etc. but they also commit several acts of lawlessness creating tensions among the original settlers according to media reports.

The unabated influx of immigrants has caused the demographic imbalance in the whole region due to population pressure on land and lowering labourer rates. There is no chance for balancing between the rate of population growth and the pace of economic development in the region. Hence, the whole region remains economically backward. This economic backwardness might be the cause of insurgency movements in various states in the region. It is solving the problems out of the unchecked growth of population due to both the natural increase and immigration, that the insurgency movement could be lessened in this sensitive region. Some constitutional measures will also have to be adopted to remove a sense of alienation in the minds of people living in the region and their constitutional aspiration should also be encouraged.

REFERENCES

Basic Statistics of North Eastern Region, 1987, North Eastern Council Secretariat, Shillong.

Census of India, 1991, Series-1, India.

Census of India, 1991, Series-4, Assam.

Bhattacharyya, N.N., 1991, "The Contemporary Geopolitical Problems of North East India" in *North-Eastern Geographer*, Vol. 23, No. 1 & 2.

Sharma, P.C., 1995, "Harness Brahmaputra for Survival of N.E. Region" in *The Assam Tribune*, 12th June, 1995.

7

GROWTH OF POPULATION AND ENVIRONMENTAL PROBLEMS IN THE URBAN AREAS OF NORTH EAST INDIA

PRANAY JYOTI GOSWAMI

Introduction

A careful analysis of the population pattern of North East India since 1901 reveals that the population of this region has been increasing at a rapid rate more particularly since partition of undivided India in 1947. The population of this region in 1901 was 42.7 lakh but in 1941 it became 86.2 lakh. During planning period (1951-91) the population of North Eastern region has increased about three times (Table 7.1). According to 1991 census the population of North East India was 31,547,314 out of which 4,382,005 lived in urban areas is 13.89 per cent of the total population in North East lived in urban areas as against 26.13 per cent for the country as a whole.

In spite of the fact that North Eastern region is still the least urbanised areas within the country, the urban population in this region is increasing at a much higher rate as compared with the country as a whole. Table 7.2 shows the growth rate of urban population in this region since 1901. The number of towns in MER had increased to 101 in 1971 from 30 in 1951. According to 1991 census there are 183 towns in this region. The number of class I city in this region has increased to eight in 1991 from only one in 1951.

As a result of rapid growth of population and migration of

TABLE 7.1: **Population Trends in North Eastern Region**

(Thousand persons)

Census Year	Arunachal Pradesh	Assam	Manipur	Meghalaya	Mizoram	Nagaland	Tripura	North East
1901	—	3,290	284	341	82	102	173	4,272
1911	—	3,849	346	394	91	149	230	5,059
1921	—	4,637	384	422	98	159	304	6,004
1931	—	5,560	446	481	124	179	382	7,172
1941	—	6,695	512	556	153	190	513	8,619
1951	—	8,029	578	606	196	213	639	10,261
1961	337	10,837	780	769	266	369	1,142	14,500
1971	468	14,625	1,073	1,012	332	516	1,556	19,582
1981	632	18,041 @	1,421	1,336	494	775	2,053	24,752 @
1991	865	22,414	1,837	1,775	690	1,210	2,757	31,548 *

@ The 1981 Census could not be held in Assam. The population figures of 1981 for Assam have been worked out by interpolation.

* The 1991 Census could not be held in Jammu & Kashmir. The projected population figure for Jammu & Kashmir is included.

Source: Census of India 1991-1, Paper -2 of 1992. Final Population Totals and Basic Statistics of NER, 1995, Shillong.

TABLE 7.2: **Per cent Decadal Variation of Population 1901-11 to 1981-91 (Urban Area)**

States	1901-11	1911-21	1921-31	1931-41	1941-51	1951-61	1961-71	1971-81	1981-91
Arunachal Pradesh	—	—	—	—	—	—	—	+139.63	+167.04
Assam	+20.55	+36.80	+27.58	+28.30	+65.73	+126.57	+65.01	+58.79	39.58
Manipur	+3.34	+7.17	+7.25	+16.21	-97.13	+2226.07	+108.95	+165.36	+34.67
Meghalaya	+41.76	+26.13	+54.25	+43.93	+53.20	+100.78	+25.27	+63.98	+36.76
Mizoram	—	—	—	—	—	+105.14	164.85	+222.61	+161.01
Nagaland	-21.66	+15.15	-1.11	+27.11	+17.62	+364.41	+168.28	+133.95	+73.18
Tripura	+6.48	+13.35	+23.72	+84.69	+140.74	+141.81	+57.64	+38.93	+86.69
All India	+.35	+8.27	+19.12	+31.97	+41.43	+26.41	+38.23	+46.14	+36.47

Source: Basic Statistics of North Eastern Region, 1995, NEC, Shillong.

rural people in urban areas for employment, education and business, poverty, inequalities of income and wealth, our urban environment has been changing and deteriorating rapidly during the last few decades. Though the problem is not so acute as in the Ganga Valley, however, the problem is to be taken seriously and sincerely with purposeful action plans before it is too late when remedial measures will have no effect at all.

Objectives of the Study

The present chapter aims to throw light on the effect of population growth on environment in the urban areas of North Eastern region with special reference to water, air and sound.

Water Pollution and Problem of Potable Water

As a result of rapid growth of population in urban areas and unplanned development of towns, there arises health and sanitation problems in our urban life. There are no proper drainage system in most of the towns of north eastern region. It is a common sight to see that after rainfall roadside drain water run over the street and residence of the people thereby causes health and hygenic problem.

Water pollution can occur in the cities by contamination of underground water pipes due to bad maintenance. The overflow of water from the open sewers comes in contact with water source like wells, ponds, underground tubewells etc. pollutes the source itself. Infrequent eruption of epidemics like cholera, typhoid, diarrhoea, malaria which claim a heavy toll every year is caused by drinking of unsafe water. During dry season stagnant drain water acts as a breeding ground of agents of diseases like flies, mosquitos etc.

It is known to all that the Brahmaputra and the Barak are two important rivers in North East India. Assam Pollution Control Board (APCB), Guwahati studied the Brahmaputra river system (Indian part) and the Barak (a stretch of 12 km flowing by the side of Silchar town). The study of the Brahmaputra reveals that apart from containing very little amount of inorganic/organic pollutants, the river shows itself high degree of bacteriological pollutants [1] All throughout the year and in almost the entire course of Brahmaputra (from Dibrugarh to Jogighopa, about 450 km), the water quality has been contaminated by total Coli-forms and fecal coliforms.[2] It may be mentioned here that effluent of Jogighopa Paper Mill were directly drained to the river Brahmaputra. The Nagaland Paper Mill, Jagiroad Paper Mill, Kamrup Paper Mill, Indian Carbon. Assam Carbon, Bokajan Cement Factory, Dimapur Sugar Mill etc. are discharging their effluent in the tributaries of the Brahmaputra or the Brahmaputra thereby polluting the greatest water resources of Assam as well as of North East India.[3] The study on Barak also reveals that this river stretch is highly polluted inorganically, organically and bacteriologically due to the 'assimilation of raw sewage and waste water and other pollutants like garbage and commercial solid waste.[4] Consequent upon the dissolve of effluents and toxic chemicals of H P C, Panchgram in the river Barak, water turns blackish tinge (from Panchgram to the down stream) during dry season. The poor people are bearing heavy toll by drinking unsafe water. There is an urgent need of scientific study to measure the magnitude of pollution and its adverse effect on aquatic life.

There is also a shortage of potable water in most of the urban areas of North East India. A waking group of NEC[5] observed that except for two urban centres Guwahati and Karimganj out of 22 selected towns of NER which had excess water supply in 1981, the remaining towns were deficit in this critical urban service. The extent of gap ranged from a low of 5.69 gpcd (in Silchar) and 6.02 gpcd (in Jorhat) to a maximum of 34.72 gpcd (in Tinsukia), 34.16 gpcd (in Agartala) and 33.86 gpcd (in Shillong). The total water supply gap was maximum in Shillong (5.92 MGD). This situation has not been changed much even after thirteen years of the publication of this report. The problem of potable water is more acute in slum areas where about 80 per cent of the people do not have house connection. Most of the slum dwellers are more likely to rely directly on rivers, lake and unprotected shallow wells for their water needs and are least able to bear the cost of simple preventive measures such as boiling water to make it safe for drinking.

Air Pollution

Air pollution is one of the major problems. It is caused by moving and point sources. Moving sources are represented by automobiles, ships, aircrafts and rockets. Industries and thermal power plants are example of point sources of air pollution.

The burning fossil produces oxides of sulphur, nitrogen, Carbon-di-oxide, Carbon mono-oxide and a complex mixture of organic compounds along with particulate matters (SPM) and SO_2. Air pollution is responsible for creating problems of poor visibility and respiratory diseases particularly in children and elderly persons.[6]

In North East India main factor responsible for air pollution is motor vehicle exhausts, factories using coal as fuel. There is an unprecedented growth of motor vehicles in the North Eastern region during last decade. Table 7.3 reveals that from 1985 to 1991, the number of registered motor vehicles has increased about four and half times in North Eastern states.

There is very limited road network in most of the towns of North East. So, vehicles are plying through one or two main roads thereby causing local air pollution by discharging smokes. As the roads are not being well metalled, the moving vehicles raise dust particles which creates nasal and respiratory problems to the passerby.

Assam Pollution Control Board has conducted some surveys in some important cities like Guwahati, Silchar etc. The survey of Silchar reveals that contents of Sulphur dioxide and oxide of nitrogen have not exceeded the limits of National Ambient Air Quality Standards. But SPM is much higher than the limits in consideration to limits fixed for residential and sensitive areas.[7] A survey conducted in Guwahati city also reveals that there is an increasing trend of air pollutions. The contents of oxides of nitrogen have crossed their limits at Dispur, Khanapara and Noonmati during premonsoon and Dharapur and Fatasil Ambari during monsoon.[8] Some industries e.g. Digboi refinery, different paper mills, Namrup Fertiliser Industry are also responsible for local air pollution. Unscientific and defective garbage management also aggravates the problem in certain areas.

TABLE 7.3: Number of Registered Vehicles NER, 1985-91

	Tripura	Arunachal Pradesh	Assam	Manipur	Meghalaya	Mizoram	Nagaland
All vehicles (as on 31.03.85)	9346	502	80,812	10,551	285	3,989	2,934
All vehicles (as on 31.03.91)	21,044	5,830	2,83,552	46,668	31,620	15,771	64,437

Total No. of vehicles in NER on 31.03.85 was 1,08,419 and on 31.03.91 it was 4,68,922.

Source: Basic Statistics of NER-1987 and 1991.

Noise Pollution

The main causes of noise pollution in many cities of North East India is unplanned roads and unscientific traffic. Most of the drivers of North East are untrained and many of them use vaccum horn in unjustified way. The use of vaccum horn may cause damage to a baby's eardrum and blood pressure of old persons.

Sometimes activities of ONGC at the drill sites creates unhealthy environment and noise level sometimes go beyond the limit of tolerance.[9] Use of heavy machinery in coal fields (like Namdang Ledo of Upper Assam) is also responsible for noise pollution.

A Case Study

The author studied the environmental problem of Silchar town in 1995. The main findings of his study are given below:

1. There is a shortage of potable water in Silchar town. There is only one water treatment plant with 5 mega gallon capacity. But as per national norm[10] there is need of 18.04 lakh gallons water within municipal areas and 32.9 lakh gallon within master plan area in 1991. In September, 1991, there were water tap connection in 7725 holdings and 542 street water hydrants.[11]
2. The river Barak receives more than 8000 kilo liters of urban waste water and sewage daily in addition to other household and commercial garbage.[12] As there is only one public latrine and urinal[13] in municipality area the poor people and tourists generally use river side for excretory purposes.
3. There is also the problem of air pollution and noise pollution[14] in the city (Appendix-A).
4. The author visited a slum area (Kalibari char) where 95 per cent of the people neither have house water connection nor latrine. They use river bank for excretory purposes. There is no proper drainage system

and garbage management. Even dwelling houses are not conducive for health and hygiene. The problem of pollution is the maximum in this slum area.

Conclusion

From the forgoing analysis it is clear that there must be multi-dimensional attack to control pollution. Following suggestions are put forward to improve our deteriorating environment:

(i) Control of rapid growth of population.

(ii) Environmental education may go a long way in regaining the health and vigour of corpus of environment. Environmental education may be catered to the students from primary to post graduate level through formal education. The common man may be educated through eco-development camp, theatre, posters, mela, radio, T.V., newspaper and magazine.

(iii) Improvement of bio-technology can also help to solve environmental health by creating eco-friendly micro organism.

(iv) The pollution-creating industries can minimise pollution by using pollution control devices.

(v) It is known to us that poverty is the cause as well as the effect of degraded environment. Thus the eradication of poverty and inequalities of income and wealth is the precondition for healthy environment.

(vi) Above all social participation and moral education can also go a long way to minimise pollution.

(vii) There is urgent need for proper drainage facilities and adequate supply of potable water.

(viii) People should be encouraged to take social forestry.

(ix) Publications highlighting the benefits of environmental protection should be widely circulated among the people.

The list presented above is not exhaustive, but only indicates an approach. A comprehensive planning both at the micro- and macro levels is the need of the hour.

To conclude, I like to quote a line of Gandhiji who once said, "The earth provides enough to satisfy every man's need but not for every man's greed."

NOTES

1. Assam Pollution Control Board (APCB), Assam; *Environmental Bulletin*, Vol. V, July/September, 1995.
2. APCB, Assam; *Environment Bulletin*, January-June, 1991, No. 1.
3. Hazarika, Arup Kumar, Environmental Pollution with special reference to air and water pollution in North Eastern Region (paper submitted in NEICSSR, Shillong in a seminar held on 5th June, 1993).
4. Report of Assam Pollution Control Board, Silchar.
5. Telang, D.W., Urbanisation situation in the North East and proposed strategy (in the *Journal of the NEC*, April-Sept. 1990, Vol. IX, No. 2 & 3).
6. NCERT (1991); *Population Education: A National Source Book* (Vol. I), Page 163.
7. APCB, Assam; *News letter*, Vol. V, July-Sept., 1995, No. 3.
8. APCB, Assam; *News letter*, Vol. IV, No. 4, Oct.-Dec., 1994.
9. APCB, Assam; *News letter*,January-March, 1994.
10. Kurap, K. Balachandra; Water, Sanitation and Health in *Yojana*; March 31, 1994, Page-13.
    (According to Govt. of India's guideline in urban area supply of water should be 70 litres per day per person).
11. Collected from Silchar Municipality.
12. Report of APCB, Silchar.
13. Collected from Silchar Municipality.
14. Regarding noise pollution please see Appendix-A.

APPENDIX-A

	Station	Duration	Result
1.	Rangirkhari (Near Netaji Statue)	10-15 am to 10-20 am	90 dB
2.	Sonai Road Bus Stop	10-25 am to 10-30 am	90 dB
3.	Rangirkhari Bus Stop	10-32 am to 10-37 am	87 dB
4.	Hospital Road (outside Hospital)	10-40 am to 10-45 am	85 dB
5.	Inside the Civil Hospital	10-48 am to 10-53 am	85 dB
6.	Premtala	10-55 am to 11-00 am	90 dB
7.	Shillongpatty (Near Women College)	11-05 am to 11-10 am	83 dB
8.	Shillongpatty (Near Appex Bank)	11-15 am to 11-20 am	75 dB
9.	Near AIR Silchar	11-50 am to 11-55 am	75 dB
10.	Sadarghat	12-00 noon to 12.05 am	88 dB

This result may be/can be compared with Ambient Noise Standard-log dB (A).

		Day Time (6 am to 9 pm)	Night time (9 pm to 6 am)
1.	Industrial Area	75	70
2.	Commercial Area	65	55
3.	Residential Area	55	45
4.	Silence Area	50	40

8

CATEGORYWISE POPULATION DYNAMICS OF NORTH EAST INDIA (1971-91)

S.D. NANDI

In general population studies are made with respect to large totals or aggregates. Such studies conceal many features which are relevant for the understanding of certain phenomena. Dis-aggregation of totals into identifiable categories reveal certain trends and help in understanding intricate dynamics that are taking place within the general trend. Dis-aggregation can be made on the basis of categories or over space. Hence we propose in this chapter to estimate the extent of infiltration in the North Eastern Region of India by utilising this method.

A large volume of literature is available on the issue of infiltration in the Region. Unfortunately, the materials available do not provide a clue to the actual number of such infiltrators nor they reveal the actual nature of infiltration. Many of them are partisan estimates, conjectural and emotional. On the one end of the spectrum there are opinions that deny the existence of infiltrators while on the other, assertions are made about the presence of millions of them in the region. The precise number however, eludes everyone. Interestingly, all such estimates are based on the census data which are make available at the end of every decade.

An Internal Note prepared by the Home Ministry, Government of India in March 1992 examined the issue of infiltration and observed:

"The illegal immigration from Bangladesh into the

> Eastern and North Eastern states and several other states in the country has become a serious problem."[1]
>
> "In the absence of reliable comprehensive census, the exact quantification of the extent of infiltration is not possible but the 1991 census data of both Bangladesh and India throw significant light on its magnitude."[2]

The Report of the General Secretaries of the Congress (I) to the Seventh General Conference of the North Eastern Co-ordination Committee, Guwahati, 3rd July, 1992, further observes:

> "There are infiltrations—though it is a difficult task to examine the precise number."

The infiltrations are not only by minorities of Bangladesh but also from the majority community—Muslims. In absolute terms, the number of Muslims crossing into India is likely to be much larger than that of non-muslims." (item 20.2)[3]

The above excerpts from the observations of authoritative responsible quarters clearly agree that infiltration has taken place but its precise quantification cannot be made. The two Reports are also unanimous about the fact that such infiltration has only taken place from across the borders of Bangladesh. The foreigner and infiltrator in the North East is synonymous with Bangladesh. The perception is further strengthened by the official figures of detection of infiltrators in the Eastern and North Eastern states. During the period of 1971 and 1991, the number of such Bangladeshi infiltrators detected can be seen in the Table 8.1 which is compiled from the "Note" of the Home Ministry referred to above. (1,2)

During 1971 and 1991, a total of 7,38,503 infiltrators were claimed to have been detected in the Eastern and North-Eastern States. Interestingly, all of them were Bangladeshis. It is surprising that the tiny States of Mizoram recorded the highest number of Bangladeshi infiltrators detected—the number exceeding that of West Bengal or even of Assam. It is well known that compared to other states in the East or in the North-Eastern part of India, Mizoram offers least economic incentives. As such, a massive migration reflected in Table 8.1

TABLE 8.1: **Number of Infiltrators Detected: 1971-91**

State/UT	Number	Period
West Bengal	2,40,466	Between 1972-Nov. 1992
Assam	1,35,656	23-3-1971-1991
Meghalaya	14,286	March, 1971-Dec. 1991
Tripura	29,382	1983-1991
Mizoram	3,18,731	26-3-71-31-12-91
Nagaland	Not available	
Bihar	Not available	

Source: "Internal Note prepared by Home Ministry, Govt. of India, March, 1992" reproduced in Arun Shourie, *A Secular Agenda*, ASA Publications, New Delhi-1, 1994, pp. 280-84.

defy understandable logic.

In estimating the extent of infiltration, standard statistical methods of comparing growth rates in total population in the region vis-a-vis that of the nation over the decades have been made. The census figures provide the basic data. The growth rate of total population in the country is taken as the normal rate of growth. Any abnormal deviation from this normal rate is indicative of illegal infiltration or lack of it. In 1981, census operations could not be undertaken in Assam due to widespread disturbances—chiefly on the basis of the issue of infiltration. In view of this, comparison of population growth rates can only be made between the census figures of 1971 and 1991. The Table 8.2 below shows the total population growth in India and in the North East, both in absolute and in percentage terms. The table is self-explanatory.

TABLE 8.2: **Growth of Population in India and North East (1971-91)**

	1971	1991	% growth (1971-91)
India	54,81,59,652	84,63,02,688	54.39
North-East	1,95,82,296	3,15,47,314	61.10

Source : *Basic Statistics of NER* : 1980, p. 5: NEC, Shillong. *Final Population Tables of Census of India*, 1991.

The population of North-East has grown by 61.1 per cent. Compared to that of the country, the rate of growth in the North East between 1971 and 1991 has been 6.71 per cent higher. If the growth rate of 54.39 per cent is taken as normal, there has been an abnormal increase in the population of North East. This higher rate of growth is indicative of illegal infiltration. And such infiltration, as the above quoted Reports emphasise, has taken place from across Bangladesh.

Aggregate data are no doubt necessary but are not sufficient to understand the character of infiltration. North-Eastern India is the home of a large number of ethnic, linguistic and religious groups of population. Dis-aggregating the total population into constitutionally relevant categories will be helpful in understanding the character of excess growth of population during the period. The operative part of many of the constitutional provisions depends on the availability of census data. The link between the Constitution and the census operations is intimate. All the 13 articles of Part-XVI, Scheduled Castes and Scheduled Tribes in order to become operative. Together they constitute the Reserved category. Isolating the reserved category of population from the total population will leave the population segment which is non-reserved. Further, isolating the Scheduled Tribes component from the total population will result in obtaining the number of non-tribal population. Table 8.3 shows the population in different categories in the country and their change during 1971 and 1991. This helps the useful purpose of unravelling the intricate dynamics of different segment of population during the period under study. Understandably, the growth rates in different categories will differ.

The Table 8.3 clearly shows that while the total population in the country during 1971-91 has grown by 54.39 per cent, that of the Scheduled Castes has grown by 69.94 per cent. The difference in the growth rate being 15.59 per cent. The Scheduled Tribes have shown a growth rate of 64.89 per cent which is 10.5 per cent higher than the growth rate of the total population. In both the reserved categories, the growth rates are substantially higher than the growth rate of total population. This is reflected in the annual average exponential growth rates of different categories. While the national growth

TABLE 8.3: **Changes in the Different Constitutionally Relevant Categories of Population in India During 1971-91**

(in million)

Categories	1971	1991	1971-91	% Change	Exponential Growth Rate
Total population	584.159	846.302	298.143	54.39	2.19
Scheduled Caste	81.334	138.223	56.889	69.94	2.68
Scheduled Tribes	41.092	67.758	26.666	64.89	2.53

Source: (1) *Basic Statistics of NER*, 1980, p. 3, NEC, Shillong.

(2) O.P. Sharma, *Scheduled Castes*, Kar Kripa Publications, New Delhi, 1990, p. 9.

(3) *Census of India*, 1991 Final Population Tables.

rate of total population is 2.19 per cent during the period, that of the Scheduled Castes and Scheduled Tribes have been 2.68 per cent and 2.53 per cent respectively. The growth pattern also shows that the rate of growth of Scheduled Castes have been higher than that of the Scheduled Tribes. This is the National pattern.

Coming to the rates of growth of the remaining categories of population, Table 8.4 shows the total non-reserved and non-tribal population and their variation during the period. Table 8.4 is derived from Table 8.3.

TABLE 8.4: **Non-reserved and Non-tribal Population in 1971 and 1991 and their Growth During the Period in India**

Categories	1971	1991	1971-91	% Change	Ex.Gr
Non-reserved	425.733	640.321	214.558	50.4	2.06
Non-tribal	507.067	778.544	271.477	53.54	2.16

Source: Derived from Table 8.3.

The rates of growth in non-reserved and non-tribal categories have been 50.4 per cent and 53.54 per cent respectively which are substantially lower than that of the reserved categories. The growth rate of non-reserved category has been lower than that of the total population by 3.99 per cent while that in the non-tribal category is slightly higher by 0.14 per cent. Compared with the Scheduled Caste category, the growth rate of non-reserved category has been 19.94 per cent lower while it is 14.49 per cent lower than that of the Scheduled Tribe category. The Non-tribal growth rate has been 16.4 per cent lower than the Scheduled Castes growth rate and 11.35 lower than that of the Scheduled Tribes growth rate. It is significant that the population categories which do not receive the benefit of protection, have been showing declining trend in growth rate while the protected categories have shown an increasing trend. The average annual exponential growth rate in the non-reserved and thus, non-protected category has been lower than any of the protected categories. The point that should not be missed is that the non-tribal category also contains the Scheduled Caste component.

The foregoing analysis will not be completed unless the composition of the population is taken into account. Table 8.5 shows the population composition for the country on the basis of the above categories and their variation over the same period. This is necessary because infiltration is not only reflected in the growth rates in the totals but also in the change in composition of population.

TABLE 8.5: **Category-wise Composition of Total Population and their Variation between 1971-91 in India**

(in percentages)

Categories	1971	1991	Variation (1971-91)
Scheduled Castes	14.83	16.33	+ 1.50
Scheduled Tribes	7.49	8.00	+ 0.51
Reserved Category	22.32	24.33	+ 2.01
Non-Reserved	77.68	75.67	– 2.01
Non-Tribals	92.50	91.99	– 0.51

Source: Derived from Table 8.3.

Between 1971 and 1991, the castes and tribes components in the total population have gained 1.5 per cent and 0.51 per cent respectively. The total gain in the protected category is 2.01 per cent. The gain in the reserved category is a loss in the non-reserved category. Between tribal and non-tribal categories, the tribal category has gained 0.51 per cent and that is precisely the loss in the non-tribal category. Between the Scheduled Castes and Scheduled Tribes, the gain is higher for the Castes than for the Tribes. The caste component has gained three times more than that of the tribes.

The electoral implications of the change in composition will not be missed by anyone. The reservation of seats in the Legislatures are based on the composition of Scheduled Castes and Scheduled Tribes in 1971. It is on the basis of that, reservation of 15 per cent and 7.5 per cent of seats in the Legislatures and also that in the public sector jobs are given. The next round assessment of such seats is expected to be made according to Article 332 of the Constitution, "on the basis of the first census after the year 2000." Re-adjustment in pursuance with Article 170 in the seats in the Legislatures will, therefore, follow from the figures of census that will take place in the year 2001. Interestingly, if adjustments are made on the basis of 1991 data, at least six more seats will be gained by the Scheduled Castes and two more by the Scheduled Tribes in the Lower House of the Parliament. In analysing the demographic politics of North East, this crucial point is overwhelmingly important. This is so for the simple reason that in the North East it is not the quantum of growth of total population that makes the subject matter of the debate but the composition of population that is of more vital significance.

The growth rates and composition of population in the North East are studied on the basis of this methodology. Table 8.6 summarises the picture by showing the total population and its dis-aggregation into various components in 1971 and in 1991.

The total population registered a growth rate of 61.10 per cent during the period. As noted earlier, this is 6.71 per cent higher than the national growth rate and is indicative of illegal migration into the region. Almost all the literature available on the subject advance this growth rate as the only piece of

TABLE 8.6: **Change in the Different Constitutionally Relevant Categories of Population in the North East During 1971-91**

(in million)

Categories	1971	1991	% Change	Exponential Growth
Total population	1,95,82,290	3,15,47,314	61.10	2.41
Scheduled Castes	11,26,440	21,61,448	91.88	3.31
Scheduled Tribes	43,46,197	81,42,624	87.35	3.38

Source: Basic Statistics of NER, 1980, *op.cit.*
Final Population Table 1, 1991, *op.cit.*

evidence, in addition to claiming that such infiltration is only by way of Bangladeshi immigrants.

The growth of Scheduled Castes population during the period under study has been 91.88 per cent. Clearly this is 30.78 per cent higher than the regional growth rate in total population. The national rate of growth in the Scheduled Caste category is the highest. It is also the highest among all categories in the North East. The national pattern holds. In terms of growth rates of this category in the country and in the region, the growth rate of the region is higher by 21.94 per cent. There is no justifiable reason as to why the Scheduled Caste population in the region should grow at a much higher rate than that in this nation. This expansion of higher growth rate in the region must be sought not in higher birth rate, nor in lower death rate but in immigration. Immigration of Scheduled Caste can be either from across the country or from other parts of the country into the region. The only possible country from where such immigration can take place, besides the other states of the Union, is Bangladesh. Therefore, the entire foreign infiltration in this category cannot be justified.

In the case of Scheduled Tribes, the growth rate in the region has been 87.35 per cent. This is 26.25 per cent higher than the growth rate of total population in the region. This category registered the second highest rate of growth both in the national and in the regional level. In this category the regional growth rate is higher by 22.46 per cent than the national growth rate. This is higher than that of the Scheduled Castes compared to the nation. It is doubtful whether this rate in the category is due to natural growth rate alone. There must have taken place immigration from outside. There is no known concentration of North Eastern tribal communities elsewhere in the country from where they might have come into the region. The only other possibility is that they must have infiltrated from across the borders from Bangladesh and also from Burma where large concentration of such tribal population exist.

All these growth rates are reflected in the annual average exponential growth which is 2.41 per cent for the total population and 3.31 per cent and 3.18 per cent for the Scheduled Castes and Scheduled Tribes respectively. These growth rates are substantially higher than the rates for the nation.

On a perusal of Table 8.4 and Table 8.6 it becomes evident that the pattern of growth in each of the components both at the national as also at the regional level is similar; although the quantum of regional growth exceeds that at the national level. The highest growth rate is recorded in the Scheduled Caste component, followed by the Scheduled Tribes.

The growth rates in other categories i.e. in the non-reserved and non-tribal categories can be seen in Table 8.7.

TABLE 8.7: **Changes in the Non-reserved and Non-tribal Components in the Total Population in North East During 1971-91**

Categories	1971	1991	% Change	Exponential Growth rate
Non-reserved	1,41,09,659	2,12,43,242	50.56	2.06
Non-tribal	1,52,36,099	2,34,04,690	53.61	2.16

Source: Ibid.

The Table 8.7 indicates that the growth rate of non-reserved category of population during 1971 to 1991 is 50.56

per cent as against the 61.10 per cent growth rate of total population. This is 10.54 per cent less. Surprisingly, the growth rate in this category fits well with the national growth rate in the same category (50.4% Table 8.4). A look at the annual exponential growth rate will also show that the national rate tallies completely with that of the regional level in this category. The inescapable conclusion that can be drawn is that there has neither been any exceptional growth nor is there any possibility of this group contributing any share in the excess growth of total population in the region.

In the non-tribal group, the growth rate in the region is 53.61 per cent and this is 7.49 per cent less than the growth of total population in the region. This rate also fits favourably with the national growth rate (53.54%). The annual average exponential growth rate is identical both at the national and at the regional level. Obviously, this category also cannot have any contribution to the excess growth of population in the region. Table 8.4 and Table 8.6 together conclusively maintain that in the excess growth of population in the region, these two categories cannot have any contribution. The responsibility of this enhanced growth, therefore, must lie squarely in the reserved components alone.

It is natural that the composition of total population has undergone substantial change during the period under study. The following Table 8.8 gives the change in the composition in the region during 1971-91.

TABLE 8.8: **Category-wise Composition of Total Population in the North East During 1971 and 1991**

(in percentages)

Categories	1971	1991	Change 1971-91
Scheduled Castes	5.75	6.85	+ 1.10
Scheduled Tribes	22.19	25.81	+ 3.62
Reserved Category	27.94	32.66	+ 4.72
Non-reserved	72.05	67.33	– 4.72
Non-tribals	77.80	74.19	– 3.61

Source: Ibid.

It is seen in the Table 8.8 that the Scheduled Castes component which constituted 5.75 per cent of the total population at the beginning of the period has gone up to 6.85 per cent at the end of the period. The Scheduled Tribes component has advanced from 22.19 per cent to 25.18 per cent, thereby registering a rise of 3.62 per cent. The reserved category as a whole advanced by 4.72 per cent consequently causing an identical percentage loss in the non-reserved category. Again, the Scheduled Tribes have gained 3.62 per cent. The pattern is similar to that of the national variation in composition. The only exception to the national pattern is that the change in the Scheduled Tribe component has been more than three times that of the Scheduled Caste component for the region. The change in the composition shows that both in the non-reserved and in the non-tribal categories there have been erosion in percentage composition. Such a situation does coroborates the earlier finding that these categories have contributed little or nothing to the excess growth of population in the region.

It has been observed earlier that the total population in the region has shown an excess growth rate of 6.71 per cent over the national rate of growth. Reducing these percentages into actual numbers, estimates can be made about the contribution of each of the categories to this excess growth. This is done in Table 8.9.

TABLE 8.9: **Estimated Contribution of Categories of Population in the Excess Growth During 1971-91 in the North East**

Categories	Actual growth	Estimated growth	Difference
	1	2	3
Total population	1,19,65,018	1,06,50,611	13,14,207
Scheduled Castes	10,35,347	7,87,595	2,47,742
Scheduled Tribes	37,96,427	28,20,247	9,75,180

Source: Ibid.

Column (1) shows the actual growth of total population, Scheduled Caste population and Scheduled Tribe population during 1971-91. Column (2) is estimated on the basis of the growth rates in each category, had they grown at their respective national rates of growth. Column (3) is the difference between the actual and the estimated growth in these categories. The above estimate is carried at on the assumption that there is no plausible reason as to why the regional growth rates in different categories would so eloquently differ from the national growth rates in respective categories.

The above estimate clearly reveals that if the total population had grown at the same rate as that of the nation, i.e. at 54.39 per cent, the net increase in head count would have been 1,06,50,611 during the period. But in actuality it came up to 1,19,65,016 persons. The difference between the estimated and the actual population registered a gap of 13,14,207 persons. This is the figure of estimated infiltration into the region during 1971-91. The excess growth in Scheduled Caste population is 2,47,742 while the Scheduled Tribes have shown an excess of 9,75,180 people. Together these two reserved categories have shown an excess growth of 12,23,932.

In terms of percentage contribution to excess growth of population over the national growth rate, the Scheduled Castes account for 18.85 per cent while the Scheduled Tribes contributed 74.28 per cent. Together they contributed 93.13 per cent in the excess growth and cnly 6.87 per cent is contributed to the non-reserved categories. The evidence is loud and clear.

NOTES

1. Internal Note prepared by the Home Ministry, Government of India, March, 1992 reproduced in Arun Shourie, *A Secular Agenda*, ASA Publications, New Delhi-110 001, (1994), pp. 280-84.
2. *Ibid.*
3. *Ibid.*, Report of the Secretaries of Congress (I) North East India Co-ordination Committee, Guwahati, July 3, 1992.

REFERENCES

Basic Statistics of North Eastern Region, 1980; North Eastern Council Secretariat, Shillong.

Census of India, 1991: *Final Population Tables*.

O.P. Sharma, *Scheduled Castes*, Kar Kripa Publications, New Delhi, 1990.

9

POPULATION GROWTH AND FEMALE LITERACY IN INDIA WITH SPECIAL REFERENCE TO NORTH EASTERN STATES

PHILOMATH PASSAH

Introduction

It is generally believed that women in India suffered an inferior and oppressed life for more than 2000 years. Their suppression began with the law of Manu and prevailed right upto 1950.[1] It was during the 1950s that a number of Hindu Family laws were enacted with a view to liberating the Indian woman from the age-old bondage of social customs and practices and granting them certain rights and equality. During the period of 2000 years, an Indian woman was denied all kinds of rights and always suppressed. The patriachal joint family system, the custom of polygamy, the child marriage, the custom of *sati* or state of permanent widowhood, all had hampered the liberty and the development of the Indian women. There was practically no education for women. Girls were given in marriage before they became eight years old and the longevity of women till 1930 was only 25 years. This means women on an average died at the young age of 25 without any care and affection.[2]

It was the American mission which began the pioneering work in setting up schools for girls in India. The mission first started a school for girls in Bombay in 1824. Getting inspiration from this mission, an Indian Society was formed in 1851 to establish schools for girls.[3] And, it was due to the efforts of great social reformers like Raja Rammohan Roy, Rabindranath Tagore, Mahatma Gandhi and others, a congenial environment was created in India for women's education.

The Gandhian era and the post-Independence period have witnessed tremendous changes in the status of women and so also the female literacy. The all-India women literacy rate from 1901 to 1991 is shown in the following Table 9.1 along with the population growth rate:

TABLE 9.1: **Female Literacy and Population Growth Rates in India (1901 to 1991)**

Census Year	Female Literacy Rate (%)	Total Literacy Rate (%)	Population Growth (%)
1901	0.6	5.3	—
1911	1.1	5.9	+5.75
1921	1.8	7.2	–0.31
1931	2.9	9.5	+11.00
1941	7.3	16.1	+14.22
1951	7.9	16.7	+13.31
1961	12.9	24.0	+21.51
1971	18.7	29.5	+24.80
1981	29.85	43.67	+24.66
1991	39.19	52.19	+23.85

Source: (1) O.P. Sharma and Robert D. Retherford, *Recent Literacy Trends in India*, Occasional Paper No. 1, of 1987, Office of the Registrar General and Census Commissioner of India, New Delhi, pp. 6-7.

(2) Census of India 1991, *Final Population Totals: Brief Analysis of Primary Census Abstract*, Paper 2 of 1992, p. 98.

The above table clearly shows that during the last three Censuses, the female literacy had tremendously improved. While the population growth rate declined relatively though at a very slow pace, the female literacy increased by more than 11 per cent from 1971 to 1981 and more than 9 per cent from 1981 to 1991. But the population growth rate declined by 0.14 per cent only from 1971 to 1981 and 0.81 per cent from 1981 to 1991.

The National Scene

There is a relationship between female literacy or illiteracy and the decadal growth of population in India. While female literacy and population growth are inversely related, female illiteracy and population growth are directly related. During the last decade 1981-91, it has been found that the decadal growth rates of population continue to be quite high in the four large states in the country namely Uttar Pradesh, Bihar, Madhya Pradesh and Rajasthan (constituting 40 per cent of India's population) where female illiteracy rates are high.

We give in the Table 9.2 below the female literacy and the growth rates of population in these states along with a few other states:

TABLE 9.2: **Female Literacy and Growth Rates of Population in the Four Large States and Other 5 States**

Sl. No.	States	Female literacy 1991 (%)	Population growth 1981-91 (%)
1.	Uttar Pradesh	26.02	25.16
2.	Bihar	23.10	23.49
3.	Madhya Pradesh	28.39	26.75
4.	Rajasthan	20.84	28.07
5.	Kerala	87.00	13.98
6.	Punjab	49.72	20.26
7.	Tamil Nadu	52.29	14.94
8.	Goa	68.20	15.96
9.	Karnataka	44.31	20.69

Source: Census of India 1991.

It is clear from the Table 9.2 that the lower the female

literacy, the higher is the decadal growth rate of population and *vice versa.* Hence in the first four large states, the population growth rates are quite high due to low female literacy. But in the last five states, population growth rates are low due to high literacy rates. This was also the finding of the International Institute for Population Sciences, Bombay. In the case of Kerala, it has been argued that large scale out-migration was also responsible for the lower decadal growth rate of the population of the state. But the contrary may also be true according to Davis' theory of multi-phase response.[4] That is to say, the more the population becomes literate, the more mobile it also becomes. Again large-scale out-migration of the females of the state also speaks of their enterprising spirit which they can acquire as they become literate.

The North Eastern States

We may now look at the North Eastern States to see whether the same pattern and relationship between population growth rates and female literacy are tenable. The North Eastern Region of India comprising the seven states of Arunachal Pradesh, Assam, Manipur, Meghalaya, Mizoram, Nagaland, and Tripura has a total geographical area of 2,55,083 sq. kms accounting for 7.7 per cent of the total area of the country. The total population of the Region according to the 1991 Census is 3,15,47,314 which is 3.8 per cent of the total population of the country. The density of population in the 7 states is given in Table 9.3.

The Table 9.3 shows that Assam's density of population is higher than All-India figure. It is the most populous state with 71 per cent of the total population of the Region. Arunachal Pradesh is the biggest state in terms of area but has the lowest density of 10 persons per sq. km. Thus Arunachal Pradesh is very sparsely populated.

Trend of Population Growth

The trend of population growth in the North Eastern Region during the last three decades is shown in Table 9.4.

TABLE 9.3: **Density of Population in the N.E. States**

States	Number of Population	Area in sq. kms.	Density per sq. kms.
Arunachal Pradesh	8,64,558	83,743	10
Assam	2,24,14,522	78,438	284
Manipur	18,37,149	22,327	82
Meghalaya	17,74,778	22,429	78
Mizoram	6,89,756	21,081	33
Nagaland	12,09,546	16,579	73
Tripura	27,57,205	10,486	262
N.E. Region	3,15,47,314	2,55,083	123
All India*	83,85,83,988	32,87,263	267

*Excluding Jammu & Kashmir.

Source: Census of India, *Final Population Tables,* Paper 2 of 1992.

TABLE 9.4: **Trend of Population Growth in the N.E. States (1961-91)**

States	1961-71	1971-81	1981-91
Arunachal Pradesh	38.91	35.15	35.86
Assam	34.95	23.36	23.58
Manipur	37.53	32.46	28.56
Meghalaya	31.50	32.04	31.80
Mizoram	24.93	48.55	38.98
Nagaland	39.88	50.05	56.86
Tripura	36.28	31.92	33.69
All India	24.80	24.66	23.50

Source: Census of India, Final Population Tables from 1971 to 1991.

The above table shows that the population growth rates in

all the N.E. States during the decade 1961-71 were higher than the All-India average. The state of Nagaland had the highest decadal growth rate of 39.88 per cent.

During the decade 1971-81 all states again exceeded the All-India average of population growth rate. There was no Census in Assam in 1981 and the figure given in the table is an interpolation from the previous figure and may not obviously reflect the actual rate of growth. Nagaland's population again shot up to more than 50 per cent growth rate. Mizoram's population too increased tremendously with more than 48 per cent growth rate.

Once more in the decade 1981-91 all the N.E. states exceeded the All-India figure of average population growth rate. Nagaland witnessed a further rise of almost 57 per cent in the growth of population. It returned the highest growth rate of 5.7 per cent per annum in the country as a whole.

Taking all the three decades into consideration, Manipur is the only state where the trend of growth is declining while Nagaland shows a sharp rise. Taking the last two decades, three states of Manipur, Meghalaya and Mizoram witnessed a declining trend in the growth rate of population.

Trend of Literacy

The trend of literacy in the N.E. states during the last three Censuses is shown in Table 9.5.

It may be seen from the Table 9.5 that in 1971, four states—Manipur, Meghalaya, Mizoram and Tripura—had literacy rates which were above the national average. In 1981, again four states (but not the same as in 1971)—Manipur, Mizoram, Nagaland and Tripura—exceeded the All-India average of literacy rate. There was no Census in Assam. The literacy rate in Meghalaya declined below the national average. In 1991, Arunachal Pradesh and Meghalaya were the only 2 states whose literacy rates were below the all-India average.

Co-relation Between Female Literacy and Population Growth

The Table 9.6 gives us the Female literacy rates in the N.E.

TABLE 9.5: **Trends in Literacy in N.E. States**

(Percentage)

N.E. States	Male/Female	1971	1981	1991
Arunachal	Persons	13.18	25.54	41.22
Pradesh	Male	20.53	35.11	51.10
	Female	4.39	14.01	29.37
Assam	Persons	33.94	No Census	53.42
	Male	43.72	—	62.34
	Female	22.76	—	43.70
Manipur	Persons	37.76	49.61	60.96
	Male	52.74	64.21	72.98
	Female	22.43	34.61	48.64
Meghalaya	Persons	34.56	42.02	48.26
	Male	39.86	46.62	51.57
	Female	28.29	37.15	44.78
Mizoram	Persons	72.26	74.26	81.23
	Male	88.49	79.37	84.06
	Female	54.88	68.60	78.09
Nagaland	Persons	31.02	50.20	61.30
	Male	39.30	58.52	66.09
	Female	21.33	40.28	55.72
Tripura	Persons	35.03	50.10	60.39
	Male	45.55	61.48	70.08
	Female	24.02	38.01	50.01
India	Persons	34.45	43.56	52.11
	Male	45.95	56.37	63.86
	Female	21.97	29.75	39.42

Note: Percentage of literacy was computed on the number of population aged 5 and above for 1971 and on population aged 7 and above for 1981 and 1991.

Source: (1) *Census of India*, 1971, 1981, 1991.

(2) *Census of India*, 1981, Primary Census Abstract, Series-I, Part B (i).

States together with their population growth rates during the last two Censuses 1981 and 1991.

TABLE 9.6: **Female Literacy Rates and Population Growth Rates in the N.E. States (1981 & 1991)**

States	Literacy Rates (%)		Growth Rates	
	1981	1991	1971-81	1981-91
Arunachal Pradesh	14.01	29.37	35.15	35.86
Assam	22.76*	43.70	23.36*	23.58
Manipur	34.61	48.64	32.46	28.56
Meghalaya	37.15	44.78	32.04	31.80
Mizoram	68.60	78.09	48.55	38.98
Nagaland	40.28	55.72	50.05	56.86
Tripura	38.01	50.01	31.92	33.92
All India	29.75	39.42	24.66	23.50

*Figures for Assam are those of 1971 as there was no Census in 1981.

Source: Census of India 1981 & 1991.

From the above table, it is evident that three out of the seven states have witnessed a declining trend in the population growth during the last two decades with the increase in the female literacy rates. But in spite of the tremendous increase in the female literacy rates in Nagaland, Tripura, Assam and Arunachal Pradesh, the population growth rates have shown sharp rise in the case of Nagaland and Tripura while in Arunachal Pradesh and Assam the rates recorded a slight percentage change of +0.71 and +0.22 only respectively. There was, however, no Census in Assam in 1981 and the projected figure may not correctly reflect the actual rate.

Conclusion

Owing to the low female literacy, women in many states in India marry at quite a young age. This was the finding of the International Institute for Population Sciences, Bombay. According to this Institute, the percentage of those marrying below the age of 20 years is still more than 60 per cent in the four large states mentioned in the earlier sections as compared to only 14 per cent in Kerala, 23 per cent in Tamil Nadu and 38 per cent in Maharashtra.

The three states in the North Eastern Region too have shown the same trend whereby the population growth rates have witnessed a decline along with the increase in the literacy rates. Though the same trend was not followed in the other four states, yet women literacy together with better health facilities would certainly become a major force in reducing the population growth rates in these states too in the near future.

NOTES

1. Bijaylakshmi Baruah, "Changing Face of Female Literacy" in *Sunday Assam Tribune*, August 4, 1996.
2. *Ibid.*
3. *Ibid.*
4. Kingsley Davis, *The Theory of Change and Response in Modern Demographic History*, Population Index 26.

REFERENCES

Census of India 1991: *Final Population Totals: Brief Analysis of Primary Census Abstract*, Paper 2 of 1992.

Census of India, Final Population Total of 1971, 1981 & 1991.

O.P. Sharma and Robert D. Retherford, *Recent Literacy Trends in India*, Occasional Paper No. 1 of 1987, Office of the Registrar General and Census Commissioner of India, New Delhi.

10

COMPOSITION AND PATTERN OF INTERNAL MIGRATION IN ARUNACHAL PRADESH
A District Level Study

A. MITRA

Migration is a process through which people move from one place of residence to another. The change of residence results in redistribution of population both at the place of origin and at the place of destination. It is not only an important component of the structure of the population but also an important factor in the economic development of a region or a state. In developing countries, migration has been recognised as an important factor in determining plans for social and economic development. Kuznets[1] data indicates that economic growth is accompanied by a gradual reduction in the relative share of agriculture and an increase in the relative share of industry and services on total output and labour force. Thus it will lead to a movement of population from agricultural to non-agricultural areas. From this point of view, internal migration seems to be an integral part of economic development. In this chapter attempt has been made to study the relationship between internal migration and economic development of Arunachal Pradesh.

The process of development in Arunachal Pradesh (The land of the rising sun) started after Independence of the country in 1947. Before Independence no developmental activity was initiated here, even the population census, which was carried out in other parts of the country was not conducted in the

Arunachal Pradesh. The first census in Arunachal Pradesh was conducted in 1961. It was administered by the Ministry of External Affairs with the Governor of Assam acting as an agent to the President. The administration head was the adviser to the Governor and his secretariat was situated in Shillong, where he was assisted by a number of advisers and heads of departments.[2] It came into being as an Union Territory on 20th January, 1972, under the provisions of North East Areas (Reorganisation) Act, 1971, which was a significant step towards the development of economic life of the people. Ultimately Arunachal Pradesh attained its statehood on 20th February, 1987.

In Section-I, I will first analyse the population growth and migration component in the North Eastern Region of India over the past two decades (only 1971 and 1981). In this connection it should be noted that suitable migration statistics of this region, are available from 1971 census onwards. It would have been interesting if the work could be done for 1991 census also but unfortunately 1991 census data have not been published till today. In Section-II, an attempt has been made to analyse the composition of internal migration of Arunachal Pradesh, both in the 'place of birth' and 'place of last residence' concept. In Section-III, an attempt has been made to find a linkage between internal migration and natural resources, social services etc. and then the conclusion follows.

SECTION-I

Analysis of Population and Migration

The North Eastern Region has experienced much higher growth rate of population than the rest of the country. For example, the average annual growth rate of population of all the states of North Eastern Region (3.62 and 3.56) is much higher than the all India average (2.47 and 2.35) during 1981 and 1991 respectively. Since there is no evidence that the natural increase in this region is higher than the rest of India, the difference can only be accounted by in-migration. The migration trends of the North-Eastern Region is presented in Table 10.1.

TABLE 10.1: **Percentage of Total Migrants to Total Population in North Eastern Region of India, 1981 (Place of Birth)**

State	Total Migrants ($M_0 + M_1 + M_2 + M_3$)	Migrants within the state ($M_0 + M_1$)	Migration from other states (M_2)	Migration from outside India (M_3)	Annual Percentage growth rate of population
1	2	3	4	5	6
1. Manipur	14.01	11.66	1.19	0.40	3.25
	(18.73)	(15.23)	(2.34)	(1.16)	
2. Meghalaya	23.93	14.67	5.93	3.33	3.20
	(29.98)	(18.41)	(5.39)	(6.08)	
3. Nagaland	25.48	14.96	8.92	1.60	5.01
	(17.91)	(8.32)	(7.27)	(2.29)	
4. Tripura	36.14	11.81	1.66	22.67	3.19
	(47.15)	(11.46)	(1.62)	(33.96)	
5. Arunachal Pradesh	41.26	21.45	14.13	5.68	3.52
	(37.28)	(22.35)	(9.48)	(5.45)	
6. Mizoram	44.13	37.34	5.06	1.73	4.48

Notes: (1) Figures in the bracket indicate the percentage of total migrants as a percentage of total population.

(2) Census could not be undertaken in Assam in 1981.

(3) In 1971, Mizoram was included as part of Assam.

Sources: (1) *Census of India*, 1971, Series-I, Part-II D (i) Migration Tables.

(2) *Census of India*, 1981, Series-I, Part-II Special Report and Tables Based on 5 per cent Sample data

Table 10.1 shows that the percentage of mobile population has increased in all the states of North Eastern Region except Nagaland in 1981 as compared to these figures in 1971. From the Table, we also find the percentage share of migrants to total population is the highest in Mizoram in 1981 (44.13%) closely followed by Arunachal Pradesh (41.26%) and Tripura (36.14%). The migrants within the state (i.e. intra-district and inter-district) is highest in Mizoram (37.34%) in 1981. Looking at the figures of the migrants from other states

(M_2), Arunachal Pradesh tops the list with 14.13 per cent of the total population in 1981. The figures of migrants from outside India are highest in the case of Tripura (22.6%) of the total population.

Internal Migration in Arunachal Pradesh

Internal migration is a very important component in the population structure of Arunachal Pradesh. According to the 1971 Census, the percentage of internal migrant population was 31.83 per cent of the total population of the state and it has increased to 35.58 per cent of the total population of the state in 1981.

TABLE 10.2: **Percentage of Internal Migrants in Total Population of Arunachal Pradesh, 1971 & 1981 (Place of Birth)**

Year	Migrants within the State ($M_0 + M_1$)	Migrants from other State (M_2)	Total Internal Migrants ($M_0+M_1+M_2$)
(1)	(2)	(3)	(4)
1971	22.35	9.48	31.83
1981	21.45	14.13	35.58

Source: (1) *Census of India*, 1971, Series-1, Part-II, D (i), Migration Tables.
(2) *Census of India*, 1981, Migration Tables, Arunachal Pradesh Part V A & B, Series-25.

Table 10.2 shows that in 1981 the internal migration as a percentage of total population has increased but there is a rapid increase of inter-state migrants which has led to rapid growth of population in the state. The reasons for the high percentage of migrant population may be attributed to (i) the centrally planned push to accelerate the development process through rapid expansion of the territary sector, (ii) the policy of NEFA administration which was formulated to develop the territory within the politico-administrative 'main stream' without disturbing the tribal ethoes and sentiments and bringing all types of working hands from outside the state, (iii) large inflow of military personnel in the border districts of the state after Indo-China War in 1962, and (iv) the fast development of the state and the implementation of various developmental projects after emerging as a Union Territory in 1972.

However, this summary picture conceals the variations of the share of total internal migrants and male migrants which are more important from the economic point of view. So, an attempt has been made to go to the district level. In Arunachal Pradesh, the share of total internal migrants varies between 28.73 per cent in West Kameng to 47.87 per cent in Dibang Valley district, (Appendix-I). The share of male migrants to total migrants varies between 33.50 per cent in Upper Subansiri to 58.95 per cent in East Siang district. (Appendix-II). It also reveals that generally the foothills district like East Siang, Tirap, Lohit etc. have a high share of male migrants because foothill lands are more fertile and have other infrastructural facilities, attracting migrants on account of economic reasons. For example, both East Siang and Tirap districts enjoy the fertile foothill plain lands and bumper crops are grown in these two districts of Arunachal Pradesh. Further, the intensity of leased area is highest in Changlang sub-division (at present Changland District) of Tirap District (46.60% of total leased-in area) followed by East Siang district (11.75%). The higher percentage of leased-in area of Tirap district is because of a large number of migrants from Assam like Kachari, Deori etc. who are normally progressive cultivators, depending mainly on agriculture. There are a good number of migrant Chah Mazdoors and Nepalee cultivators in East Siang district who cultivate the area leasing from the local people.[3]

On the other hand, the districts like Upper Subansiri and east Kameng which are lacking in fertile land and infrastructural facilities, have failed to attract male migrants. However, this explanation does not held good in case of Dibang Valley district which may have fertile land but a large part of the district remains inaccessible due to its hilly terrain and lack of proper communication facilities. Thus, unlike Upper Subansiri district, this district was having a high percentage of total and male migrants. This may be due to reasons like large inflow of military personnel in this border district etc. However, the most important reason seems to be that the total population in this district was very low with only 30,978 persons in 1981. Therefore, the percentage change figures also tend to magnify the position both in the case of total migrants and male migrants which we are aware of.

From Appendix-III, we observe that the share of inter-district migration is low, both in the case of total and male migrants in all the districts of Arunachal Pradesh. The reasons for this low inter-district migration may be attributed to the fact that (i) Most of the districts are scattered and intersected by innumerable turbulent rivers. (ii) The road communication between districts is very poor. For example, the state does not have lateral road connecting the district headquarters of almost all the districts of the state.[4] Generally, the roads run vertically connecting places of Assam with the places of different head-quarters. (iii) The local people inhabiting the state belong to a number of tribes and sub-tribes, having diversified customs and dialects. This has reduced the inter-district mobility of tribals in the state.

Regarding the inter-state migration (M_2), it is the only component of internal migration which influences the population structure of the state. So, an attempt has been made to discuss the interstate migration component in details. The total migrants into Arunachal Pradesh from other states and union territories were 89,274 in 1981, i.e. 14.13 per cent of the total population of the state. Out of which, male migrants were 58,865 (65.94%) and female migrants were 30,409 (34.06%). The migrants coming to Arunachal Pradesh from different states are given in Table 10.3.

Table 10.3 shows that out of the total inter-state migrants (M_2) 89,274 in 1981, 51,526 i.e. 57.72 per cent are coming from the bordering state of Assam alone. From the non-bordering states, the largest numbers are coming from Bihar (11,436) followed by U.P. (7,250). Arunachal Pradesh also received a sizeable number of migrants from Meghalaya (2,287) which may be due to the shifting of capital as well as administrative offices from Shillong to Itanagar.

TABLE 10.3: **Migrants from Major States of India to Arunachal Pradesh, 1981**

State	Total	Male	Female	Sex-Ratio
(1)	(2)	(3)	(4)	(5)
1. Assam	51,526	31,646	19,880	628
		(63.94)	(34.06)	
2. Bihar	11,436	9,430	2,006	213
		(16.02)	(6.60)	
3. U.P.	7,250	5,156	2,094	406
		(8.75)	(6.89)	
4. West Bengal	4,060	2,598	1,463	563
		(4.41)	(4.81)	
5. Meghalaya	2,287	1,275	1,012	794
		(2.17)	(3.34)	
6. Kerala	2,237	1,552	685	441
		(2.64)	(2.23)	
7. Other States	10,478	7,209	3,269	453
		(68.81)	(38.19)	
	89,274	58,865	30,409	516

Note: Figures in the bracket indicate the percentage distribution of total male and female inter-state migrants.

Source: Computed from Census of India, 1981, Migration Tables, Arunachal Pradesh, Part V A & B, Series-25.

Now if we analyse the concentration of inter-state migrants (M_2) into various districts of Arunachal Pradesh, it is found that (i) the economically attractive foothills districts like Lohit (62.17% and 70.31% of total and male internal migrants), Tirap (48.36% and 54.83%) and East Siang (46.63% and 53.47%) and (ii) The sensitive international border district like Dibang Valley (65.09% and 53%) and West Kameng (47.95% and 55.64%) have a larger proportion of both total and male inter-state migrants (Appendix-III).

In the first category of districts, the economic condition is relatively sound. This is because in these districts like East Siang, Lohit and the Changland subdivision of Tirap district, there is a vast area under settled cultivation. The intensity of leased-in area is also quite high particularly in Changland sub-division of Tirap district (46.60%), Lohit (21.19%) and East Siang (11.75%). On the other hand, in Lower Subansiri district, the percentage of inter-state migration is also high (32.45% and 46.94%) and is expected to be higher in 1991 Census due to the location of state capital. For example, migration may be most effective in and around Itanagar because of the construction of the new capital complex.

Another important aspect to observe from the Table 10.3 is that the sex ratio among the inter-state migrants is quite low (516 females per 1000 males). This low sex-ratio among the inter-state migrants reflects the fact that they are not permanent in nature as they have left their families at their respective home places. Therefore, it can be inferred that the migrants from other states basically come to Arunachal Pradesh with an economic motive to earn their livelihood specially in the Government services. The major attraction for the Government jobs are possibly, free furnished accommodation facilities, higher salaries and other benefits which are rare in many parts of India. Many of them also migrate to earn their livelihood as wage earners at various construction projects. Naturally, in such type of temporary jobs, it was difficult for them to maintain their families due to the high cost of living as compared to that of their home towns. Although 1981 Census is silent over the economic classification of the migrants, but 1971 Census figures show that the tertiary sector is the most important one for the inter-state migrant workers. For example, more than 70 per cent of the inter-state migrant workers were employed in the tertiary sector in 1971.

So far we have studied the pattern and volume of total and male migrants on the basis of 'place of birth' only. The migration data in 'place of birth' concept has certain limitations. Some of the limitations have been overcome by taking into account 'the last residence' concept. If we analyse in the context of duration of residence in the place of enumeration, we find that a larger percentage of total and male migrants do not usually settle down in the place of enumeration. An attempt has been made to calculate Karl Pearson's co-efficient of correlation for inter-state total migrants and migrants with duration of residence for less than 10 years. It is interesting to note that there exists a high correlation between these two variables and the value of 'r' was found to be +0.72, which is statistically significant at 95 per cent level of confidence. Therefore, we can say that interstate migrants do not usually settle down permanently in the place of destination. This may be due to the existence of inner line permit, restrictions in acquiring landed property by non-tribal etc. (Appendix-IV).

Finally, an attempt has been made to mention a few lines about out-migrants from Arunachal Pradesh i.e. migration from Arunachal Pradesh to other states.

However, the information is not easily available and can be compared only after the scrutiny of census reports of all other states. If we look into the out-migration of Arunachal Pradesh to the neighbouring North Eastern States, it appears that except Nagaland (279) and Meghalaya (267), the out-migrants from Arunachal Pradesh to other North Eastern States are negligible. Thus, it seems that by and large, the tribal people of the state are reluctant to migrate to other state. This is particularly due to climatic and social factors. However, there is an exception among the tribal people of Tirap district who were found to work in the neighbouring tea-gardens of Assam.[6] Any way, this type of migration is only seasonal. During winter, local tribal population had no work on their farms or Jhums and migrated to tea gardens of Assam for working as wage labourers and returned after nearly two months.

SECTION-II

In this section, an attempt has been made to find a linkage between migration stream and natural resources, social services etc. i.e. whether internal migration has burdened the natural resources, social services etc. It is difficult to have a direct linkage of internal migration and burdening of natural resources. However, it can be said that inter-state migration, which is quite high, has led to a rapid growth of population of

Arunachal Pradesh. Since the natural growth rate of population is not so high, it is due to interstate migration that the population has been growing by more than 3 per cent per annum during 1971-81 and 1981-91. So, naturally, the rapid growth of population has put more pressure on natural resources. For example, the requirement of food of the state has increased from 58.3 thousand tonnes in 1960-61 to 148.8 thousand tonnes in 1990-91. In order to meet the requirement the food production of the state has increased from 40.3 thousand tonnes in 1960-61 to 207.6 thousand metric tonnes in 1990-91. The increase in food production is no doubt due to the increase in agricultural productivity but also may be due to conversion of more forest land into agricultural land with its serious implication for the ecological balance of the state.[7]

The data also supports the fact that the net area sown in Arunachal Pradesh has increased by 26.29 per cent during 1980-81 to 1983-86. In a hilly state like Arunachal Pradesh, this increase in net area shown may be mainly due to the increase in agricultural land which is at the cost of area under forests. Although the Government of Arunachal Pradesh has tried to control the shifting cultivation but statistics shows that the forest land due to shifting cultivation is around 70 sq. km. during 1991-93 according to "Forest Survey of India", Dehra Dun, 1993. The population pressure has also contributed to deforestation by increasing the demand for firewood which is the major source of energy in the absence of adequate supply of commercial energy at reasonable rates.[8]

Further, it is found that internal migration seems to be an important component of the urban population of the state in 1981. It is comparatively low in the existing towns like Bomdila (56.19%), Passighat (55.93%) and comparatively high in Itanagar (66.74%). Of all the towns in Arunachal Pradesh, the inter-state migration component is very high (more than 60%) except Bomdila in 1981. So, it can be inferred that internal migration in general, and inter-state migration in particular, has led to the rapid growth of urban population which is quite high (139.63% in 1971-81 and 152.98% in 1981-91). This rapid growth of urbanisation has created more pressure on natural resources apart from causing ecological damage and environmental hazards. This is because more forest land has been destroyed for construction of roads, buildings etc. as well as creating urban amenities.

Moreover, the fast growth of urban population would impose a heavy burden on basic services like housing, sanitation, supply of water and electricity. For example, in Itanagar, the capital of Arunachal Pradesh which has experienced the highest growth rate of urbanisation in the state, one has to put up with very frequent load-shedding and acute scarcity of water supply particularly in winter season. So, in future there will be no surprise that under these circumstances dust and pollution may become normal features of the urban areas of the state, despite all the hills and green-land that surround them.

Conclusion

Thus the present study reveals that the share of mobile population of Arunachal Pradesh is not uniform at the district level. It varies from 47.87 per cent in Dibang Valley district to 26.41 per cent in Tirap district of Arunachal Pradesh. However, Arunachal Pradesh shows a contrasting pattern as far as the direction of male migrants is concerned. For example, in this state as distance increases, the share of male migrants is reduced first and then increases at inter-state level. Hence Lee's theory regarding the distance covered by migrants does not hold good in this hilly state. Another peculiarity is that the inter-district mobility among the people of Arunachal Pradesh is quite low in spite of the creation of a number of district in the state between 1971 and 1981.

It is also found that inter-state migration is high in Arunachal Pradesh (14.23% of the population). This high rate may be partly due to centrally sponsored planned development and the policy of NEFA administration when almost all types of working hands were mobilised from outside the state. However, it should be gradually reduced when the people of the state acquire the desired skill and ability. Therefore, it is necessary to invest a large amount in human capital for improved productive capabilities in the form of (i) provision of improved medical and health care for improving their capability, (ii) arrangement of more on-the-job training facilities in specialised institutions, and (iii) introducing vocational education. In fact, the inter-state migration problem can be reduced to some extent through proper manpower planning and formation of skill and entrepreneurial ability of the local people.

So far relationship between internal migration and natural resources and social services are concerned, it is difficult to connect the direct relationship between the two components. However, it can be said that internal migration in general and inter-state migration in particular has increased the population growth as well as the rapid growth of urbanisation in the state which in turn has adversely affected the natural resources and social services of the state. This deserves the serious attention of the authorities dealing in development and urban planning. It should be noted that the problem of urbanisation in the hilly areas is different from those in the plains. While in the plain area, a vast area of flat land is available for further expansion, but this is not possible in the hilly areas. Hence, it is suggested that instead of population conglomerating in one or two large towns, it is better to have more small and medium towns in different districts of the state which will have less pressure on natural resources and social services.

NOTES AND REFERENCES

1. Kuznets, S., *Modern Economic Growth-rate, Structure and Spread*, New Haven and London, Yale University Press, 1966, pp. 1-5.
2. Elwin, V., *A Philosophy for NEFA*, Published on behalf of Adviser to the Governor of Assam, Shillong, 1964, p. 4.
3. *Report on Agricultural Census*, 1980-81, Published by Directorate of Agriculture, Government of Arunachal Pradesh, Naharlagun, pp. 28-29.
4. Chatterjee, S.K., *Emergence of a Dynamic Economy*, Associated Publishing House, New Delhi, 1986, p. 167.
5. Sebastian, A. , "Migration in North East Region of India" in Datta Ray, B. (ed.), *The Pattern and Problems of Population of N.E. India*, Uppal Publishing House, New Delhi, 1986, p. 79.
6. *Techno-Economic Survey of NEFA, National Council of Applied Economic Resources*, New Delhi, 1967.
7. *Ibid*., p. 103.
8. The State of Forest Report, 1991, Government of India, Ministry of Environment and Forest, Dehradun, p. 70.

APPENDIX-I

PERCENTAGE SHARE OF TOTAL INTERNAL MIGRANTS TO TOTAL POPULATION IN THE DISTRICTS OF ARUNACHAL PRADESH, 1981

Sl. No.	Districts	Share of Migrants to Total Population
1.	West Kameng	28.73 (18,187)
2.	East Kameng	38.51 (16,458)
3.	Lower Subansiri	42.95 (48,387)
4.	Upper Subansiri	35.14 (13,849)
5.	West Siang	36.86 (27,340)
6.	East Siang	32.52 (22,910)
7.	Dibang Valley	47.87 (14,829)
8.	Lohit	41.53 (28,863)
9.	Tirap	26.41 (33,973)

Note: Figures in bracket indicate the absolute figures of total internal migrants.

APPENDIX-II

PERCENTAGE SHARE OF MALE INTERNAL MIGRANTS TO TOTAL MIGRANTS IN THE DISTRICTS OF ARUNACHAL PRADESH, 1981

Sl.No.	Districts	Share of Male Migrants to Total Magrants
1.	West Kameng	52.09 (9,474)
2.	East Kameng	34.05 (5,604)
3.	Lower Subansiri	45.59 (22,060)
4.	Upper Subansiri	33.50 (4,640)
5.	West Siang	45.34 (12,396)
6.	East Siang	58.95 (13,505)
7.	Dibang Valley	58.34 (8,651)
8.	Lohit	54.35 (15,687)
9.	Tirap	58.43 (19,850)

Note: Figures in bracket indicate the absolute figures of male internal migrants.

APPENDIX-III

TOTAL AND MALE MIGRANTS CLASSIFIED BY DISTANCE COVERED IN THE DISTRICTS OF ARUNACHAL PRADESH, 1981

(In Percentage)

Sl.No.	Districts	Intra-district	Inter-district	Inter-state
1.	West Kameng	47.79	4.23	47.98
		(47.01)	(4.35)	(55.64)
2.	East Kameng	75.68	7.38	16.94
		(56.78)	(8.58)	(34.64)
3.	Lower Subansiri	62.59	4.96	32.45
		(47.54)	(5.51)	(46.95)
4.	Upper Subansiri	80.03	6.97	13.00
		(63.32)	(8.04)	(28.64)
5.	West Siang	67.23	5.90	26.87
		(52.18)	(6.36)	(41.46)
6.	East Siang	42.23	11.14	46.63
		(35.93)	(10.10)	(53.97)
7.	Dibang Valley	33.64	13.36	53.00
		(22.76)	(12.15)	(65.09)
8.	Lohit	33.18	4.65	62.17
		(25.22)	(4.47)	(70.31)
9.	Tirap	46.14	5.49	48.37
		(39.95)	(5.22)	(54.83)

Note: Figures in bracket indicate the percentage distribution of male migrants.

TOTAL MIGRANTS CLASSIFIED BY DISTANCE COVERED ACCORDING TO PLACE OF LAST RESIDENCE AND PERCENTAGE DISTRIBUTION OF MIGRANTS BY DURATION OF RESIDENCE IN ARUNACHAL PRADESH, 1981

Sl.No.	District	Share of Internal Migrants to Total Population	Intra-district	Inter-district	Inter-state	Duration of Residence in place of Enumeration		
						Less than 10 years	More than 10 years	Period not stated
(1)	(2)	(3)	(4)	(5)	(6)	(7)	(8)	(9)
1.	West Kameng	34.75	58.89	6.91	34.20	76.18	20.46	3.36
2.	East Kameng	40.15	77.74	10.64	11.62	58.48	40.54	0.98
3.	Lower Subansiri	45.50	67.62	6.80	25.58	68.53	29.73	1.54
4.	Upper Subansiri	36.44	82.70	9.23	8.07	51.63	45.32	3.05

(Contd.)

Appendix-IV *(Contd.)*

(1)	(2)	(3)	(4)	(5)	(6)	(7)	(8)	(9)
5.	West Siang	38.64	72.37	8.09	19.54	59.11	38.27	2.62
6.	East Siang	35.21	52.05	14.11	33.84	67.94	28.46	3.60
7.	Dibang Valley	53.66	44.81	13.97	41.22	74.92	23.85	1.23
8.	Lohit	45.36	46.59	7.38	46.03	60.26	37.58	2.16
9.	Tirap	35.67	62.96	6.65	30.39	74.12	24.80	1.68

11

POPULATION PRESSURE ON THE AGRICULTURAL LANDS IN THE HILL AREAS OF ASSAM

A Case Study on Karbi Anglong District of Assam

A.K. BORAH and A.K. SACHAN

Karbi Anglong which is one of the two hill districts of Assam, physiographically covers the extended portion of the Shillong plateau (Das, 1995). The elevation of the hills varies approximately from 100 metres to 1000 metres. The total geographical area of Karbi Anglong is 10,33,000 hectares out of which 2,74,000 hectares are forest land. Further barren and uncultivable lands covers an area of 6,33,000 hectares, (SHBA, 1987). Thus approximately 1,26,000 hectares are available for human habitation and for agricultural use both for shifting cultivation (commonly known as *Jhuming*) and for settled cultivation.

As per 1991 Census, the total tribal population of the state of Assam is 28,74,441 out of which the total Karbi population is 2,90,000 approximately constituting 11.02 per cent (Das, 1995, p. 4) of the total tribal population of the state. But the population of the district does not include only the Karbi tribe, other tribes like Boro Kachari, Dimasa, Garo and non-tribal plains population are found in the district. The tribe-wise breakup of the population is not available after 1991 Census. The district contains a total of about 5,00,000 persons covering both tribals and non-tribals. The density of population varies with the different topographical settings of the district. The high hills are thinly populated while the plain areas are densely populated.

One can find the Karbi cultivators are shifting their areas of cultivation as they shift their dwelling habitations in the hills. In the immediate foothill of the district—Bokajan, Namborhabi village, Mohongdijua (popularly known as Manja), Diphu, Bokulia, howraghat, Centre Bazar etc. the population is alarmingly increasing and now it is spilling over in various parts of the plains areas of the district.

The population pressure on land specially on the agricultural land, in this district comes from two groups of people viz. Karbi shifting cultivators and the plains men specially the refugee population which was settled in this district after the partition and which is swarming like bees on the plains lands owned by the Karbis and grabbing every cultivable plot of land from the latter under different devices which would be later described in this chapter.

Taking the first group of the people who have caused great pressure on land, i.e. the Karbi shifting cultivators, it has been found that originally as reported by the Karbi people themselves, the *Jhum* cycle was 15-20 years. But now it has been reduced to only 3-5 years. Owing to the increase of population in geometrical progression even among the Karbi shifting cultivators as generally observed by these authors, the Karbi shifting cultivators are presently cultivating only once a year in the said *Jhum* lands. They are no longer interested in raising crops more than once a year in the *Jhum* areas as the fertility of the *Jhum* lands is alarmingly decreasing leading to the reduction of the *Jhum* cycles and lesser yield and productions per year (Bordoloi, 1995). This has become a very serious problem because the reduction of the *Jhum* cycle has already caused large scale denudation of forests and a serious disturbance of the ecological settings of the *Jhum* areas resulting into rainfall scarcity in the whole district of Karbi Anglong. The district did not face such a situation in the past. If it is not controlled immediately, *Jhum* cultivation may, within a decade from now, turn the whole hill areas of the Karbi Anglong district into a mere barren land devoid of any vegetation and the concept of sustainable eco-system would remain a myth rather than a reality.

Speaking about the pressure on land by the plains men on the immediate foothill district like Bokulia, Howraghat, Centre Bazar, Parokhowa, etc. and in particular the plains areas of the district which fall under the Howraghat Tribal Development Block, the erstwhile East Bengal (Now Bangladesh) refugees (Bordoloi, 1991: 216) whose population is increasing in geometrical progression, it has been noticed that these people have deviced some methods by which to cleverly snatch away the fertile plains areas from the Karbi people who are settling in the Howraghat and other fertile plains area. From the field evidences that we had collected, it has been found that the plains dwellers among the Karbis of Howraghat Development Block were forcibly alienated from their fertile cultivable lands by the erstwhile East Bengal refugees who have been already referred to above. The Karbis of these areas were economically very weak and taking advantages of this, the refugees manufactured certain devices (Bordoloi, 1991) by which they could gradually and methodically grab arable lands from the former's possession. These devices are briefly discussed as under:

Paikas System

Under this system a non-tribal cultivator offered monetary advances to a tribal land owner or settlement holder. In consideration of the advance the tribal land owner let out the land to the non-tribal cultivator for a period of one or two years. After stipulated period was over, the non-tribal cultivator was supposed to return the land to the tribal land owner. But in practice it never so happened. What actually happened was that before the period came to an end the tribal settlement holder takes further money advances from the non-tribal cultivator leading to further extension of the stipulated period. This process continues and eventually the tribal land owners lost their lands to the erstwhile non-tribal refugees through the clever device of the latter. According to Bordoloi (1991: 216) the non-tribal (refugees) cultivated the land held on *Paikas* and reaped the harvest while the actual (tribal) owner got nothing but the advance received in cash which was in fact (only) one-eighth of (or even less than) the value of the produce obtained from the *Paikas* land (words within brackets are our emphasis).

Though the ownership of the land under this system did not get transferred from the tribal owner to the non-tribal actual cultivator, yet the former became a mere spectator while the latter continued to cultivate the land and produce the crops year after year as if he was the real owner of the land (Bordoloi, 1991: 216-217). As time passed, the ownership of the land ultimately got transferred from the real owner to the actual cultivator.

Sukti Bandhak

This system is in operation in certain plains areas and more specially in Centre Bazar area under Howraghat Development Block. Under this system, land is taken on rent for cultivation by non-tribal people from tribal land owners at the annual rate mentioned in the formal agreement signed between them. According to Bordoloi, "the term *Sukti* means agreement and *Bandhak* literally means mortgage. During the period of agreement the land owner shall have no right to cultivate his land or question its utility. The person who takes the land from his tribal counterpart becomes virtual owner of land like the *Paikas* holder" (1991: 217). As the non-tribal cultivator repeatedly renews the *Sukti* with his tribal land owner for the land taken earlier for cultivation, the tribal land owner virtually loses his ownership over his land.

Khoi Bandhak

Under this system a non-tribal refugee takes the land from the tribal land owner for a period of 5 years against the cash payment of a certain amount of money calculated at certain annual rate per bigha of land. The entire amount in cash is paid to the tribal settlement holder only once at the beginning. Before the period is over the cultivator again lures the tribal settlement holder with money thereby makes the latter enter into an agreement for another five years. However, this system is not always followed now.

Mena

As stated in the preceeding paragraphs, the density of the Karbi shifting cultivators in the hill areas or in semi-hill areas are low. As such, there are unreclaimed virgin lands adjacent to Karbi villages which, after reclamation, would become favourable for cultivation. The non-tribals take the land for reclamation and cultivation from the tribal people under the agreement that after a period of 3-5 years a portion of the reclaimed land would be given back to the tribal owners. This system is known as *Mena*. The system is in vogue presently in Sapong areas of Duardisa mouza of Phulani circle. This area also falls under Howraghat Development Block.

Adhiar System

The *Adhiar* is nothing but a share cropping system. This system was not liked by non tribals earlier. But after the declaration of *Paikas* system as illegal by an amendment to the Land Transfer Act mady by Karbi Anglong District Council during the tenure of Uoyanta, Rongni as Chief Executive Member, the non-tribal refugees have to cultivate the land of the tribal people under this system which does not threaten the tribal ownership of the land.

The foregoing discussion has clearly brought to light that the settlement of the erstwhile refugees in Assam has resulted into the alienation of the hill tribal lands to the refugees in Karbi Anglong district through various devices. The important point to be noted is that the tribal people are alienated from their lands by non-tribals under various devices against which the tribals are incapable of resisting. Time is soon coming, however, that owing to the rapid increase in the number of population among the non-tribal refugees, heavier pressure on the cultivable lands alienated from the tribal settlement holders would occur thereby causes serious conflicts among the non-tribal people themselves. This would definitely happen in no distant future for which no solution exists. The Karbi Anglong Autonomous District Council along with the law machinery of the state may still save the Karbis from being alienated from their lands by the land-hungry non-tribal population through legislation under the sixth Schedule of the Indian Constitution.

Acknowledgement

The authors are grateful to Prof. M.M. Das, Head of the Department of Geography, Gauhati University and to Dr. B.N. Bordoloi, former Director, Assam Institute of Research for Tribals and Scheduled Castes and presently Advisor, National Institute of Rural Development, N.E.R. Centre, Guwahati, for the various information received in the discussion with them for the preparation of this paper.

REFERENCES

Bordoloi, B.N., 1991, *Trsnsfer and Alienation of Tribal Land in Assam* with special reference to the Karbis of the Karbi Anglong District, Chandan Nagar, Guwahati.

Directorate of Economics and Statistics, 1987, *Statistical Hand Book of Assam,* (SHBA), Guwahati.

12

POPULATION GROWTH AND ITS IMPACT UPON THE LAND RESOURCES OF ASSAM

KEYA SENGUPTA

In the present day society any kind of discussion relating to developmental work, would remain unconvincing and one-sided without its reference, directly or indirectly to the population growth and its impact on the natural resources. In fact formulation of plans and policies connected with economic development has always been based on long term perspective of population growth. Changes in population growth trends may even warrant changes in governmental policies and programmes.

Again a study on the structure of population should touch upon both its quantity and quality. After all it is the effort and hard work of the population of a nation that determines its economic growth. All attempts at developmental work would not only be fruitless, but also meaningless without the people for whom it is meant. Hence, all the developmental works are by the people and for the people. The right size of population can go a long way in helping capital formation process and supplying manpower for economic development and also creating demand for goods and commodities produced in the country.

However, just as population is an imperative factor of economic development, under certain circumstances, it can also be a great obstacle to economic development. This is particularly so in a capital-poor and a technologically backward country. According to Prof. Meier, "Contrary to the stagnation theory, population growth, if it is in a backward country, does not induce capital widening investment or innovations. Instead it diminishes the rate of capital accumulation, raises costs in extractive industries, increases the amount of disguised unemployment and a large part, simply diverts capital to maintaining children who die before reaching the productive age. In short, resources go to the formation of population not capital."

In an agriculturally dominated country or region with the concentration of the masses in the rural areas, an uncontrolled increase in population growth can adversely affect the land-man ratio. The per capita availability of land for cultivation may decline, thereby retarding the development of the economy. However, if the productivity of land is increased, the per capita availability of foodgrains may increase. The experience of most agriculture based economies with the tremendous growth of population, reveals that a fall in the average land holding reduces the income of the farmers, who are not in a position to introduce any kind of modern technology for the purpose of agricultural development, thereby reducing the possibility of increasing the per capita availability of foodgrains. This results in raising the level of poverty, giving rise to the problems of unemployment as well as underemployment. Over-population, further, gives rise to the problem of congestion, lack of space for house and other constructional work. It is in this context that the present study makes an attempt to analyse the situation in Assam, focussing attention on the per capita availability of agricultural land as well as per capita availability of agricultural crops, particularly the main staple food crop of the region i.e. rice. The period chosen for the purpose of the study is from 1980-91. The data for the purpose of the study has been obtained from the *Basic Statistics of the North Eastern Region*, 1990 and the *Statistical Handbook of Assam*, 1993. From the data available, we have calculated the per capita availability of agricultural land and per capita availability of rice, the estimates of which are given in Table 12.1.

The Table 12.1 reveals that the two variables of per capita availability of agricultural land as well as per capita availability of rice, have a tendency to move in the same direction. However, a proper grasp of the situation, prompts us to use the Sign Test, so as to be able to support our hypothesis with the conclusion that can be drawn from the Test.

TABLE 12.1: **Per Capita Availability of Cultivable Land and Rice**

Year	Population (per '000)	Total area available for cultivation (hect.)	Production of Rice (kg per hec.)	Per Capita availability of agricultural land	Per Capita availability of Rice
1980	178928	2275	2522	.0127	.0141
1981	182509	2278	2235	.0124	.0116
1982	186168	2301	2583	.0124	.0139
1983	189926	2322	2540	.0122	.0133
1984	193799	2324	2438	0.119	.0126
1985	197811	2464	2846	.0123	.0144
1986	201981	2287	2385	.0113	.0118
1987	206336	2336	2715	0.112	.0132
1988	210900	2311	2789	.0109	.0130
1989	215701	2469	3085	.0114	.0143
1990	220770	2526	3270	.0115	.0148
1991	224143	2572	3197	.0115	.0143

Source: *Basic Statistics of North Eastern Region,* 1990, North Eastern Council Secretariat, Shillong.

The underlying null hypothesis of the Sign Test is that the signs of the direction of changes of per capita availability of agricultural land and availability of rice in the parent population are randomly distributed. The significance of the test will therefore, signal that there exists a systematic relation between the direction of changes between the two variables. If both these variables increase or decrease together, the paired changes are described as uni-directional and a plus sign will be allotted to it. If, however, changes in the two variables are in opposite direction, a negative sign will be allotted to the paired changes. The panel data reveals that only 3 out of 11 signs allotted to such paired changes are negative. This refutes the null hypothesis. Only the years 1982, 1987 and 1991 are exceptional years when in the former case the per capita availability of land is constant, though there has been an increase in the per capita availability of rice. This may be due to favourable monsoons or may be due to the increase in the use of fertilizers. The analysis, therefore, reveals the crucial fact that as the agricultural land holdings decline, it is bound to have its effect on the per capita availability of foodgrains, highlighting a very disturbing reality that the consumption of rice actually declines which may adversely affect the health and nutritional levels of the population.

The above estimates further reveal that the per capita availability of land has been showing a continuous downward trend from 1980 to 1988, thereafter increasing marginally from 1989 onwards, when the average had actually shown an upward trend. All these happened in spite of the fact that there has been an increase in absolute terms in the total availability of land for the purpose of agriculture. The analysis, therefore, proves that the increase in the population is at a rate which is much faster than the increase in the area of land under cultivation.

Similar disturbing trend is also displayed by the per capita availability of rice production, which has also been showing a declining downward tendency. The few exceptional years are 1982, 1985, 1987, 1989 and 1990. However, for most of these years, there has been a slight increase in the availability of area per capita. This clearly reveals that the availability of more land per person also gives rise to more foodgrains per person, just as a decrease in the availability of land per person, due to the tremendous pressure of population, leads to an immediate fall in the foodgrains availability per person.

The fall in the availability of foodgrains has to be met by bringing foodgrains from other states, thereby not only increasing the dependence of the state on the other states, but also results in wastage of the scarce resources for feeding the unnecessary increase in the population sacrificing the development of the state to that extent.

Our estimates above further reveal that though per capita availability of agricultural land and foodgrains is decreasing every year, the total area under cultivation is actually increasing in terms of absolute area, focussing attention to the fact that every year the pressure of population compels additional land being brough under cultivation. This often necessitates the depletion of forests, often at the cost of environmental welfare of the society.

Consequently, it is quite evident that though population is considered to be the ultimate means of transforming an economy, the uncontrolled increase of population is actually acting as a big hindrance for the development of the economy. In other words, instead of working for their betterment, the people are working unconsciously for their own downfall. No country or region like the industrially under-developed state of Assam can ill afford to do so. The rich natural resources of the state instead of being utilised for the development of the state, is wasted away in feeding her own population. It is therefore, not always correct to speak about financial resources for the transformation of the economy. In spite of financial and other resources, unsystematic and uncontrolled increase in population may result in structural distortion of the economy, thereby throwing all plans and programmes of development out of gears.

The improper and inadequate attention by the social workers and the policy-makers may only mean that the state is heading for a dark future. It is in this context that the role of the policy-makers assumes importance. There have been numerous measures adopted for population control in India but none of them is a success. In most simple connotation, a population policy is a "legitimate act by a governmental authority that aims to influence the growth, decline, size, composition or distribution of a population". In the Indian case, politics has often shaped the population policies. The politics of population policies are reflected by the wish to gain or retain power, economic interests, racial and ethnic, ethical, moral theological and ideological relations. Consequently, without relying much on population policies, which keep on changing with time, greater effort should be placed on the people themselves to understand the magnitude of the problem as it is. Educating the public and also trying to raise the literacy rate may be the first step in this direction. Then the negative aspect of population increase should be given wide publicity. Reliance can be placed on the motivation of the people for voluntarily reducing the size of the family. Compulsion of any nature in this respect may be met with misunderstanding and antagonism and may even give negative results. Coupled with this, some disincentive in mild form for families with more than two children should be a must just as reward for a small family can also be introduced as an additional feature. It may, therefore, be expected that consciousness for small families by the people themselves coupled with some mild doses of incentives and disincentives may perhaps help to reduce the magnitude of the problem even if it cannot totally be eliminated.

REFERENCES

Basic Statistics of North Eastern Region, 1990, North Eastern Council Secretariat, Shillong.

Meier, G.M., *Leading Issues in Economic Development,* Oxford University Press, 1983.

13

POPULATION TREND AMONG THE KARBIS IN A CENTURY (1872-1971)
An Overview

R.P. ATHPARIA

Introduction

The Karbis or the Mikirs constitute a major tribe of Assam. They are mainly concentrated in Karbi Anglong district. They are also found in some pockets of Nowgaon, Kamrup, Darrang, Golaghat, North Cachar Hills of Assam as well as in Arunachal Pradesh, Meghalaya and Nagaland.

A study of the physical aspects of the Karbi land has shown that the Karbi habitations are considerably diverse particularly in respect of physiography, vegetation etc. This diversity in the geo-physical structure has formed a distinctive ecological background that has greatly influenced the settlement pattern, economy, population as well as socio-political life of the people. There prevails cool climate on the higher elevations of the hills and plateaus and warm and humid climate in the plains and low-lying areas. Vegetations vary from thick forests in the Dhansiri and Kopili valleys in the higher elevations bordering Nagaland and Meghalaya to the thin forests in the Brahmaputra plains.

It is in this physical setting that the Karbis came to inhabit in the present habitat long before the coming of the Ahoms in the early thirteenth century. The Karbi linguistic and socio-cultural affinities with other Tibeto-Burman families and their myths and legends form sufficient ground to accept the view that the Karbis immigrated into the present Karbi Anglong district crossing over the hill ranges lying between Southern Nagaland and Northern Manipur, and further proceeded through North Cachar Hills to their present habitat. Here, the Karbis come into contact with the historically powerful principalities of the Kacharis, the Jaintias and the Ahoms. Much later they come into contact with the British. It is in the Ahom and the British periods that Karbis spread themselves territorially covering the major part of their present habitat. Their relation with the Ahoms was cordial and that with the British was somewhat indifferent, if not inimical, and this especially encouraged them to settle in the foothills and the plains. During the British period, the Karbis came under the influence of modern administrative system, and as a result social and political consciousness and sensitivity developed to an appreciable extent. They were so much influenced that they developed an aspiration to have a separate administrative entity for themselves, which they could manage to achieve in the form of a separate autonomous district in the post-Independence period.

The Karbi Land

During the British period the present Karbi Anglong district was included partly in Nowgaon and Sibsagar districts and partly in Khasi and Jaintia Hills district. The areas inhabited by the Karbis were called 'Partially Excluded Area' and 'Excluded Area'. The provisions of the 'Partially Excluded Area' order operated in the districts of Nowgaon and Sibsagar. The Karbi settlement in the Khasi and Jaintia Hills came fully under the provisions of the 'Excluded Area' order.

After Independence, the areas inhabited by the Karbis were carved out from the districts of Nowgaon, Sibsagar and United Khasi and Jaintia Hills and added to what was formed as the new United Mikir and North Cachar Hill District. On 2nd February, 1970 Mikir Hills was declared as a separate administrative district, and renamed as Karbi Anglong on the 14th October, 1976.

The Karbi Anglong district is bounded on the north by Nowgaon and Golaghat districts, on the south by the North

Cachar Hills district, on the east by Golaghat district and State of Nagaland and on the west by the State of Meghalaya. It lies between latitudes 25°30' and 26°41' N and between longitudes 92°7' and 93°52' E. The district has a total geographical area of 10,332 sq. km. There are three Civil Sub-divisions—Diphu, Hamren and Bokajan. The Bokajan Sub-division came into existence on August 15, 1989. There are six police stations in the district, namely Diphu (2009 sq. km.), Baithalangso (1030 sq. km.), Bokajan (2263 sq. km.), Howraghat (1985 sq. km.), Hamren (2005 sq. km.) and Khereni (1040 sq. km.).

According to 1971 Census, there were seven National Extension Service Blocks (NES) in the district (Table 13.1).

TABLE 13.1: **NES Blocks with their Area and Headquarters**

Name of the Block	Area in Acre	Headquarters
Rongkhang	1,92,019	Donkamokan
Bokajan	1,43,360	Bokajan
Howraghat	6,25,020	Howraghat
Lumbajong	5,90,060	Manja
Nilip	69,306	Chokihola
Amri	2,62,640	Ulukunchi
Socheng	1,16,846	Jirikindim

Source: Census of India, 1971, *District Census Handbook.*

From the above Table 13.1, it is seen that the Howraghat Block is the biggest in area. The smallest Block is Nilip. Apart from these blocks, there are some other blocks which are called the Integrated Tribal Development Blocks (ITDB) with all ancillary facilities. In the true sense, these are not full-fledged blocks as they are under the management of one or the other of the aforesaid seven parent blocks for overall supervision and management. The ITDP Blocks in the district are Chinthong with Headquarters at Hamren, Samelangso with Headquarter at Samelangso and Rongmongwe with Headquarters at Rongmongwe.

Karbi Village

Generally, the Karbis live in homogeneous villages. According to 1971 Census, the total number of Karbi villages in Karbi Anglong was 1451 (Table 13.2).

TABLE 13.2: **Police Station-wise Distribution of Villages**

Police Station	No. of Villages
Baithalangso	503
Howraghat	318
Bokajan	377
Diphu	253

The Baithalangso Police Station now includes both the Baithalangso and the Hamren Police Stations while the Diphu Police Station includes both Diphu and Kheroni Police Stations.

The Karbis exhibit a peculiar habitual custom of not settling down at a place for a considerable length of time. Permanent habitations are, therefore, rarely seen. Villages are frequently shifted from place to place within a definite territorial limitation. The causes for this kind of shifting are diverse. The death of the village headman, the epidemics or the scarcity of water, all or one of these may cause the shifting.

The Agro-Economic Research Centre for North East India, Jorhat, undertook a survey at Kanther Terang, a Karbi village, in March, 1961 and also in 1966. The survey found that the previous site of the village was just at the periphery of Diphu town where it remained for more than ten years. By 1966 the village was shifted to a distance of about two and half miles from Diphu (Saikia, 1968:1).

Occasionally, under certain circumstances mostly economic and socio-cultural, a section of the village might break away and set up a new village.

A Karbi village is thus socio-cultural and socio-economic in nature rather than a political unit. The households in a village are bound by social and economic bonds. The village headman, the *Sarthe*, occupies an honourable place in the social set up of the village.

The naming of the village after the name of the headman is a long established custom. The death of the headman may warrant a change of the name of the village. Therefore, recording of the names of the villages for official purposes sometimes runs into difficulties.

Population Trend

Lyall (1908: 1) mentioned that the number of Mikirs was 87,046 in the 1901 Census, and the speakers of the Mikir language was 82,283. Thus there was a discrepency in the two figures. The author further observed that in no districts the number of speakers was identical with the number of those returned as Mikirs. It was indeed remarkable that more persons were returned as speakers of the language of the tribe than belonging to the tribe. On the other hand, in the North Cachar Hills none of the 1446 Mikirs were shown as the Mikir speakers who were manifestly absorbed. The figures of the Census 1901, regarding as Mikirs as a tribe and as speakers of one's own language was quite interesting as can be seen in Table 13.3.

TABLE 13.3: **Mikirs as a Tribe and as Speakers**

District	Mikir by race	Speaking Mikir
Cachar Plains	717	728
Sylhet	156	166
Kamrup	10,581	8,026
Darrang	2,646	3,108
Nowgaon	33,732	34,278
Sibsagar	22,909	22,803
North Cachar	1,446	Nil
Khasi & Jaintia Hills	12,840	13,142
Elsewhere	13	37
Total	87,046	82,283

Source: Lyall, 1908: 1.

From the Table 13.3, it is clear that in Kamrup, Nowgaon and Sibsagar the Mikirs or the Karbis have returned numerically higher than the other places. Lyall (1908: 1-2) assumed that the Mikirs returned as speakers also spoke some other language (probably Assamese), being bilingual like other non-Aryan races in Assam; and the 809 persons in Darrang, the Khasi and Jaintia Hills, and elsewhere, returned as speaking Mikirs, though not as Mikirs by tribe, must really have belonged to the tribe. The author further opined that since 1891, when the number of Mikirs was returned as 94,829, there has been a considerable falling off, due to the terrible ravages of the disease called *Kalaazar* in the Nowgong and Kamrup districts.

The above observations of Lyall (1908) gives us an idea of the Karbi populations trend which is peculiar in the present context. The author has highlighted that the district is malarious and unhealthy for unacclimatized persons, with a very moist climate, and is wanting in the breezy amenities of the higher plateaus of the Khasi and Jaintia Hills; but (save during the recent prevalence of *Kalaazar*) the inhabitants appear to have acquired some degree of immunity against the noxious influences of the locality (Lyall, 1908:3).

During the first even Census of 1872 under the British, the total Karbi population was 47,328. Separate figures for males and females were not shown. By 1881, their number rose to 77,765 over the previous census population figure accounting for the decadal growth rate of 64.12 per cent. It was observed that this almost abrupt decadal growth was perhaps due to the reason that the enumeration in the first year was not so comprehensive as the next enumeration was. In the following decade there was an increase of the Karbi population figure which returned 94,829 showing a decadal growth of 31.94 per cent.

During the decade 1891-1901 the total Karbi population showed a marked fall by 7.90 per cent. This sharp fall could not be accounted for by the records in the relevant census. However, as has already been mentioned by Lyall (1908) it must have been due to the terrible disease of *Kalaazar* in the Nowgong and Kamrup districts.

The Censuses of 1872, 1881 and 1891 have shown

considerable increase of Karbi population in the districts of Kamrup, Nowgaon, Darrang, Sibsagar and Lakhimpur. It is to be noted that Nowgaon district showed the highest growth of Karbi population (36%) during 1872-1881. This is mainly due to the fact that what was shown as Naga Hills in 1872 later came to be included in the Nowgaon district where Karbi population concentrated. Further, the large increase of Karbi population in Darrang, Sibsagar, and Lakhimpur was shown to be due to immigration of the Karbis most probably from Nowgaon district where they lived in large concentration.

The Karbis living in Goalpara district did not appear in 1881 Census. It was perhaps due to their emigration to other districts. Till 1891, the Karbi population continued to increase considerably in the district of Khasi and Jaintia Hills and Darrang at the dacadal growth rate of 81.75 per cent and 79.69 per cent respectively. The high growth rate in the Khasi and Jaintia Hills is perhaps due to more careful census enumeration, and in Darrang, due to immigration from the Southern bank, especially from Nowgaon district, which recorded a slight increase (0.81%). However, North Cachar and Kamrup districts recorded a decrease during the decade of 1881-1891. The decrease in the former was 49.91 per cent and in the latter it was 12.56 per cent. This is due to the emigration. There was also a slight decrease in Cachar and Sibsagar districts.

The disappearance of Karbi population from Lakhimpur is interesting, the reason being the suspected confusion of the Census enumeration of the Mikirs (Karbis) and the Niris (Mishings). The Karbis must have been recorded as the Mishings. This, therefore, accounts for the surprisingly high numerical figure for the Mishings and a small figure for the Karbis in the Census of 1891.

In the decade 1901-11, the growth rate of the population was 21.67 per cent. During the 1911-21, there was an epidemic outbreak of influenza besides *Kalaazar* which both swept over Kamrup, Nowgaon and Sibsagar districts. This again resulted in a very low growth rate of 5.05 per cent of the Karbi population during the decade. In the following two decades, the growth rates recorded was 16.28 per cent (1921-31) and 15.37 per cent

(1931-41) respectively. The Census of the succeeding decade indicated a fall in the growth rate to 1.86 per cent (in 1941-51) which was perhaps due to the separation of Sylhet district from India. Following the partition in 1947, a large number of the Karbis who also lived in that district went over to the then East Pakistan (now Bangladesh).

In the 1961 Census again there was a sharp fall of the Karbi population to the tune of 20.62 per cent. This surprising fall, however, was not because of any epidemic or such natural calamity but because of the Government Modification Order on Scheduled Castes and Scheduled Tribes in 1956 which excluded all the Karbi population living outside the autonomous hill district, namely, United Khasi and Jaintia Hills, United Mikir and North Cachar Hills, Garo Hills and the Lushai Hills. This involved the exclusion of a good number of Karbis living in the plains districts of Assam.

The figure shown against 1971 Census gives a 58.04 per cent decadal growth over 1961 Census. This clearly indicates a quite high growth rate of Karbi population during the decade. This decadal growth was perhaps due to the migration of the Karbis from the plains districts to the autonomous district of Karbi Anglong.

Conclusion

To sum up, it can be said that growth of population among the Karbis according to the earlier Censuses of 1891-1901 was slow. The negative variation shown in 1901 Census was chiefly due to the effect of natural calamities such as the outbreak of black fever and other epidemics which had done ravages to most Karbi inhabited areas. The negative variation in 1951-61 was due to the Government Notification on the constitution of the autonomous District Council under the provision of the Sixth Schedule to the Constitution that excluded all Karbi population living outside the autonomous district of United Mikir and North Cachar Hills. By 1971, Karbi population showed a considerable upward trend. This has happened due to the migration of the Karbis from plains districts to the autonomous district of Karbi Anglong.

However, it is observed that in all the Censuses, the growth of male population was more than that of the females.

REFERENCES

Chari, R.B., 1975: Census of India, 1971 Series-I, Paper I, *Scheduled Castes and Scheduled Tribes*, Tables-C, VIII Parts A & B, New Delhi: Government Publication.

Lyall, C., 1908: *The Mikirs*, Lodon: David Nutt.

Lyndoh, F.B. and B.K. Roy Burman, 1972: Census of India 1961, Vol. I, Monograph Series, Part V-B, *Mikir of Assam*, Delhi: Manager of Publication.

Saikia, P.D., 1968: *Changes in Mikir Society*, Jorhat: Agro-Economic Centre for North East India.

14

ENVIRONMENT AND SOME ASPECTS OF POPULATION STRUCTURE OF MEGHALAYA*

D. TYAGI

The environment, which is indispensable for man's survival, plays an important role in shaping demographic structures. They are so intimately interlinked that all development programmes must take the major demographic dimension into consideration. Because "the study of demographic features provide the correct understanding of resource features and an appreciation of regional differences" (Kayastha 1964:304). Population studies can be traced back to 391 to 269 B.C., when Kautilya suggested how to conduct population, economic and agricultural censuses. The interdependency between man and environment is well known and in view of this, we present the ecology alongwith some demographic aspects, such as population structure, density, sex-ratio, occupation etc. of Meghalaya.

Meghalaya (Megh=cloud; alaya=abode)—the abode of clouds, one of the smallest states of India; a tribal dominated state. This majestic mountainous state of North East India lies between 25°47'N to 26°10'N latitude and 89°45'E to 92°47' longitude. It has an area of 22,489,00 ha. It is bounded by Bangladesh (a nation that has emerged one month perior to the formation of the state) on the south and one fourth of western border and the rest is bounded by Assam. It is an eastwest extension of Peninsular plateau region of India seperated from the main block by a gap, subsequently the area is filled with the alluvial deposits of the Ganges and the Brahmaputra. Meghalaya is situated on the Shillong plateau, renamed as Meghalaya Plateau. 'This plateau is an example of structural platform bordered by a steep scarp in the south which detaches the Surma Valley from it and gently sloping towards Brahmaputra Valley in the north'. It is full of highly dissected and irregular terrain, but on western and southern boundary it has regular and steep fall, whereas the northern boundary is difficult to describe. Meghalaya is a land locked region with mountainous terrain, dense forest, enchanting streams and rivulets have given rise to relative isolation. "Meghalaya plateau, with maximum height upto 1961 m above m.s.l. lies across the path of the south west monsoonal winds as an imposing barrier. The moisture laden winds strike first of all to its southtern steep . . . the area between Mawsynram and Cherrapunjee receives highest orographic rainfall in the world." (Husain 1984:70). Due to these, the vegetation is luxuriant and extends from a variety of savannah grass and bamboos in the valleys to dense pine and evergreen forests on the hills. The area is rich in minerals, like coal, iron ore, quarts, sillimanite, glass, uranium etc. In spite of "more or less flat erosinal surface have formed giant steps, which make the road transport easier with gentle climb, whereas in ridge and valley topography of the Himalayas road transportation faces difficulties with steep climb..." (*Ibid.*:74). The area is well known for *Jhum* cultivation, which is practised in loamy soils on the hill slopes. However, settled cultivation is also practised in river valleys and on terraces. The horticulture and plantation crops, such as banana, oranges, arecanut etc. are grown in coarse loomy soils. It is said that climatically Meghalaya is suitable for sericulture and animal husbandry.

Meghalaya, in spite of having rugged topography, extremely moist and inhospitable claimate and dense vegetation, is picturesque and beautiful. Then Meghalaya was formed in 1972 out of the two hill districts of Assam—namely the Garo Hills and Khasi-Jaintia Hills, at present there are seven districts (East Garo Hills, West Garo Hills, Bagmara, Jaintia Hills, East Khasi Hills, West Khasi Hills and Nongpoh). In Meghalaya only 9.93 per cent of the total land is under cultivation (i.e. 2,23,370 ha under cultivation, out of total 22,48,900 ha). "On the basis of geomorphology, altitude, soil and climatic factors Meghalaya has different agroclimatic regions. The Garo Hills due to lower altitude, comparatively high temparature, low gently undulating rolling plains, loamy soils etc. are more suitable for agriculture than rest of the Meghalaya." (*Ibid*:70). The Garo Hills region is an intensively dissected part with an average alevation of 600 metres above (m.s.l.). The two important physiographic features of the region are Tura range and the Simsag Valley. The Garo is the main tribal group which inhabit the Garo Hills. According to one legend they are the descendants of Torua—a province in Tibet. They are said to be a part of Bodo-ethnic stream. They speak a dialect of Tibeto-Burman group. The Garo Hills District had 35.49 per cent of area of the state but it shares 48.78 per cent of its total cropped area; 52.29 per cent of area is sown more than once, 55.42 per cent of the total cropped area is under food grains and constitutes 52.36 per cent of the total food grain production in the state. (Husain, 1984:72). Crops cultivated in the Garo Hills are rice, pulses, cotton, tobacco, oil seeds, chillies etc.

The Khasi-Jaintia Hills region is a true plateau. At micro level it constitute, the undulating hills in the north, upland topography in the central and precipitous face of upland in the south. The region occupies 63.59 per cent of the total area and has higher population, in comparison to other region. The region is the represented by two tribal group, i.e. Jaintia and Khasi, which also forms the majority population of the region. It is believed that the Khasis and Jaintias are the remnant of the Monogolian overflow into India. The Khasi language belong to Mon-Khmer family of languages.

Population, Growth and Sex Ratio

The population of Meghalaya is 17,74,778 (1991 Census) constituting 0.22 per cent to the total population of India (1991 Census) it was 0.20 per cent in 1981. The Scheduled Tribes population has increased from 2.09 per cent in 1981 to 2.34 per cent in 1991 in relation to population of India. The corresponding figures of Scheduled Caste is negligeable to 0.01 per cent (in 1991). This reveals that the Scheduled Tribe and Scheduled Caste population has increased in relation to all India figures. But for 'other' it is 0.05 per cent in 1981 and became 0.04 per cent in 1991 (Census of India 1991). The Census of 1991 reveals that in the state, the Scheduled Tribe population is 85.53 per cent (rural = 90.82%; urban = 62.36%), and Scheduled Caste population is 0.51 per cent (rural = 0.34%; urban = 1.24%) and remaining 13.96 per cent (rural = 8.84%; urban = 36.39%) is non-S.T./S.C. population. The growth rate during last decade is quite high in S.C. population (total = 65.19%; rural = 68.54%; urban = 61.25%) followed by S.T. population (total = 41.03%; rural = 39.18%; urban = 54.05%) and negative growth in non-S.T./S.C. population (total = –2.44%; rural = –14.20%; urban = 14.20%). The overall growth is 32.86 per cent (rural = 32.00%; urban = 36.70%). The Sex Ratio is highest (997) in S.T., followed by S.C. (821) and non-S.T./S.C. (739) giving a overall Sex Ratio of 955.

The population of Meghalaya was 340,524 in 1901 and grew to 1,744,778 by 1991 (Table 14.1), showing an increase of 21.19 per cent. The population increased over every decade, but there were fluctuation in growth rates in different decades this increase was less than 20 per cent before 1951 (prior to Independence). But, after Independence there is a constant increase in growth rate and during the last decade it was 32.86. Another noteworthy feature is the high percentage of female upto 1921 and thereafter a constant decline in the sex ratio (Table 14.1). The sex ratio constantly declined from 1036 in 1901 to 937 in 1961 (After 1961 the sex ratio in Meghalaya has shown improvement). Splitting the population into rural and urban there is a wide variation in sex ratio. Comparatively, sex ratio is always higher in rural area than urban area. This situation is expected, because in urban areas immigrants come in search of jobs, leaving their family behind. This is one of the major factors for a low sex ratio in urban area. But a deeper analysis of sex ratio reveals that from 1971 onwards, trend has slightly changed, the data indicates a higher sex ratio than what was during the earlier decades. With constant increase in population the density has increased from 15 (in 1901) to 79 (in 1991), but, it is lower than the national average or Assam. The literacy in Meghalaya has increased to 49.26 per cent

TABLE 14.1: **Population Distribution, Sex Ratio and Growth in Meghalaya (1901-1991)**

	Population			Growth Rate	Sex Ratio			Density
	Total	Male	Female		Total	Rural	Urban	
1901	340,524	167,256	173,268	—	1,036	1,047	725	15
1911	394,005	195,706	198,299	15.72	1,013	1,024	757	18
1921	422,403	211,216	211,187	70.21	1,000	1,009	809	19
1931	480,837	243,993	236,844	18.83	971	989	697	21
1941	555,820	282,666	273,154	15.59	966	991	683	25
1951	605,674	310,706	294,968	8.97	949	967	784	27
1961	769,380	397,288	372,092	27.03	937	971	764	34
1971	1,011,699	520,967	490,732	31.50	942	958	853	45
1981	1,335,819	683,710	652,109	32.04	954	965	904	60
1991	1,774,778	907,687	867,091	32.86	955	966	910	79

(rural = 41.05%; urban = 81.74%). The male population has a higher literacy rate 51.57 per cent than female 44.85 per cent Meghalaya has a total area of 22429 sq. km., out of which 99.31 per cent is rural and remaining 0.69 per cent urban, 81.40 per cent of the population lives in rural areas, thereby giving a very higher density to urban area (2145.67 person per sq. km.) in comparison to rural area (64.86 person per sq. km.). There are 5.24 persons per household (rural = 5.44%; urban = 5.34%) and the variation in urban and rural is very little. The state is predominately inhabited by Scheduled Tribes, as 85.53 per cent accounts for S.T. population and of which 86.44 per cent lives in rural area and remaining (13.56%) lives in urban areas.

The population structure of Jaintia, Khasi and Garo show slight variation. Out of total population of Meghalaya 62.31 per cent lives in Jaintia-Khasi hills and remaining (37.69%) lives in Garo hills. In both the regions the population in the rural area is significantly higher (above 99%), it is slightly more in Garo region than Jaintia-Khasi region (Table 14.2). The analysis of persons per household of the two regions reveals a slightly higher number of persons in Jaintia-Khasi hills (5.50%) than in the Garo hills (5.30%). It is worth mentioning that in the rural areas of Jaintia hills person per household (5.57%) are more than in the urban area (5.29%), whereas in the Garo area (rural = 5.27%; urban = 5.63%) the picture is reverse. The Scheduled Tribe population to the total population of the area is more or less similar. However, the S.T. population of the region to the total Meghalaya S.T. population, we find that 62.46 per cent lives in Jaintia-Khasi region and 37.54 per cent lives in Garo region. The respective rural and urban area figures are 60.20 per cent; 76.85 per cent and 39.80 per cent; 23.15 per cent respectively. The variability is seen in the literacy rate of the two regions. It is high in Jaintia-Khasi (42.74%) than Garo (32.37%). The literacy is high in urban areas, as well among males as is clear from Table 14.2.

The workers are divided into various categories and they are presented in Table 14.2. There are 2.35 per cent marginal workers in Meghalaya and majority in rural areas and only 0.66 per cent of marginal workers are in urban areas. The

TABLE 14.2: **Occupational Categories in Two Regions of Meghalaya**

	Meghalaya			Jaintia-Khasi			Garo		
	P	M	F	P	M	F	P	M	F
	(1)	(2)	(3)	(4)	(5)	(6)	(7)	(8)	(9)
Marginal Workers									
Total	2.35	0.53	4.26	0.90	0.25	1.59	4.75	1.01	8.65
Rural	2.74	0.60	4.95	1.15	0.25	1.83	5.11	1.09	9.27
Urban	0.66	0.23	1.13	0.49	0.22	0.79	1.34	0.27	2.53
Main Workers									
Total	40.32	49.52	30.67	40.66	49.59	31.29	39.75	49.44	29.65
Rural	42.30	50.42	33.90	43.19	50.42	35.70	41.07	50.41	31.40
Urban	37.64	45.78	16.10	32.68	47.04	16.95	27.28	40.56	12.50
Cultivators									
Total	55.31	50.75	63.02	44.22	39.52	52.04	74.07	69.15	82.10
Rural	64.16	61.01	69.00	54.31	51.01	59.06	78.53	74.89	84.57
Urban	3.55	2.78	6.11	2.13	1.69	3.49	10.53	7.70	21.04

(Contd.)

TABLE 14.2 *(Contd.)*

	(1)	(2)	(3)	(4)	(5)	(6)	(7)	(8)	(9)
Agri. labourers									
Total	12.15	11.60	14.03	13.19	12.92	15.61	10.10	9.41	11.29
Rural	14.12	13.49	15.08	16.71	16.24	17.40	10.33	9.68	11.41
Urban	3.08	2.76	4.06	2.33	2.01	3.30	6.78	6.33	8.38
Livestocks									
Total	6.39	6.37	6.43	9.71	9.61	9.88	0.78	0.98	0.43
Rural	7.15	7.25	6.99	9.80	11.90	11.20	0.62	0.78	0.35
Urban	1.96	2.26	1.03	1.74	2.06	0.78	3.04	3.21	2.43
Others									
Total	26.15	31.28	16.52	32.88	37.95	22.47	15.05	20.16	6.18
Rural	14.57	18.25	8.93	19.18	20.85	12.34	10.52	14.65	3.67
Urban	91.41	92.25	88.80	93.80	94.24	92.43	79.65	82.76	68.15

(Contd.)

TABLE 14.2 *(Contd.)*

	(1)	(2)	(3)	(4)	(5)	(6)	(7)	(8)	(9)
Preliminary workers									
Total	74.81	69.51	83.75	68.69	63.15	77.90	78.77	80.11	93.92
Rural	86.01	82.55	91.31	83.50	80.36	88.10	89.65	85.59	96.40
Urban	9.27	8.46	11.81	6.89	6.49	8.11	21.12	17.87	32.88
Secondary workers									
Total	3.73	5.17	1.54	4.61	6.30	1.79	2.09	2.93	1.11
Rural	2.04	2.62	1.14	2.30	3.00	1.28	1.64	2.09	0.90
Urban	13.71	16.35	5.42	14.24	17.19	5.28	11.07	12.41	5.24
Tertiary workers									
Total	21.46	25.32	14.71	26.70	30.55	20.31	11.64	16.96	4.97
Rural	11.95	14.83	70.55	14.20	16.64	10.62	6.43	12.31	2.70
Urban	77.02	75.19	82.77	78.87	76.32	86.61	67.81	69.72	60.88

regionwise analysis reveals that Garo region has a high percentage of marginal workers (4.75%) than in Jaintia-Khasi (0.90%) region. Irrespective of region and area, the female as marginal workers are more than males as marginal worker. The main workers are further sub-divided into cultivators, agricultural labourers, livestocks etc. and 'others' (cf Table 14.2). A large number of people (55.31%) are engaged in cultivation and only 12.15 per cent are working as agricultural labourers and 6.39 per cent are engaged in livestocks. It is seen that a higher number (63.02%) of females are engaged in cultivation, whereas only 50.75 per cent of males are cultivators. Similar is the situation with the rural females and only 3.55 per cent of urban population is engaged in cultivation. A large number of Garo people (74.07%) are engaged in cultivation in comparison to Jaintia-Khasi (44.22%). It is higher in rural areas than urban areas. Irrespective of area and region the females percentage engaged in cultivation are more than their counterparts. Agricultural labourers are low (12.15%) in Meghalaya. It is lesser in males and urban areas. The comparative analysis of two regions reveals that agricultural labourers are high in Jaintia-Khasi (13.19%) in comparison to Garo (10.10%). In this occupational category the females percentage are more than males, irrespective of area and region. In livestock occupation category 6.3 per cent are engaged. It is high in rural area than urban area. Similar is the situation in Jaintia-Khasi, whereas the people in this category are 9.71 per cent (rural = 9.80%; urban = 1.74%). But in Garo region the situation is just reverse to Jaintia-Khasi, as only 0.78 per cent people pursue this occupation, in Garo region and it is high in urban areas (3.04%) than rural area (0.62%). A sexual variation is also observed among Garo people, but not so in Jaintia-Khasi region.

The various occupational categories as given in census of India are clubed into three major occupations, i.e. Primary, Secondary and tertiary workers. An analysis indicates that primary workers are in majority in Meghalaya (74.81%), followed by tertiary (21.46%) and secondary (3.73%). The female primary workers (83.75%) are more in comparison to male primary workers (65.91%) and similar is the case in rural and urban areas. But in urban areas their percentage is quite low. The secondary and tertiary workers are more in urban areas than rural areas. At the same time the male percentage dominates over female percentage in primary and secondary workers category except in tertiary worker of urban area where we find a high frequency of females. Similar is the situation in Jaintia-Khasi region, where the secondary and tertiary workers are 4.61 per cent and 26.70 per cent respectively. In Garo region more or less the situation is same except in this female percentage is lower than male and the frequency percentage is low in comparison to Jaintia-Khasi region. On the basis of comparative analysis of two regions, we find more or less similar trend with few exceptions in population structure which goes with the variation in environment between the two regions. It also reveals that the Scheduled Tribes constitute the bulk of the population of state and regions. It is also clear from the discussion that agricultural activities are the most resourceful of all types of economic pursuits prevalent in Meghalaya. The Industrial growth is also slow and mainly concentrated in Jaintia-Khasi region, but in recent past the other region—Garo is also inching towards industrial growth. At present the growth and progress in two regions are more or less similar, except in few areas such as industrialization, literacy, urbanisation etc.

Note: In primary, cultivation; agricultural labourer; livestock, forestry, fishing etc. and mining and quarrying are included. In secondary manufacturing, processing, servicing, repairs are included. In the tertiary remaining occupations are included. The figures given are as per Census of India.

REFERENCES

Census of India 1991 Series I, India, Paper 2 of 1992, Final Tables: Brief Analysis of Census Abstract.

Census of India 1981, Meghalaya.

Husain, Z. 1984, Ecological Implications of Environmental Factors in the Meghalaya Plateau Ecosystem. In *Status of Ecology* ed. by I.J.S. Jaswal, Petide: Punjab Publishing House, pp. 69-77.

15

POPULATION GROWTH AND NATURAL RESOURCE BASE IN MEGHALAYA

SUTAPA DATTA

The population in any nation or that of its societies, and its growth over time maintains a direct relation with the resource base of the country. This relation may be smooth or strained, depending on the population resource ratio being high, low or balanced (Ackerman, 1970). It is only in developed countries or societies, that the population resource ratio becomes either high or balanced. In developing and underdeveloped nations, however, due to a rapid growth of population over a shorter span of time, the man-resource ratio is usually low and imbalanced. The imbalance is not simply caused by population or by resource alone. The factors as economy of the country or society, the stage of technological development and level of expectations of its people, should also be given due consideration. However, the number of population and its change over time is usually considered as the point of beginning in any assessment of population-resource relationship.

It is quite difficult to hold a proper relationship between population and resources, both of which have varying quantity and quality over space and time. Even then, it is essential to have a clear idea about such a relationship in the context of growing population and economic and social development. The term 'resource', as has been conceptualised by geographers and other social scientists, may be any object or substance, having certain function and can satisfy certain want or demand of human being. Thus a variety of natural object may be there to frame the resource base of a country. In the present context, however, the impact of population growth on resources is assessed from the point of view of man-land ratio, which has particularly affected density and distribution pattern on the one hand and the coverages of forest on the other.

It is in this backdrop, the chapter analyses the population-resource relationship in Meghalaya. This kind of study for Meghalaya becomes far more significant, since the population in the state (though only 0.2 per cent of country's total) show an appreciable annual and decadal rise of 2.80 per cent and 31.8 per cent respectively (1981-91), compared to 2.1 and 23.5 per cent of those of the country. This high rate of growth of population is sure to create pressure on the limited amount of land (0.68 per cent of country's total) in the State. Again, a considerable part of land in the State being rough and rockey, puts increased pressure on arable land to obtain at least the subsistence products, and at the same time leads to large scale depletion of forest coverage, by unplanned and un-economic use of them for shifting cultivation. Thus the basic resources of the state (land and forest) more than being gainfully extracted and utilised (due to a relatively low level of technology), are being deteriorated by population growth.

The chapter has been worked out basing on secondary source of data as Census and other Government reports, books and research articles. A few simple statistical techniques have been used to analyse the data for their interpretation. However, non-availability of data at several instances has limited the scope of the work in further detail.

II

The population in Meghalaya shows a positive trend of growth from 1901-91. This is more or less common in other States of the North Eastern Region (Table 15.1). However, the growth rate in Meghalaya (471.03% in 1901-91), though quite high in relation to that of the national average (254.00%), yet when compared to regional level, remains much lower than those of Mizoram and Nagaland.

TABLE 15.1: **Population Growth in North Eastern Region, 1901-91**

State/Region/Country	Percentage share of population	Growth 1981-91	Growth 1901-91
(1)	(2)	(3)	(4)
Arunachal Pradesh	2.37	35.86	154.60+
Assam	71.77	23.58	577.71
Manipur	5.82	28.56	542.16
Meghalaya	5.61	31.80	471.03
Mizoram	2.19	38.98	732.44
Nagaland	3.87	56.86	1097.02
Tripura	8.75	33.69	1483.63
N.E. India	3.71*	21.87	630.02
All India	100	23.50	254.00

* Relates to share to total Indian Population.

+ Related to the period 1961-91.

Sources: *Basic Statistics of NER*, 1992.

A look at the population growth in Meghalaya, reflects two distinct patterns i.e. pre-Independence growth pattern (1901-51) and post-Independence growth pattern (1951-91). The former is characterised by a low and fluctuating rate of growth on the whole, whereas the latter shows a moderately high and steady growth rate (Table 15.2).

The population growth in Meghalaya, as reflected in Table 15.2, reveals that, prior to 1951-61, the growth pattern was highly fluctuating. This could be attributed to factors like natural increase and emigration (Kar, 1986) on one hand (1901-11 and 1921-41), and the effects of war, famines, epidemics, and reorganisation of the hill districts of Assam through separation of Mikir Hills from the Khasi-Jaintia and Garo Hills region (Census of Assam, 1951) etc. on the other (1911-21, 1941-51).

TABLE 15.2: **Decadal Change in Population, 1901-91, Meghalaya and India**

Census Decades	Meghalaya		India	
	Total Population	Growth Rate (%)	Total Population	Growth Rate (%)
(1)	(2)	(3)	(4)	(5)
1901	340524	—	238396000	—
1911	394005	15.7	252093000	5.8
1921	422403	7.8	251321000	-0.3
1931	480837	13.8	278977000	11.0
1941	555820	15.6	318661000	14.2
1951	605674	9.0	361088000	13.3
1961	769380	27.0	439235000	21.6
1971	1011699	31.5	548160000	24.8
1981	1335819	32.0	685184692	25.0
1991	1774778	32.9	836212161	23.6

Source: Calculated from Census of India, 1981 and 1991, Meghalaya, and *Basic Statistics of NER*, 1992.

The trend of population growth from 1951 onwards is quite high resulting from a high natural increase due to eradication of dreadful deseases from the region (malaria, *Kalaazar*, influenza, etc.) and immigration of people into the State who were attracted by various developmental programmes introduced in the State as well. However, the growth of population in Meghalaya, appears to be primarily due to natural growth (Table 15.3), which indicates an early second phase of demographic transition of its population.

A quite spectacular aspect of population growth in Meghalaya is its wide variation from rural to urban areas. The rural areas, though maintain a considerable rate of increase, the growth rates do not deviate much from that of the population as a whole. The urban population, on the contrary,

TABLE 15.3: **Decadal Birth and Death Rates and Population Growth from 1981-91**

(Birth and Death Rate figures are all per thousand)

Decades	India			Eastern Region*			Meghalaya		
	Birth Rate	Death Rate	Growth	Birth Rate	Death Rate	Growth	Birth Rate	Death Rate	Growth
(1)	(2)	(3)	(4)	(5)	(6)	(7)	(8)	(9)	(10)
1881-91	48.9	41.3	7.6	—	—	—	—	—	—
1891-1901	45.8	44.4	1.4	51.0	46.0	5.0	—	—	—
1901-11	49.2	42.6	6.6	49.0	44.0	5.0	—	—	—
1911-21	48.1	47.2	0.9	50.0	49.0	+1.0	—	—	—
1921-31	46.4	36.3	10.1	47.0	36.0	11.0	—	—	—
1931-41	45.2	31.2	14.0	46.0	34.0	12.0	—	—	—
1941-51	39.9	27.4	12.5	44.0	32.0	12.0	—	—	—
1951-61	41.7	22.8	18.9	45.0	26.0	19.0	—	—	—

(Contd.)

TABLE 15.3 *(Contd.)*

(1)	(2)	(3)	(4)	(5)	(6)	(7)	(8)	(9)	(10)
1961-71	38.5	16.5	22.0	44.0	20.4	23.6	—	—	—
1971-81	34.6	14.7	19.9	—	—	—	32.5	12.6	19.9+
1981-91	32.7	11.5	21.2	—	—	—	34.3	9.9	24.9

* Constituents states are: Arunachal Pradesh, Assam, Manipur, Meghalaya, Mizoram, Nagaland, Tripura, Orissa, Bihar, Sikkim, West Bengal, Andaman & Nichobar Islands.

+ Relates to 1976-81.

Source: Calculated from:

(i) S.C. Srivastava: *Demographic Profile of North East India*;

(ii) M.K. Premi: *India's Population—Heading Towards a Billion*;

(iii) Basic Statistics of NER, 1992.

shows a very high rate of growth, particularly in the decades of 1921-31, 1951-61, and 1971-81 (Table 15.4). The high urban growth in these decades was mostly associated with reclassification of new urban centres in the State. The unequal rural and urban growth in Meghalaya, however, is to be interpreted in the light of number of urban centres and their respective status. Thus, it becomes clear that, since urban areas are only twelve in number and far apart from one another, they have to cover large rural hinter-lands, which tends to increase urban population of these urban centres mainly by rural-urban migration. However, the growth of rural population, though much less than the urban growth, cannot be underestimated, when the size of the State and its proportion of the rural population are considered.

TABLE 15.4: **Growth of Rural and Urban Population in Meghalaya, 1901-91**

Census Decades	Growth Rate: Rural			Growth Rate: Urban		
	Total	Male	Female	Total	Male	Female
(1)	(2)	(3)	(4)	(5)	(6)	(7)
1901-11	15.0	16.2	13.7	2.3	39.2	45.3
1911-21	6.6	7.3	5.8	26.7	22.5	30.9
1921-31	12.1	13.2	11.0	53.1	64.4	41.8
1931-41	13.9	13.8	14.0	43.7	45.2	42.1
1941-51	5.7	6.9	4.5	55.3	44.5	66.0
1951-61	19.2	19.0	19.3	100.5	103.1	97.9
1961-71	32.6	33.5	31.7	26.2	19.3	33.1
1971-81	26.6	26.1	27.1	64.4	59.6	69.2
1981-91	30.8	31.3	30.3	36.4	36.3	36.4

Source: *Census of India*, 1981 and 1991.

III

The growth of population, as analysed in the previous paragraphs have significant bearing on its resource-base, which is limited not because of its scarcity, but also considerably due to non-extraction as a result of a low level of technology. The primary and obvious effect of population increase in Meghalaya is the changing nature of its population density which has increased from only 15 persons in 1901 to 79 persons per sq.km. in 1991. However, the general density in Meghalaya is much less compared to the national (267 persons) or North East regional (823 persons) densities. But in the context of proportionate share of land of the States in India, a density of 79 persons becomes quite impressive in a state whose total land share is only 0.2 per cent of the country's total and a major share of this being not available for cultivation.

The real pressure of population on land in any area is better understood by man-land ratios. These ratios become more meaningful in a state like Meghalaya, where majority of people depend directly on land to eke out their living. Though there has been a considerable increase in net cultivated area from 174 thousand hectares in 1970-71 to 203 thousand hectares in 1989-90, which means about 17 per cent of increase in cultivated land, the population over this period has increased by 75 per cent and agricultural population by 37 per cent. Thus compared to its general density, both physiological* and agricultural** densities are much higher in Meghalaya (Table 15.5).

In Meghalaya, as is reflected in Table 15.5, the increasing population leads to an increased pressure on agricultural land which again tends to lower the productive capacity of land. Since shifting cultivation is widely practised in the State, the increased population also means a fall in the duration of

---

* $$\text{Physiological Density} = \frac{\text{Total Population}}{\text{Net sown area}}$$

** $$\text{Agricultural Density} = \frac{\text{Total Agricultural Population}}{\text{Net Sown Area}}$$

When, Agricultural population includes both cultivators and agricultural labourers.

TABLE 15.5: **Average, Physiological and Agricultural Densities in Meghalaya 1970-71 to 1989-90**

Decades	Population		Density (per sq.km.)		
	Total	Agricultural	Average	Physio-logical	Agricultural
(1)	(2)	(3)	(4)	(5)	(6)
1970-71	1011699	353109	45	581	203
1980-81	1335819	420909	60	733	232
1990-91	1774778	485296	79	874+	239+

+ Net sown area according to 1989-90 figures.

Source: Calculated from Census of India, 1991, *Basic Statistics of NER*, 1992; and Land Utilisation Statistics of Meghalaya, 1970-71 to 1989-90.

Jhum cycle* (5-7 years at present) and thus the supporting capacity of land reduces.

The other important resources of Meghalaya, which is directly affected by increased population, is the forest cover of the State. It has been recently estimated that there has been a decrease of about 106 sq. km. of forest cover in the state during the last two years. If the same trend of decrease continues unchecked, it not only will disturb the ecological balance of the region severely, but will also bring down the resource potential of the state to a great extent.

The reduction of forest cover in the state, as assessed by FSI is primarily due to deforestation by the practice of shifting cultivation incurring a loss of about 110 sq. km. forest land in 1991-93. This is a loss which is measured only in open forests of the state, accounting for about 950 sq. km. of area. However, no proper assessment is made of the reduction in those forests owned by private traditional ownerships.

IV

From the discussion held in preceding paragraphs, it appears that the existing population-resource ratio in the State is not a

* The fallow period in years that is required to replenish the lost fertility of land.

smooth one, and it requires some immediate and sincere steps to improve the situation. As it has been mentioned earlier, Meghalaya, with an early second phase of demographic transition, has a long way to go to achieve some kind of stability in its population number. Thus, to check the birth rate or control the natural increase in population may not be suggested at this juncture.

Since, the rural areas of the state are most affected by any increase in population, some strategies of economic development should be chalked out, which will more effectively reduce or divert the pressure of population on land. Thus, it may be suggested that, all agricultural practices in the state should have a cropping pattern with maximum possible diversification. At the same time, non-farm rural economies should be promoted with necessary improvements made in rural infrastructure, as roads and communication, water supply, electricity, facilities of marketing etc. An attempt can and should be made to enhance the rural employment potential by introducing rural transport and repair services, rural construction and agro-based processing industries.

In the social sector too, a sincere attempt is required to improve the housing and health services in the rural areas. Above all, it is the need of the hour to improve rural literacy of the region, so that people in rural areas are able to use their talent to earn a living.

REFERENCES

Ackerman, E.A., "Population, Natural Resources and Technology" in *Population Geography: A Reader,* ed. G.J. Demko, *et al.*, McGraw-Hill Book Company, New York 1970, pp. 476-87.

Heer, D.M.,: *Society and Population,* Prentice Hall of India (P) Ltd., New Delhi, 1987.

Kar, B.,: "Socio-Economic Implications of the Migration-Dominated High Population Growth Rates of N.E. Region", in B. Datta Ray (ed.) *The Patterns and Problems of Population in North-East India,* Uppal Publishers, New Delhi, 1986, pp. 285-96.

Census Reports on Meghalaya, 1971, 1981, 1991.

Census of India, 1951, Vol. XII, Assam, Manipur, Tripura (Part-I A).

Basic Statistics of NER, 1980, 1985, 1992.

The Shillong Times, Tuesday, 14th March, 1995.

The Sentinel, Thursday, 16th March, 1995.

16

IMPACT OF POPULATION GROWTH ON THE PRESENT CIVIC AMENITIES WITHIN THE SHILLONG URBAN AGGLOMERATION

SUBRATA PURKAYASTHA

Shillong, the capital of Meghalaya is a picturesque hill station situated at an altitude of about 1500m above mean sea level.

Shillong has grown as an enclave in the midst of a rural society catering to the administrative and educational needs of the surrounding areas. It has emerged as an important administrative, educational and tourist centre of the North Eastern Region. Over the years trade and commerce has developed and today Shillong may be regarded as an important nodal centre of the North Eastern Region perhaps second only to Guwahati.

As in other urban centres of the country Shillong too has faced urbanisation and growth of population at a very rapid pace. From a mere 1363 people in 1874, when it was declared as the capital of Assam, Shillong now records a population size of about 2,23,366 (sources as per 1991 census).

When one takes into account the urban population of Meghalaya, it is seen that about 68 per cent of the total urban population of the state is concentrated within this capital city. Shillong as an urban centre grew up without much planning. Hence the question arises whether the present civic amenities can sustain this enormous size of population.

As far as roads are concerned, it is extremely inadequate in relation to the amount of traffic plying in these roads. It covers only about 14 per cent of the total developed area of Shillong which also includes the parking areas. To quote the Urban Affairs Report on Shillong Master Plan 1991-2011, it is stated that "Continuing growth of population and resultant Urban expansion could not keep pace with the increased demands. With each passing day traffic condition in Shillong is becoming increasingly hazardous."

Thus our present planners need to concentrate more on the development of main roads and by-passes as well as fly-overs so that traffic congestion can be minimised. But this again calls for a proper understanding of the physiography of the region. For Shillong being a hill station, indiscriminate felling of trees for construction purposes may in turn result into environmental degradation.

In regards to water supply, the situation is worse. About 25 lakh gallons of water is supplied per day for a population size of more than 2 lakhs. Of this total amount of water supplied much of it is wasted through leaking pipes. Moreover, the supply is not uniform in all the localities of Shillong. According to the National Commission on Urbanisation, the average water supply to a Class I city is about 125 litres per capita per day. Thus Shillong Urban Agglomeration, in spite of being situated in a rainfed area, suffers extremely from water scarcity.

When one looks at the sanitation aspect of Shillong, it is seen that the sewerage discharge is thrown directly on the open streams and drains of Shillong especially those streams lying just outside the Shillong Municipality. This causes pollution and ultimately health hazard for the people of Shillong. Closely linked to the water supply is the question of sewerage and drainage and when sewerage is disposed of in the streams which are again the source of water, it is indeed an alarming situation.

The open bins and drains are also places of breeding of harmful insects and flies, which not only pollute the surface, but also the ground water and the soil itself.

With the over increasing population of the city, today's Shillong has a number of slums coming up. The Urban Affairs Department of Government of Meghalaya have identified 23 slum pockets within the Shillong Urban Agglomeration, where the conditions are more depressing than the rest of the city. Here there is an acute lack of not only water supply and other basic sanitary facilities but also approach lanes, electrification and housing facilities. As these areas are inhabited by the economically deprived sections of the society, these areas suffer from inadequate educational and health facilities. They are usually the pockets of unemployment and underemployment. Thus poverty often drives these sections of the society into participating in criminal activities.

These slums often turn into dens of criminal and anti-social activities. Moreover, with the ever increasing migration of the surrounding rural population into the Urban Centre of Shillong, the slums are growing larger in size. These recent migrants usually prefer to be in these depressed areas before they can eke out a better standard of living and usually in this competitive world, these migrants can never realise their aspirations and, therefore, ultimately resort to anti-social activities to support themselves and their families.

The slums are thus overcrowded and in the absence of proper civic amenities, these areas are usually highly polluted and become detrimental to the society at large.

The scene is same in the case of housing. Shillong is faced with the problem of housing. It is seen that the ever increasing population size has resulted into acute shortage of housing facilities thereby affect the population at large. The Residential Areas in some localities are extremely congested. Moreover, there is the problem of ever increasing rent as the Government of Meghalaya has no proper rent control policy.

The ethnic disturbances from time to time within the city has resulted in the concentration of different communities in particular localities. It is observed that the rents are higher in Lachumiere, Laitumkhrah, Laban, Oakland, Police Bazar areas than in Mawkhar, Mawlai, Jaiaw, Umsohsun, Riatsamthiah, Wahingdoh and Mawprem.

All these problems, therefore, call for the Government attention. Similarly, other civic amenities like electrification, public health, public distribution system, etc. need to be streamlined and remedial measures have to be taken not only for minimising these problems, but also for ensuring efficient and effective functioning of all the above important amenities falling within the parameters of Urban Development.

REFERENCES

Buch, M.N., *Environmental Consciousness and Rural Planning*, Orient Longman, Delhi, 1993.

Directorate of Urban Affairs, Meghalaya, Shillong, *Master Plan of Shillong 1991-2011*, Shillong.

Provisional Population Total, Rural-Urban Distribution Series, Paper 2 of 1991, Vol. I & II, 1991.

17

BIRTH RATE AND DEATH RATE IN MANIPUR (1971-89)
A Study of the Time Series

DIPAK KUMAR ADAK and R.TH. VARTE

Introduction

The birth and death rates are two major demographic components related with population growth in any region. According to the theory of demographic transition (Notestein and Thompson, 1953), the reason for rapid population growth in any developing country is due to significant fall in the death rate which is not immediately accompanied by such decline in the birth rate. In India, the birth rate has fallen slightly, whereas the death rate has come down drastically. As these two components vary in different geographic regions among cultural groups and also among the people of various economic status, there is a need to undertake a study on the birth and the death rates in different parts of the country.

For a systematic study on the birth and the death rates, the complete, reliable and detailed time series data are helpful. The time series analysis helps in understanding of past behaviour, in planning future operations and in evaluating current accomplishments as it facilitates comparison (Gupta, 1981). In this context our study is very specific. Attempt have been made to use the time series data i.e. from 1971-1989, of birth and death rates in Manipur. The data of the present study is solely based on the *Basic Statistics of North Eastern*

Region, published by the North Eastern Council Secretariat, Shillong (1992). At the end we discuss the impact of population on food supply in the perspective of Manipur.

Trends of Birth and Death Rates

The estimated data on annual birth and death rates in Manipur are given in Table 17.1. It reveals that both the birth and death rates are undergoing changes with the passage of time. It holds good for both rural and urban areas. The death rate exhibits a very lower level than the birth rate which is lesser than one-third of the birth rate of total, rural and urban population. This combination of high birth rates and very low death rates clearly indicates the imbalance between the two which could be considered as one of the principal causes of rapid population growth in Manipur. Throughout 1901-91, population growth in Manipur is much higher than the national average.

It goes without saying that high fertility and rapid population growth have serious socio-economic consequences and tend to offset the benefit of development in backward areas. It results in family frustration, dependency burden and unemployment problem. More people means more mouths are to be fed or more men, women and children are to be provided with potable water to drink, pollution free air to breath and houses to live in and so on.

In 1971 the total, rural and urban birth rates in Manipur were respectively 33.3, 34.0 and 26.4 while the death rates in the same year were 6.9, 7.1 and 5.1 respectively. After 18 years i.e. in 1989 the birth rate in Manipur had come down to a considerable level but it is interesting to note that the death rate remains almost same as those in 1971. In 1989 the total birth rates (rural and urban) in Manipur were 22.8, 24.8 and 16.5 while the death rates were 6.8, 7.0 and 6.1 respectively.

Although the death rate of Manipur does not exhibit a declining trend with the passage of time, its lower level since 1971 is noteworthy. If we compare death rate in Manipur with national average, we find Manipur exhibits a progressive trend in this regard. In 1971 the total, rural and urban death rates in India were 14.9, 16.4 and 9.7 while in 1989 they were 10.3,

TABLE 17.1: **Estimated Annual Birth Rates and Death Rates in Manipur**

Year	Birth Rate			Death Rate		
	Total	Rural	Urban	Total	Rural	Urban
1971	33.3	34.0	26.4	6.9	7.1	5.5
1972	31.2	32.1	21.9	9.0	9.1	7.8
1973	28.7	29.2	24.1	7.8	7.9	6.5
1974	25.0	25.1	23.6	8.3	8.3	8.0
1975	24.5	25.3	18.7	5.6	5.6	5.5
1976	25.3	25.7	21.2	6.9	7.1	5.4
1977	26.6	27.3	19.4	6.3	6.4	4.5
1978	32.2	31.9	25.5	7.6	7.8	5.7
1979	28.6	29.2	23.0	6.7	7.0	3.5
1980	30.9	31.6	24.1	6.3	7.4	4.6
1981	26.6	26.8	24.4	6.6	6.8	4.5
1982	N.A.	23.3	N.A.	N.A.	7.1	N.A.
1983	28.0	30.0	24.7	7.0	7.3	6.1
1984	29.1	29.7	27.1	6.2	6.4	5.8
1985	27.5	28.9	23.4	7.4	7.6	6.8
1986	25.3	27.0	19.9	6.6	7.1	5.1
1987	25.9	27.7	19.9	5.6	5.9	4.5
1988	25.8	27.7	19.6	6.8	7.3	5.3
1989	22.8	24.8	16.5	6.8	7.0	6.1

N.A.: Not available.

Source: Sample Registration Bulletins.

11.1 and 7.2 respectively. The probable reasons behind this disparity may be due to the fact that the health status of the people in Manipur is comparatively better as they are comparatively more health conscious and avail themselves more medical facilities.

For a visual representation, the trend lines are fitted alongwith the actual data separately for the birth and death rates. This has been done by following the least square method.

The trend lines of birth rates exhibit a downward trend with the passage of time. This trend is very slow in case of death rates. However, it appears that although the birth rates of total, rural and urban population of Manipur have started declining since 1971 and have come down to a considerable level in 1989, the declining trend is not uniform particularly in the year 1974, 1975 and 1978 in total populations, in 1974, 1975, 1978 and 1982 in rural populations and in 1975, 1977 and 1984 in the urban populations. In these years, comparatively a higher deviation of actual data are seen from the trend lines. It is interesting to note that the birth rates of Manipur exhibit a sudden increase in the interval of 1977 to 1978. In 1977 the total, rural and urban birth rates of Manipur were 26.6, 27.3 and 19.4, whereas in 1978 they have suddenly increased to 32.2, 32.9 and 25.5 respectively. However, the reason behind this is totally obscure to us.

Thus, it appears that though the birth rate in Manipur had come down considerably with the passage of time (i.e 1971-89) and the low level of death rate remains almost constant since 1971, the gap between the two has not been narrowed. Therefore, it can be assumed that social and economic factors might have exercised as an important influence on the decline of fertility in Manipur.

However, to further reduce the growth of population to a considerable level in Manipur it can be suggested that the family planning efforts need to be geared up intensively in the state. In this context, the younger generation can play a greater role as they enter the reproductive age.

Natural Growth Rate

The difference between the birth and death rates indicates the natural growth rate. Table 17.2 exhibits such data on rural and urban sectors for the years 1971-89. It reveals that both the rural and urban sectors are undergoing through changes with the passage of time. It is true that the rate of natural growth in rural sector is much higher than that in urban sector. However, the declining trend in both the sectors is very much perceptible.

TABLE 17.2: **Sector-wise Natural Growth Rate for the Years 1971-89**

Year	Natural Growth Rate	
	Rural Sector	Urban Sector
1971	26.9	20.9
1972	23.0	14.1
1973	21.3	17.6
1974	16.8	15.6
1975	19.7	13.2
1976	18.6	15.8
1977	20.9	14.9
1978	25.1	19.8
1979	22.2	19.5
1980	25.2	19.5
1981	20.0	19.9
1982	16.2	—
1983	22.7	18.6
1984	23.3	21.3
1985	21.3	16.6
1986	19.9	14.8
1987	21.8	15.4
1988	20.4	14.3
1989	11.8	10.4

Source: NEC. Basic Statistics, 1992.

Impact of Population on Food Supply

In the country as a whole, during the last forty years, population has doubled, while food supply has almost tripled. In the hill areas of North East India, food production fluctuates due to the practice of shifting cultivation. Hence the estimate of food production in the region may not give the true picture (Neog, 1994).

TABLE 17.3: **Per Capita Foodgrains Production (in kg) in Manipur (1972 to 1991)**

	1972-73	1980-81	1990-91
Manipur	159	205	155
India	172	190	208

Source: *Economic Surveys* (various issues), *Census Reports of India*, and NEC, *Basic Statistics of N.E.R.*

The above Table 17.3 presents the per capita foodgrain production in Manipur at three points of time during the last two decades. It is seen that in Manipur the per capita production is considerably lower than the national average during 1972-73 and 1990-91 but not so in 1980-81. However, in the last decade (1980-81 to 1990-91) a declining trend is very much perceptible in Manipur. This suggests that the economy of Manipur stands as a "Locus Classicus" of the Malthusian dilemma.

Impact of Population on Employment

The spread of education and higher rate of population growth are two important contributing factors to serious unemployment, in the State. In our country, unemployment is rising in spite of job reservation for SC's and ST's, which is a cause for concern (Neog, 1994).

Table 17.4 shows the number of persons unemployed on the live Register of Employment Exchanges in Manipur. It appears that the number of unemployed persons belonging to SC is much lower (i.e. 1.6 thousand) than those belongs to ST (i.e. 53.2 thousands). This finding corroborates with the 1991 figures i.e. SC 2.02, ST 34.41 and others 63.57. However, these figures do not exhibit the similarity with the national average.

Concluding Remarks

"Since the ancient times, India has had the legacy of a thickly

TABLE 17.4: **Number of Persons (in thousand) Unemployed on the Live Register of Employment Exchange**

	Total in 1993	SC & ST in 1992	
		SC	ST
Manipur	229.9	1.6	53.2
All India	36,275.5	4,801.9	1,256.5

Source: Ministry of Labour, DGE&T.

settled population" (Davis, 1968). In our country, population density varies according to geo-climatic variation in different regions. The whole of North East India is characterised by low population density as compared to the national average though the plains of Assam and Tripura are thickly populated. "If we look into the population figures of Manipur since 1901 to 1991, we find decadewise percentage variation in Manipur is always higher than our national average" (Chaudhuri and Adak, 1994). "Though the population density of Manipur is considerably less but in comparison to the available land it becomes already high. In the face of limited availability of land, expanding population has led to fragmentation and subinfeudation in agriculture, constructing the scope for application of capital and improved technology" (Mitra, 1978). It can be concluded that the per capita foodgrain production in Manipur is considerably lower than the national average. Again, the number of unemployed persons on the basis of live Register of Employment Exchanges also shows a dissimilar trend with the national average. Thus for sustainable economic development of Manipur, the reduction in population growth rate through family planning is necessary. This will help attain the national goal of net reproduction rate of one corresponding to 1.2 per cent annual population growth rate before population stabilises.

REFERENCES

Chaudhuri, S. and D. Adak, "Population Growth and Literacy Trends in Manipur (1901-91)" in *Demographic Profile of North East India* (ed.), Omsons Publication, New Delhi, 1994.

Davis, K., *Population of India and Pakistan*, Princeton University Press, New York, 1968.

Gupta, S.P., *Statistical Methods*, Sultan Chand and Sons, New Delhi, 1981.

Mitra, A., *India's Population: Aspects of Quality and Control*, Vol. II, New Delhi, 1978.

Neog, A.K., "Population Dynamics of the North Eastern Region", in *Journal of the North Eastern Council*, Vol. 14, No. 4, 1994.

North Eastern Council Secretariat, *Basic Statistics of the North Eastern Region*, Shillong, 1992.

Notestein and Thompson, *Population Problem*, Mc Graw Hill Book Company, New York, 1953.

18

WHAT CAUSES POVERTY?

P.K. MISRA

Gandhiji had once said that there was enough for every one's need in this world but not enough for every one's greed.

Preface of Eighth Five Year Plan states that 1/3 of the population in India live below poverty line. 43 NSS survey (1987-88) states that 90 per cent of the rural poor in Andhra Pradesh, Maharashtra, Orissa, West Bengal, Uttar Pradesh, Rajasthan, Tamilnadu and Karnataka live below poverty line.

In this chapter, I propose to focus the discussion on the causes of mass poverty. The issue is at once relevant for not only the people of India but for all the people in the world. For the problem of poverty in a country of the size of the Indian population cannot be set aside as its local problem. The size of the population identified as poor in India, even if the lowest estimates are taken would be about 200 million.

Poverty Line Debate

India adopted a policy of planned development through Five Year Plans. Gradually in these plans, programmes of poverty alleviation started appearing which experimented with a variety of strategies. In spite of all these efforts a vast number of the people in this country are poor and very poor. Of course there has been a difference of opinion as to what exactly is the proportion of poor people in the country, but there has been a general agreement that the poverty is widespread and its number is not appreciably decreasing if not increasing. The debate on this issue has become some what weird after scholar turned politician, Dr. Manmohan Singh announced in the parliament, later also on T.V. as part of the election manifesto of his party, that the proportion of the poor has been brought down to 19 per cent as a result of the policy of liberalisation followed by his government. These estimates are being revised by the present establishment as a result of which the number of the people below the poverty line has suddenly gone up. Mehta writes, "The choice of a dramatic decline of the poverty level to 19 per cent of the population is highly controversial. There was admittedly an increase in the number of those below the poverty line in the first two years of the post-reform period. There is evidence also to show that even if this adverse trend had been halted in 1993-94, it reappeared in 1994-95. Real wages for unskilled agricultural workers too declined in 1994-95. According to the estimates of the *Economic Times*.... real wages of farm workers in 1994-95 fell by 2.5 per cent. Increase in GDP in itself does not automatically reduce poverty as is assumed by the reformer's lobby. The distribution of the gain of growth is neither fair nor equitable in India. This is further highlighted by the fact that the prices of essential articles of consumption have been rising at a higher rate than prices in general. This hurts the vulnerable sections of the population most cruelly' (1996:35). In the same issue of *Mainstream*, Prasad has demonstrated that the real income of the wretched 245 million workers has been falling by 7.5 per cent. It is obvious that the statement of Singh about the number of the people below the poverty line is not acceptable. Of course as pointed above these figures are no more acceptable to the present establishment, however this point would become further clear, if we look at the debate on poverty issue of the past decades.

Years of intensive programming and implementation of community development schemes and other programmes under Five Year Plans had brought home the point that poverty in India was widespread and is not amenable to easy solutions. This realisation led to raise questions, such as how many people were actually below poverty line and how acute was their poverty. Some excellent studies were conducted like that of Dandekar and Rath (1971), Bardan (1973), Dantwala (1973), Djurfeldt and Lindberg (1975), Retzlaft (1978) etc.

These studies confirmed the worst fears that the poverty was very much widespread and acute.

In order to measure poverty in the Indian condition it was found that 2250 calories per capita per day would be adequate for normal nutrition. Dandekar and Rath calculated that to obtain that many calories an expenditure of Rs. 170 per head for the rural population and Rs. 271.70 per head for the urban population was essential. On the basis of national income of 1960-61, it was calculated that about 33 per cent of the rural population and 50 per cent of the urban population could not afford that amount of money. The study group of the Government of India had suggested a national minimum of Rs. 240.00 (at 1960-61 prices) per capita per year. According to that in 1960-61, 40 per cent of the rural population and 50 per cent of the urban population lived below the desirable limits. Since there were severe regional imbalances and the distribution of income in different states was uneven, it was estimated that the number of people actually living below the poverty line in some of the states would be much higher. In terms of absolute numbers, the people living below the poverty line was staggering 220 million at 1971-72 prices. These figures generated debate among the scholars as regards the scale of measurement of poverty and on the other side made the planners realise the enormity of the problem at their hands. Numerous workshops, seminars, studies, conferences were organised all over the country to get a correct picture of the poverty and also on the designs to eliminate it. It was not that the country was starting from a scratch on this subject, there were already so many programmes of development in operation but what was becoming apparent was that they were not good enough to make an impact on poverty. The problem was complex. Sharma called it web of poverty; he wrote, 'this web is insidious, or else how do we explain the persistence of poverty and emergence of phenomenal affluence at the same time notwithstanding a commendable record of development after the Independence and our commitment to the establishment of an egalitarian social order' (1989:1).

Rural Poverty

Jain *et al.* found 86.4 per cent of the population in a village in

Purnea district in Bihar was below the poverty line by income and about the same proportion (88.02%) by household expenditure in 1981. This was the village which was covered by almost every conceivable programme of development since 1956 (1985:99). The findings of the Anthropological Survey of India were no different. It had conducted an all India study to find out the situation of the poor in the rural areas of India. Intensive study of at least one village in each state was conducted between 1972-74. The studies showed that the poverty was very extensive in the villages of India. Morab found 80 per cent people in a village in north Karnataka below poverty line. On all counts he found that the Harijans and the Waddars, the two lower most castes in the village were decisively weak. Some of the households of the village belonging to upper castes were decisively dominant. The communities maintained social distance at all levels of interactions in the village situation (1993:543). Misra found 80 per cent of the Harijans and almost 58 per cent of the people in a village in Tamilnadu lived on income below Rs. 360 per head per year. She too found that the communities maintained social and cultural boundaries among themselves which had its repercussion in the economic arena. More than in Karnataka the divide between the Harijans and others in Tamil Nadu were more clearly pronounced. The Harijan settlement was far removed from the main village. In 1972, they were not allowed to use water of the canal, which was the main source of water supply in the village (1993:554). Sen Tapno found that 88 per cent of the Kharura and Sankhari families in a village in Orissa earned less than Rs. 40 per month (1993:155). Choudhury found 69.57 per cent households of a village in South Bengal very poor (1993:95). Sen Gupta found that the situation of the poorest in a village in Uttar Pradesh was hopeless and their condition had become worsened since Independence (1993:355). These case studies confirmed that very large number of people in the villages of India suffered with extreme poverty. Except for a few places, the study showed a correlation of poverty with lower and lower middle strata of the Hindu caste hierarchy. Poor were landless and marginal farmers. Literacy was poor among them. It was also noted that the poor belonging to lower castes continue to suffer with a variety of social disabilities. These studies very clearly indicated close interlinkages between economic, social and cultural factors. These interlinkages, of course work to the advantage of the dominant sections of the village and to the disadvantage of the weaker sections. These disadvantages continuously keep on further eroding their physical and social capacities. For instance when children of the poor cannot go to school for education, and instead have to work in the fields of landlords and look after their cattle, there are very slim chances that such children when they grow up will be able to break the vicious circle of poverty in future. First, by working in the fields of their landlords they have provided cheap labour to them and have further strengthened their position to intervene in their lives in a variety of ways. Second, they have denied themselves education and learning of new skills which would have enhanced their capacities. They grow up as ignorant persons in a modern society which is bursting up with information. This creates a big gap which is difficult to fill later in the life. Third, they become critically dependent upon their employers for their sustenance and also in course of time indebted them. Fourth, living on barely sufficient diets, their nutritional level is low to very low and thus have very little capacity to take any risk in terms of looking for alternative sources of income generation, or in participating in any kind of movement to protest against their exploitation. Generally such populations have rarely been mobilised for any collective action.

Causes of Poverty

With this discussion in the background we may return to the basic question we had raised and that is, what causes poverty and allowed its persistence. So long as we do not have a proper understanding of what causes poverty, we may not be able to find appropriate clues to remove it.

In 1969 Galbriath outlined the following factors which were considered to be probable causes of poverty:

(1) The people are poor because they prefer it that way.
(2) The country is naturally poor.

(3) The country is poor because of colonial oppression.
(4) Poverty is the consequence of class exploitation.
(5) Poverty is caused by insufficient capital.
(6) Overpopulation is the cause of poverty.
(7) Poverty is caused by incompetent policy.
(8) Poverty is caused by ignorance.

He took the above factors one by one for detailed discussion and negated them by citing evidences to the contrary from different parts of the world. He came to the conclusion that the poverty was not caused by a single factor but was a product of plurality of causes which may vary from country to country depending upon the historical antecedents and culture of the country. He cautioned that the convenient remedies have to be avoided. He said that it was easy to provide seeds and fertilizers but it was extremely difficult to bring land reforms. It was easier to instal a steel plant but to impart elementary education to all was an altogether a different proposition. His final conclusion was that illiteracy was number one cause of poverty.

Bureaucracy

Jain *et al.* reviewing the community development programme in India since its inception in 1952 and about its failure to achieve the task of poverty alleviation wrote, 'the foremost reason for this unfortunate state of affairs is that the people themselves have no place in rural development, every available inch is occupied by the bureaucracy' (1985:194). According to Jain *et al.*, the people at grass-root levels were not involved in the governance of development plans. The task of bringing change was entirely left to bureaucracy. The bureaucracy as we know in India was designea by the British with very specific objectives such as to maintain law and order, to collect revenue, not to trust people in general administration (so many check points were designed) and to maintain absolute authoritarianism of the higher officials who were 'Sahibs'. They were the law by themselves. They were the symbols of power. They had to be shown extreme deference. Short of crawling, literally people had to do every thing to keep a 'Sahib' well fed, well kept and in good humour. This style of functioning of bureaucracy never changed even after Independence. The brown man easily slipped into the shoes of his predecessor. It is often not realised that this style of bureaucracy is enacted at all levels down to the peon. The buck stops only at the level of people. The only difference that took place was that bureaucracy was given additional charge of welfare and development. The two roles, the role of authority demanding all the deference and submission down its own hierarchy and in relation to the people, and other of a friend concerned with the welfare of the people were incongruent but nonetheless were thrown together. Here I cannot go into this aspect in detail except to say that bureaucracy has not given up its authoritarian style, development and welfare tasks have only enhanced its value and have made it deadly. It has become more paternalistic and demands more submission from the people. Whatever, this attitude may have done to bureaucracy, it has certainly harmed the development in a significant way. People do not think that the development programmes are theirs; they think that they are of the government and for the government. Aiyar writes 'a bureaucracy that has become one gigantic mafia that loots the exchequer and people with impunity. No political party has dared to reform the bureaucracy. . . . Every petty functionary, no matter how corrupt or inefficient, plies his trade safe in the knowledge that he cannot be sacked. And yet minister after minister proposes new schemes to be handled by the very tribe of parasites that already makes off with untold of thousands of crores' (1994:16).

In the development process, bureaucracy tends to develop a vested interest in the development *per se* rather than in achieving the results. It allows them to have more resources at their command and also to expand. In course of time it becomes its own rational, notwithstanding the fact that its reach to the target groups particularly the poor is least or nil. Since targets have to be fulfilled without having a will for it or commitment, corruption is most likely the result. Jain *et al.* write, 'despite these known constraints the extension staff continues to induce the poor to acquire milch cattle because of the high subsidy involved and their ability to pocket it with ease' (1985:200). The popular joke has been that the same milch cow goes again and again to a number of recipients yielding more subsidies than milk. 'One can add many more such cases from the field experiences. However, there is another side of the story and that is when the development becomes its own logic and compulsion. A very good illustration of it comes from Andaman Islands. There is a small tribe called Onges. There is no doubt that they have been on the verge of extinction. At some stage the administration decided to step in and save them. A group of them were settled in a separate Island. They were provided with houses. The administration also decided to provide them with free ration, clothing etc. Now the rest of the story can be anticipated. Soon clerks moved in to maintain stocks and to distribute goods. In course of time, the administration had to buy a ship to supply the goods. The ship had to have its crew and own paraphernalia. Meanwhile, it was suggested that the island should have its own electricity and therefore a generator was installed there. In order to run the generator and maintain it, machine men were employed. The story goes on. At the time I visited the island as a member of a team to enquire into the affairs of the 'primitive tribes' of the Island, each Onge house had a fan but the Onge leader was demanding fan in each room. I do not know how much of the demands being put to us was coming from their own or on prompting from others but their houses had some incompatible things such as suitcases, gumboots, raincoats, tins of powder milk etc. The leader of the Onge told me in no uncertain terms that his house has to be made bigger like that of Lt. Governor. In order to be certain as to what he was asking, I asked him, "would you draw a sketch of the type of the house he was wanting". He gladly accepted the offer and took pen and paper from me and retired in a corner. He gripped the pen in his palm and painstakingly drew a sketch. Of course, what he drew was only a series of irregular lines, joined here and there. But he was clear in his mind that his house had to be big. On being asked whether he would want that type of house for other Onges in the Island. His answer was emphatic, "no". He wanted a helipad too in his Island, so that he can commute between his Island and Port Blair. He was one of the members of the Council of Andaman and Nicobar Islands. He was reflecting what he had seen of the other leaders, more concerned about themselves rather than with the problems of the people. Leaving aside the individual aspirations of a leader, in the so called development activities of the island the vested interests of the development workers were involved. They had grown in size as well as in their influence over the decision making process of the administration. In this game the interests of the Onge in general whose number was not more than 100 were peripheral.

The very failure of the development programmes may also be attributed to the belief that the brilliant ideas would bring the desired results without changing the machinery through which the ideas will be delivered.

Democratic Decentralisation

In order to correct all this it was rightly thought that democratic decentralisation of the power was essential so that people were in control of the resources, will participate in the decision-making process and will be responsible for their own action. Panchayat act were enacted but the same were not allowed to function. At many places panchayat elections were not withheld, or wherever established they were given limited role particularly with regard to development. However, in 1995 a new act on Panchayat Raj was passed. It is in the process of implementation.

Urban Bias

Lipton is of the opinion that continued existence of mass poverty in spite of all development and accelerated expansion of science and technology is owing to urban bias in development process. He writes, 'The most important class conflict in the poor countries of the world today is not between labour and capital. Nor is it between foreign and national interests. It is between the rural classes and the urban classes. The rural sector contains most of the poverty and most of the low cost sources of potential advance; but the urban sector contains most of the articulateness, organisation and power' (1980:13).

Web of Poverty

Sharma thinks that there is a vicious circle of poverty. He

writes, 'The forces responsible for poverty have a web like structure. The person coming under the sway of any of these forces gets caught in the web and becomes subject to the other adverse forces as well, one by one. He is gradually drawn to its centre where the effect of the adverse forces taken together is maximum' (1989:1). It would be pertinent to ask how this web is constructed and how it is maintained. This understanding is necessary if the objective is to demolish this web so that the people are not caught in it.

Poverty Production

It should however be emphasised here that the web of poverty is not a thing given by nature. It is constructed. It is produced by the human beings in the process of development. There was no poverty in the primitive society even though the people in such societies had fewer goods. According to Sahlins, 'poverty is the product of the kind of relationship human beings establish among themselves' (1972:37). Colonialism brought growth, wealth, breakthroughs in science and technology but for the colonised it brought subjugation, misery, disease, famines, etc. People in the vast areas of the world such as North America, South America, in Island societies of the Caribbean, lived in a relative affluence till the Europeans landed there and established a relationship in which the former indigenous populations most of whom were converted into subjugated population and many of them as slaves produced affluence for the populations of the west European countries misery and poverty for themselves. The producers of the wealth themselves lived only on that much which was just enough for their survival. They had no right on what they produced. They were made to understand that the customs, practices and religion of their societies were inferior. This is the beginning of absolute mass poverty in India. The instruments through which the west Europeans established their hegemony were political subjugation, economic exploitation and cultural super imposition. The populations subjected to these instrumentalities for a long period of time tend to internalise them and reproduce them in a variety of ways. The point would become clear if we look back into the history of last 200 years of India epistemologically.

Like many other countries India too was politically subjugated by a European power. It was mercilessly exploited. Its natural resources and products of human labour were drained off. The entire framework of the Indian society was disturbed. Its agricultural economy was shattered. Its manufacturing industries were destroyed. The primary producers and artisans in spite of the hard work they put in earned very little. India which was a leading country in terms of production technology became a backward country troubled by cycles of famines and epidemics. It became a dependent country in all senses of the term, politically, economically and culturally. After the country became independent it was thought that through a process of planned development it would be able to establish a society based on equality and justice. Development did take place but its fruits were cornered by a small section of the population. Majority of the rest were left in abject poverty. How did this happen? It may sound simplistic but the fact remains it is the result of the continuation of the same kind of relations which were established during the colonial period, but within a different frame work. Call it neo-colonialism or by whatever name, the relationships which were established between developed regions and under-developed regions, between haves and have nots, between industry and agriculture, between capital and labour, between urban and rural classes have not changed. Why? Answer to this crucial question may enhance our understanding of the persistence of mass poverty in India. It would amount to tautology if it is stated that the people who could have changed this kind of relationship were those who were adversely affected by them, and not by those who were the beneficiary of those relationships. The beneficiaries, so to say have internalised the colonial values. Like the white colonisers, the brown too think what they are getting is owing to the fact that they are God's chosen people and those who work and toil are getting what they deserved. They systematically thwart all attempts to change the relationship on which their own position is based. Let us have a quick look at some of the hard evidences.

After the country became independent it was decided to go in for planned development in order to come over its acute economic problems. However, the entire development machinery to this day has remained highly centralised, in spite of severe criticism of this. People were not involved in the process of planning. They remained passive recipients of the planned projects.

In spite of all the fanfare and repeated assurances the village self rule has remained a distant reality. The masses in the village have not been empowered. Peasants to this day have remained unorganised. Through a complex manoeuvring and shifts they have been endlessly divided into castes, sub-castes and communities. Differential assessment of wages without defining the basis of it continues. It is strange in independent India that there is vast gap between highest paid and lowest paid within governmental organisation itself and between organised and unorganised labour. How it can claim to bring equality of some sort. The wages earned by unorganised peasants continue to be woefully low as compared to what the organised labour of the industry earns in the industry. This results in continuous outflow of people from rural areas to urban areas. Although this increases the population of the slums in the cities, it helps the city dwellers in getting the cheap labour. Such employment does not help the migrant labour not only because of their low income but in the cities there are any number of suckers who practically live on the income of such labourers. It also does not help the people whom they have left back in the villages. In the absence of the adult male workers, their agriculture cycle gets disrupted which makes them more vulnerable.

There has not been any attempt to systematically empower and activate the community for equitable and just development. For this it is absolutely necessary that the community is made to realise what are its responsibilities, power and what are the pitfalls they should avoid. For this the community has to be properly educated and made to realise what are the sources of its problems, what is sustainable and what is not, and so on. Instead what has been so for attempted is to give emphasis on individual solutions. That is let the structure and ideology remain the same but allow some individuals to cross the threshold of poverty. It is obvious such measures are going to be patently inadequate. The problem of mass poverty is the problem of structure and values of the societies. They need to be radically changed. Any other effort would be cosmetic and palliative.

REFERENCES

Aiyar, Swaminathan Ankleshwaria, 1997: "The Real Path to Social Justice" *Times of India*, 27th April 1997.

Choudhury, Chandrima, 1993: "Pitambara: A Village in South Bengal" in ed. by S.C. Sinha, *Anthropology of the Weaker Section*. Calcutta, Anthropological Survey of India.

Dandekar, V.M. and Nilakantha, Rath, 1991: *Poverty in India*, Poona, Indian School of Political Economy.

Dantawal, M.L., 1973: *Poverty in India: Then and Now 1870-1970*, Delhi, Macmillan Co. Ltd.

Djurfeldt, Goran and Stafen Lindberg, 1975: *Behind Poverty: The Social Formation in a Tamil Village*, Scandavian Institute of Asian Studies, Monograph Series.

Galbraith, J.K., 1969: *Economic Development*, Harvard University Press.

Jain, L.C., B.V. Krishnamurthy and P.M. Tripathi, 1985: *Grass Without Roots: Rural Development Under Government Auspices*, New Delhi, Sage Publications.

Lipton, Michel, 1980: *Why Poor People Stay Poor*, New Delhi, Heritage Publishers.

Mehta, Balraj, 1996: 'Rhetoric and Reality', *Mainstream*, Vol. XXXIV, No. 15.

Morab, S.G., 1993: 'Vithalgera: A village in north Karnataka' in ed. by S.C. Sinha, *Anthropology of the Weaker Section*. Calcutta, Anthropological Survey of India.

Misra, Rajalakshmi, 1993: 'Palayasivaram: A village in Tamil Nadu' in ed. by S.C. Sinha, *Anthropology of the Weaker Section*. Calcutta, Anthropological Survey of India.

Prasad, Pradhan H., 1996: 'Red Face of Non-Development Syndrome', *Mainstream*, Vol. xxxiv, No. 15.

Retzlaft, R.H., 1978: 'Structural change: An approach to poverty in Asian rural development', *Economic and Political Weekly*, Vol. XIII, No. 51.

Sem Topno, 1993: 'Balipatna; A village in Orissa' in ed. by S.C. Sinha, *Anthropology of the Weaker Section*. Calcutta, Anthropological Survey of India.

Sengupta, Sadhan, 1993: 'Pehar; a village in eastern Uttar Pradesh' in ed. by S.C. Sinha, *Anthropology of the Weaker Section*. Calcutta, Anthropological Survey of India.

Sharma, B.D., 1989: *The Web of Poverty*, Shillong, North-Eastern Hill University.

19

DECONSTRUCTING POVERTY

B.S. BUTOLA

I am a women
Whose hands have been lacerated
By the sharp daggers of pain
Whose body has been broken
By your endless, humiliating, grinding toil
Whose skin is a veritable desert
And whose hair smell
Of the factory smoke . . .
A woman whose life blood
Satisfies the thirst of vampire
Whose dripping blood
Adds to the profit of the capitalist . . .
And yet you shamelessly contend
That my hunger is an illusion
And my nakedness a dream.

—*Marzieh Ahmadi Oskooii*

Primitive humans were haunted by fears of natural disasters of flood, drought and earthquakes, whose incidence he could not predict and against whose terrors he could but propitiate his gods[1] and humans the beauty of the world and also the paragon of the animals brought about a brutalising worship of nature, and the sovereign of nature fell down on his own knees in adoration of creatures like Hanumana the monkey and Sabala the cow.[2] The modern humans are haunted by the misery and squalor in which millions of his fellow beings live.[3] The causes of which have always been obscure to the majority though sometimes due to lack of knowledge (as was the case with the primitive people) and sometimes due to ideological and philosophical hold of the ruling classes over the poor which forces the majority (both through the use of force as well as persuasion) to accept the unjust social order along with their exploitation and appropriation as a legality of the class rule (mostly common in all the class society). The ideological hold of the ruling classes over the subaltern classes is exercised and carried through by creating false consciousness in the minds of the oppressed and reinforced by creating and circulating numerous myths for justifying the practice of exploitation on the one hand and blunting their ability to find out the real causes of their misery and poverty on the other. In this way the prevalence of poverty is always accompanied by constructing and circulating numerous myths in every class society. In this chapter attempts have been made to critically evaluate some of these myths and then deconstruct these one by one.

The Population Myth

Though, the *Population Myth* has existed for a long time but, it was most systematically developed and elaborated by Sir Thomas Malthus[4] in the 18th century. The most condensed form of this myth is:

(a) The world's resources including food are limited;
(b) There are two many people in the world and every one knows that the poorest countries have the highest birth rates, and
(c) It is the poor who are consuming most of the World's resources.[5]

According to Malthus "all animals, according to known laws by which they are produced must have a capacity of increasing in a Geometrical Progression".[6] In case of human population the rate of "progression may be safely asserted . . . when unchecked increases in a Geometrical Progression of such a nature as to double itself in every twenty year".[7] These conclusions of Sir Thomas Malthus were based on his two important postulates of:

(a) Food is necessary to the existence of man, and
(b) The passion between the sexes is necessary and will remain nearly in its present state.[8]

Based on these two postulates he argues that "the power of population is indefinitely greater than the power in the earth to produce subsistence for man".[9] Therefore, the resultant outcome will be that "the population when unchecked increases in Geometrical Ratio and subsistence increases in only in an Arithmetical Ratio".[10] Therefore, there is always an in built imbalance and condition for the occurrence of poverty. The solutions that Malthus suggested are of two types:

Natural Category

(a) Preventive Checks like the foresight of the parents in identifying the difficulties in attending and rearing of a family, and
(b) Positive Checks like the actual distress of some of the lower classes by which they are disabled from giving the proper food and attention to their children.[11]

But, when human beings fail to check the population growth through these checks and create imbalances between the two rates of progression then the imbalance is allowed to grow and this brings in operation the Prescriptive Checks, which according to Malthus "all these checks may be fairly resolved in to misery and vices".[12] The possible way out of this according to him is "moral restraints".[13] Thus, according to the Malthussian population myth the cause of poverty is when the superior power of population keeps its pressure on the low levels of means of production and moreover moral restraints as well as positive and prevent checks also fails in checking the population growth then poverty takes place which is a kind of negative check on the population i.e. checks by vices and checks by misery or poverty.

The anti-human misanthropic construction of Malthus have been ascribed to the central theme in the discourses on population and poverty. Scholars like Arnold J. Toynbee has also been greatly influenced by such a myth. According to him "every species has the biological capacity to increase in number ad infinitum and therefore, its multiplication is bound to be increased sooner or later. The physical volume of our planet is limited and the capacity of the planet's surface for producing food for living creatures is limited proportionally".[14] Therefore, the roots of poverty are pre-existing in every social formations though in varying propensity at which these things multiply. Toynbee warns us that unless and until we regulate our birth rate voluntarily,[15] the removal or even reduction of poverty will be done by nature through any one of the *Nature's Three*[16] methods of limitation.[17] The limitless growth potentials of human population though a gift of nature yet he believed that to allow it to happen in nature's fashion or according to the law of nature is to "play into Nature's hands unnecessarily is a folly. It is also criminal. It is a kind of high treason committed against our own humanity, and this is one of the biggest issues with which mankind ever has been or (perhaps) ever will be confronted.[18] To fight against this scourge of poverty is to control the natural instinct.[19] He emphasises that "man, alone among living creatures has the choice of regulating the size of his population voluntarily".[20] Our aim and objective to fight hunger and poverty will be "maximum welfare not maximum population".[21] This objective can not be obtained unless we control our birth rate. Thus, "so long as it (success to keep low death rate) coexists with a persistent failure to regulate the birth rates to match the reduction of death rate threatens to turn into a curse instead of a blessing."[22] Apart from this most celebrated and widely held construction there are some others in circulation. The environmental myth particularly the weather, climate, soil fertility, cultural and genetic factors form part of the contemporary discourses on poverty and the myths that surrounds these.

It is basically these constructions that have surrounded the discourses on poverty for over three centuries since the expositions made by Thomas Malthus and these need to be critically judged and if possible (de)constructed.

(De) Construction

Poverty and hunger may have been the constant companions of human race, but, under capitalism such fatalistic views are held and so many myths are created and circulated for pursuing petty gains and narrow class interests at a very high cost of destitution and destruction of millions of fellow human beings that it has become imperative to explode these myths. To begin with it is an uncontested fact the poverty is created by our social actions and relations. Now, hunger or poverty is not a scourge but a scandal.[23] Poverty has become an inevitable outcome of capitalist social formation. According to the structural logic of capitalism labour is the principal source of all values and surplus. Thus it also forms an important site of locating the principal contradiction of the system as well as the arena of dominant forms of class struggle within capitalism. It is in the fitness of the interest of the capitalist classes to adopt each and every method and ways for defeating the labouring classes in their class struggle. One of such and the most powerful method is by keeping the "reserve army of proletariats (labourer)[24] for insuring that the wages remain at the lowest possible level in the class struggle and if possible at the bare minimum level of subsistence. It is history repeats itself. Just as the propertied classes of yester years opposed every reform and predicted imminent economic disaster if eight years old could no longer work in the mills so, today those groups that make profit from the poverty keep people hungry are attempting to maintain the *status quo* between the rich and the poor worlds.[25] Therefore, under capitalism in the so called unplanned free market economy poverty is systematically planned and reproduced on the basis of extended reproduction. It is observed that in a general way the chronically hungry and poverty stricken people are physically less developed and mentally less alert than those who are properly fed. They have far less resistance to diseases, more susceptible to invasion by parasites and they continue to persist in these irreversible conditions[26] down their generations which ultimately weakening the united resistance of the struggling classes against their exploiters on most systematic and persistence bases.

The Malthussian Myth of differences in the two types of Progression i.e. the Geometrical and the Arithmetical Progressions are unfortunately too much muddled up in the ruling class ideology that today Malthussians are identified with forces opposed to the principles of social distributive justice. It stresses mainly on the production rather than the distribution of the social surplus including food and other basic necessities of life. The issue of social distributive justice gains enhanced significance particularly in the Post World War Second period of Neo-Imperialism when it is unequivocally accepted that "there is no business like the agri-business."[27] Today food is not the simple item of basic human necessity. It has acquired an important position as an international commodity. It has also become an important weapon in class politics and in international diplomacy. It is an effective weapon in the national and international ideological conflicts. Furthermore, it has become one of the most powerful tools in our Negotiating Kit.[28] It was further corroborated by a Central Intelligence announcement that "increasing food grains shortage could give Washington . . . virtual life and death power over the fate of multitudes of the needy".[29] This is the transformation essence of international and the class politics. Food has become a source of profit, a tool of economic and political control, an avenue of intimidation, a means of insuring effective domination over the world at large specially over the wretched of the earth.[30]

The scourge of poverty under capitalism is not just because there lies enormous profit and surplus in poverty. But, it is more than this simple economic logic. The planned production of poverty is intricately related to the systematic and persistent decline in the human dignity. Therefore, it is just not a distribution problem either. It is also due to declining human values and ethos under capitalism that makes poverty one of the most frightening social problem of today. The decline in human value and dignity can be exemplified by the comparative preference animals receive in the developed world over the people of the developing countries. The pigs in the developed world are more important than the human beings in the developing countries. Luxuries and affluence of a few have become more important than the basic concern and assistance to the majority. According to one estimate the world food production was about 1300 million tonnes in the year 1975-76, out of this nearly 50 per cent was consumed by the developed countries though they have a population of only 20 per cent of the total world's population. The rest of the food was consumed by their animals which was sufficient to feed the population of India and China put together. This has happened when over 350 million people were unable to get two square meals a day in India alone and when nearly 1/3 of the population in the developing countries were living in ghettos, during the same years. Moreover, the comforts of life too were so different for animals and the human beings in these two worlds that the cattle and the hogs . . . and other animals never touch the ground in the developed countries. They are bred, suckled, and fed to maturity in specially designed pens[31] while, millions of people die every year in the developing countries for wants of minimum calories, safe drinking water, hygienic living conditions, minimum basic health care and personal safety. This is just one of the many ugly facets of capitalist path of development.

In its mature phases of development capitalism has succeeded in articulating its political manifestations in the form of liberal democracy which in its turn is based on the principles of supremacy of free play of market relations, freedom of individuals from the wills of others and social relations as the individual's voluntary decisions are independent of any social commitment. Now the individual is the proprietor of his own persons and capacities for which he owes nothing to society.[32] These apparent principles vary from individuals to individuals depending upon ones class position. Some individuals are more free than the others, mostly by depriving and curtailing the freedom of others. Such a construct of liberal polity is largely responsible for generating and reproducing certain types of myths about poverty namely the myth of free market relations and ocular centric notion of power. In the name of individual freedom liberal politics have always been antagonistic to planned economic development. Planning according to liberal thinkers is an infringement and intrusion on the individual's freedom. But, surprisingly this is not so and in fact liberal political system can not sustain itself without planning particularly that of planned scarcity. Though, it is beyond doubt that food is a basic human necessity but it does not mean that it is universally a basic human right too. Food is like any other commodity on which speculation can be played and capital can be generated through accumulation of profit. There are international food cartels which maintain a close links with the government on the one hand and the black marketers on the other for continuously creating planned artificial scarcity. There are various methods adopted for keeping the prices of food items in control. The most significant ones are:

(a) Not to produce surplus food under any circumstances. This has been the tactic employed by the developed country in the west.
(b) Holding of foodgrains away from supply market or circulation.
(c) By destroying the surplus food so that supply can be regulated in favour of the food cartels and their interests.
(d) By increasing the supply of cereals in the diet of cattle and animals therefore, making less food available for human consumption in the developing countries.
(e) The most effective food stock manipulation executed by the giant food traders is to have huge stock of food-grains held in the government owned buffer stocks subjects to release under certain favourable economic conditions laid down by the international cartels.

Poverty and power have always maintained an intrinsic relationship. The nature and magnitude of poverty changes with the social power relationship. Autocratic centralisation of power mobilises maximum resource for the welfare of a few at the cost of the majority. As opposed to this the crisis of legitimacy of power and its subsequent renewal by the masses will compel the holders of the power to take appropriate measures for the just redistribution of social produce. This is one of the reasons that society endowed with well developed civil society and legitimate system of governance have relatively less cases of poverty while, the supremacy of autarchic power blocks show higher incidence of poverty. But, it is not only the power in the ocular centric sense that is important as far as the relationships between power and poverty are concerned. A poor is never a poor[33] if he or she fails or deprived from getting his/her basic necessities only. Inability to obtain basic minimum necessities is necessary to be considered a poor but the totality of poverty also includes ones ideological and political domination at the same time. It is so because Freedom of individual (also the central concern of all ideological struggle) is not opposed to justice as is the case in most of the ideological constructs. Freedom is chosen today in relation to those who are every where suffering and fighting. Today, freedom and bread have got fused into single ideology and power relation. Therefore, if someone takes away some ones bread, he suppresses his freedom too at the same time. Similarly, if someone takes away some ones freedom then be sure that his bread is also threatened at the same time. Poverty increases insofar as freedom retreats and *vice-versa.*[34]

In the most acute as well as articulate forms poverty and class struggle too have intricate relationships. It would not be incorrect to state that in the ultimate analysis poverty forms the core of all the class relations. The ruling classes every where and always try to keep the majority at the level of bare minimum subsistence (poverty) for their most comfortable and successful class rule while the subaltern classes always raise their struggle for raising their living standard above the level of minimum subsistence. And poverty will remain a perennial theme of all the social conflicts so long as majority will remain deprived of the opportunity of realising the gains of their individual as well as collective endeavour for the general welfare of the last social human.

Finally to conclude the forgoing discussion it can be said that poverty is a social relationship emanating from the social production and monopolistic appropriation of social produce. Therefore, the relationships of appropriation are also the poverty relationships. And all the appropriated ones are potential target/victims of poverty. But, at a given point of time only a portion of these are the actual victims of poverty. The number of actual victims of poverty will depend upon the levels and nature of class consciousness and also the organised struggle of the appropriated/subaltern classes in striking the economic, political, ideological and legal bargain in their favour in the social power relations and also the class struggle. In this way poverty relations in its totality are also the class relations between the united appropriators and its powerful state apparatuses on the one hand and the unorganised, and low level of class consciousness among the appropriate ones. A poor is one who is economically appropriated and deprived, politically manipulated, ideologically hegemonised to accept the value, culture, signs and symbols of the exploiters and ultimately a vote bank in the quantitative liberal bourgeois democracy. Therefore, the fight against poverty is meaningful only when it involves total overthrow of the existing social structure, power relations. And any thing less than that will only be a liberal approach to handle poverty by creating more poverty along with great claims of fighting it. To begin with the subaltern must incorporate *Food as the basic human right* as the main aim of their class struggle.

NOTES

1. Peter Lloyed, *Slums of Hope? Shanty Towns of the Third World*, Penguin Books, Harmondsworth, 1979, p. 13.
2. K. Marx and F. Engels, "On Colonialism", *New York Daily Tribune*, No. 3804 June the 25th, 1853 as quoted in the book *On Colonialism*, Progress Publishers Moscow, 1978.
3. According to Arnold J. Toynbee,: "Freedom from Hunger campaign is one of the three major educational campaigns on which the human race is engaged in our times. The other two are, of course, the campaign against war and the campaign against disease. War, pestilence and famine have been the three traditional scourges of the human race." Address delivered before the opening session of the World Food Conference of the Food and Agricultural Organisation of the United Nations Organisation Washington D.C. on June the 5th 1963.
4. Thomas Robert Malthus, *An Essay on the Principle of Population and A Summary View of the Principle of Population*, Penguin Books, Harmondsworth, 1970.
5. Susan George,: *How The Other Half Dies*, Penguin Books Harmondsworth, 1980, pp. 54-55.
6. Malthus, *Ibid.*, p. 226.
7. Malthus, *Ibid.*, p. 238.
8. Malthus, *Ibid.*, p. 70.
9. Malthus, *Ibid.*, p. 71.
10. Malthus, *Ibid.*, p. 71.

11. Malthus, *Ibid.*, p. 89.
12. Malthus, *Ibid.*, p. 103.
13. Malthus, *Ibid.*, pp. 25-27.
14. Larry, K.Y. Ng and Stuart Mudd (ed.), *The Population Crises*, Arnold J. Toynbee, "Man and Hunger the Perspective of History", Indiana University Press 1965, p. 134.
15. Toynbee, *Ibid.*, p. 133. It something similar to the preventive, and positive checks and moral restraints of Malthus.
16. Toynbee Identified Nature's Three methods: Hunger (famine), war and disease of population control similar to Malthussian negative checks. Toynbee, *Ibid.*, p. 133.
17. Toynbee, *Ibid.*, p. 134.
18. Toynbee, *Ibid.*, pp. 138-39.
19. Similar to the second formulation of Malthus "the passion between the sexes is necessary and will remain nearly in its present state" Malthus, *op cit.*, p. 70.
20. Toynbee, *Ibid.*, p. 139.
21. Toynbee, *Ibid.*, p. 139.
22. Toynbee, *Ibid.*, p. 139.
23. Susan George: *How the Other Half Dies*, Penguin Books, Harmondsworth, 1980, p. 23.
24. Peter Lloyed, *Slums of Hope Shanty Towns of the Third World*, Penguin Books, Harmondsworth, 1979, p. 61.
25. Susan George, *Ibid.*, p. 23.
26. Susan George, *Ibid.*, pp. 31-33.
27. Susan George, *Ibid.*, pp. 158-191.
28. Butz, U.S. Secretary of Agriculture as cited in Susan George, *Ibid.*, p. 16.
29. Susan George, *Ibid.*, p. 16.
30. Susan George, *Ibid.*, p. 16.
31. Susan George, *Ibid.*, p. 26.
32. C.B. Macpherson, *The Political Theory of Possessive Individualism: Hobbes to Lock*, Oxford University Press, London, 1962.
33. This goes against the construct of Dada Bhai Naroji, A.K. Sen, V.K.R.V. Rao, N.K. Rath, V.M. Dandekar and Sukhatme etc.
34. Albert Camus, *Resistance, Rebellion and Death*, Hamish Hamilton, New York, p. 67, 1978.

20

PERSPECTIVE ON POVERTY

B.K. PANDA

Introduction

Poverty is a complex and multi-faceted phenomenon which involves multifarious problems and deserves proper understanding without which it will be like groping the elephant by the blind man. To fathom the giant creature one requires a clear vision and similarly problem like poverty requires to be examined from different angles and unusual perspective. Any attempt in tackling poverty thus necessitates basic understanding, situational analysis, identification of the critical issues and evolving action plan with sustainable options based on appropriate strategy. In this context, this chapter attempts to highlight certain basic features and brings out few critical issues for retrospection and parlance.

Poor, Poverty and Poverty Line

Who is poor? What is poverty? What are the criteria for identifying the poor? How poverty is measured or determined and what is poverty line? These interwoven questions are often encountered while dealing with the subject. The generic dictionery meaning of the term 'poor' is lack of means for comfortable subsistence and 'poverty' is the state of being poor. Hence, the term leaves ample scope of subjective interpretation but primarily reflects the scarcity of food which is vital for subsistence. Thus, Poverty line can be explained as the level of income sufficient to purchase the minimum standard of nutrition/food. The official estimate and prevalent method of determining poverty is based on 'consumption of calories' which is ought to be the absolute minimum requirement for subsistence. In other words, the economic condition assumes a prime position. However, analysis reveals that poverty not only reflects economic status rather entwine the overt manifestation in terms of deprivation, incapacitation and deplorable infrastructure and services.

Developing the concept of 'culture and poverty' which applies to the poor, Oscar Lewis characterises the features as 'Low wage and chronic unemployment and underemployment which lead to low income, lack of property ownership, absence of saving, absence of food reserves at home and a chronic shortage of cash, which not only reflects scarcity but reduces the possibility of effective contribution of these group to the economic and production system. While these features reflects and represents economic dimension, poverty epitomise DIRE deprivation and touches the entire fabric of social, physical, psychological and moral aspect of the group.

The prevailing unidimensional 'calorie consumption' approach is normative and insensitive to the behavioural elements, ignores relative nature of poverty, insensitive to intensity and severity, inflexible to consider the regional variation and does not capture the various aspects relating to poverty such as status of health, education, isolation, ineffective access, powerlessness and gender based disadvantages.

Any attempt to tackle poverty, thus take due cognisence to the multifarious dimension and features involved in phenomena of poverty, otherwise the attempts may continue to be superficial. It is well recognised that identification on multiple criteria is not only complex, time consuming and requires specialised service, none-the-less a systematic approach will be effective.

Economic Growth, Unemployment and Poverty

The extent of poverty in the economy as a whole depend on the degree of development. Under-development and inequality are the two prime factors of poverty. One school of thought believes that solution to poverty lies in accelerated growth rate of economy which would in turn redistribute income and reduce inequalities through trickle down process. The 'Sixth Five Year Plan' documents also partially recognised and endorsed that substantial increase in the overall rate of growth of the economy will no doubt create favourable condition for reduction in poverty and unemployment. Economic growth while considered to be pre-requisite for alleviating poverty, sole reliance on 'growth' itself may be detrimental due to uncertainty of equitable/proportionate distribution of growth and though poverty is ineluctably related to income level, it is obviously not the sole factor as explained earlier.

Poverty is ineluctably related to employment to the size of the low-skilled and unskilled population which is distributed in urban and rural areas according to economic and other considerations. Growth of population leads to growth in demand in urban areas for all factors of production including unskilled labour. The change in the proportion of unskilled workers in urban areas depends on growth in demand for urban and rural commodities and on comparative decline of traditional production in these areas. Since, traditional production is non-viable in the face of modern manufacturing, its decline may release unskilled labour to other parts of the economy. The prudent economic policy, while play an active and effective role in development of effectuating buoyant growth, statistics reveals that employment growth rates is in declining trend. The nature of employment opportunity has changed by way of decline in salaried job and increasing trend of casualisation of labour and self-employment. Those in favour of market economy advocates that unemployment rate do not show an increasing trend. On this covent it is worthwhile to note that unemployment rate does not grow much as the abject poverty group are desparate enough to choose any sort of activities as survival is key where intake of food is not filling the stomach but providing energy to strive till next day. Hence, the attempt should be aimed at accelerated growth of economy in one hand and re-insteading the poorer section as part and parcel of the productive economy.

Rural Poverty vis-a-vis Urban Poverty

Off late immense debate has been generated on the extent, magnitude and priority issue on rural poverty vis-a-vis urban poverty. Opinion differs on greater thrust and attention towards these mainly based on the extent of poverty. However, poverty being a complex phenomena can not be isolately considered as there is an intricate link between the urban and rural areas in terms of production and population specially among the poorer echeleon. Hence, any discrimination or lopsided attention to the poverty groups of particular areas would alleviate the problem at the other. Prudent and simultaneous effort is thus desirous and will avoid imbalances.

Conclusion

It will not be exagerated in pointing out that no civilised society can afford to be a silent spectator to the issue of poverty and while efforts to ameliorate and alleviate poverty reinforced, the underlying issues may be taken into consideration so that the situation of poverty trap may be avoided and sustainable development of the poor can be achieved.

21

CURRENT STATUS OF POVERTY AND ITS DETERMINANTS IN THE NORTH EASTERN REGION

KEYA SENGUPTA

The major thrust of all developmental policies to india, since the early fifties, has been the alleviation of poverty and raising the standard of living of the masses. Such policy considerations play a pivotal role for a developing and poor country, and particularly for a still highly backward region like that of the North Eastern one. The success of all economic policies and programmes, should be evaluated in terms of their ability to raise the living conditions of the masses, since all such policies are based ultimately for the betterment of the common people.

It is postulated that, just as the ultimate purpose of all developmental policies and programmes is to reduce the level of poverty among the people and raise the economic welfare of the maximum, the very existence of poverty acts as a deterrent to any kind of ambitious economic policy. This is in view of the fact that poverty gives rise to illiteracy and illiteracy in turn acts as an obstacle to stability of population growth. Studies throughout the world economy reveals that the higher population growth, higher also is the level of poverty. High level of poverty and population growth creates unemployment problems, giving rise to poverty related crimes, social deprivation and tension and pent up source of injustice. Existence of such factors, slackens the pace of economic development, and lengthens the period for the benefits of developmental policies to percolate down to the poorest of the poor. Poverty thus intensifies poverty. It is, therefore, extremely essential that no economy particularly the North Eastern one with its own special and some peculiar characteristic problems should be caught in the grip of poverty, and allow developmental plans to be hampered. This calls for a periodic review of the nature and extent of poverty in this region, and consequent change and review of the existing policies if the occasion so demands.

It is in this context that the time has arrived to take stock of the extent and nature of poverty existing in the North Eastern Region. Cruciality of this review is of particular concern to all policy-makers and researchers, working for the development of the North Eastern Region, since from the eighties till the present, a good number of special programmes and policies have been enunciated particularly for this region, and thus it is imperative to make a review of the impact of such policies on the level of poverty existing in this region. It is with this aim in view that the present chapter makes an analytical investigation into the extent of poverty existing in the North Eastern Region, so as to confront the policy-makers with empirical reality, relating to the extent of poverty prevalent in these various states.

Poverty is a relative term, a poor person in one country in terms of certain indicators of poverty measurement may be considered rich by the standard of another nation or region. Therefore, what should be the satisfactory indicator of measuring poverty? Numerous studies on poverty have taken different indicators to measure the extent of poverty. Measurement in terms of per capita income, may not always provide satisfactory results, since such measurements may conceal the concentration of income in a few hands. Per capita consumption of some basic necessities of lie, such as food, clothing, shelter even education and health, may also prove to be unsatisfactory, in the sense of being unable to capture the essence of the real measurement of poverty. This is mainly because such requirements may vary due to climate, geographical and personal requirements, depending on age, sex and taste of the persons concerned, so that these measurements may fail to provide any meaningful intra or inter regional comparison or comparisons between two periods of time. Expenditures per head too may not convey any meaningful measurement of poverty, because a person may have high income, but may not have the desire to spend, as a result of which per capita expenditure on various items of consumption may have a small value.

Consumerism in most countries of west has reached a state of vulgarism so that compairing the level of consumption in backward region with such vulgar consumerism of the developed nations, may not only be meaningless but may also prove to be misleading.

Considering all these factors, choice of indicators for measuring poverty is extremely crucial as well as difficult. The extent of poverty could be measured by the level of unemployment specially in a poverty striken over populated country like India. Higher the level of unemployment, higher is also the level of poverty. In economies characterised by a high percentage of unemployment it is a foregone conclusion that the capacity to spend and consume, would also be much lower than in other countries, where the percentage of employment is higher. This highlights the necessity and the importance of government's spending for the maintenance of such people, since they are unable to meet the costs of the various social sectors themselves such as health, sanitation etc. at their own expense. Therefore, the lower the per capita expenses on these items, higher is the level of poverty. We have, therefore, chosen such indicators as government expenditure per head on health services, education and other social services. Per capita availability of doctors, hospitals as other indicators of poverty, since it is a common experience that lower the percentage of such facilities higher also is the death rate, since it it mostly the poor people who are often the victims of diseases and epidemics of various nature coupled with the fact that they lack the financial abilities to satisfy their medical needs. Another indicator of the level of poverty, selected for the purpose of our study, has been the literacy rate, since numerous studies have revealed that there is an important corelationship between poverty and illiteracy. A nation characterised by poverty also has a low rate of literacy.

The present study, therefore, attempts to focuss attention on the extent and level of poverty of the various constituent units of the North Eastern Region, with some of the selected indicators of poverty mentioned above. The study analyses the scenario with the situation as was prevalent in 1991 so as to capture the essence of the extent of poverty of the states of the region.

Data relating to the various states of the region, reveal that the level of unemployment is the highest in the states of Assam followed by Tripura. One would normally conclude that population growth may be one of the reasons for unemployment and a consequent rise in the level of poverty. However, the growth rate of population is one of the lowest in Assam, among the North Eastern States, implying that the state has reached the saturation level as far as employment generation is concerned. However, population growth could be a possible cause of the high level of unemployment in Tripura. Using unemployment as an indicator of poverty the study reveals that the position of the other hill states seems to be relatively better, but things may go out of hand unless and until immediate steps are taken to control the growth rate of population.

Using the per capita expenses by the government on health services, data reveals that health services in terms of hospitals and doctors is the poorest in Assam, the highest per capita expenditure on health notwithstanding. Consequently, the state also registers the highest death rate in the region. Mention needs to be made about the highest death rate recorded in the region in Arunachal Pradesh in 1991. This could be due to poor medical facilities warranted by the lowest per capita expenditure on health, though the state is relatively better off in terms of the number of people served by hospitals and doctors which could be due to the sparse population of the state. Analysing similar data for the state of Tripura, the study reveals that the indicators of health services for the population are not too encouraging, and the number of hospitals in the state certainly needs to be increased.

Latest studies on poverty considers education to be a contributory factor towards increasing one's earning capacity and hence in determining the quality of life. Investment in educational infrastructure determines the facilities of education available, but such investments cannot be left in the hands of private investors as return to educational investment is long-term and more of a social rather than of economic nature. Consequently, investment in education is an important factor which is left in the hands of the government and it has tremendous potentiality to determine the quality of life available to the masses. It is revealed that Assam has the lowest per capita expenditure on education followed by Manipur and Meghalaya. Consequently, the literacy rate in the state too is one of the lowest in the region. It is important to highlight here that educational expenditure per head as well as the literacy rate is the highest in Mizoram and the state tops the list in terms of employment too. This prompts us to conclude that there is a positive corelationship between expenditure on education, literacy rate and the employment rate.

A direct fall out of poverty is the poor condition of living and shortages of houses. This gives rise to slums and unhygienic living conditions, increasing the misery of poverty, which is a feature associated more with urban poverty rather than with rural poverty. Analysis of such data reveals that housing shortage is most acute in Assam followed by Tripura.

A perusal of the trend reveals that judging from the point of view of our selected indicators, Assam emerges as the most poverty striken state of the region followed by Tripura and Arunachal Pradesh. This prompts an investigation into the possible causes for the same. Expenditure per head in terms of the state and central plans could be an important determinant of the extent of poverty prevalent in the states. The study highlights the fact that Assam spends the lowest amount of money per person, both in terms of state Plans as well as Central assistance, followed by Tripura. The two states witnesses the same trend in terms of per capita expenses on social services in spite of the fact that in poverty stricken states, the state needs to incur substantial expenses on various items of social services, in an attempt to alleviate poverty. It is interesting to note here that the highest per capita expenditure on social services, both in terms of the state Plans as well as Central assistance in the region notwithstanding, Arunachal Pradesh continues to be a poverty striken state. On the other hand such variations show a favourable trend both for Mizoram and Nagaland, the states which are most favourably placed in terms of the indicators of poverty measurement.

The above study reveals that the North Eastern region cannot be treated as a single homogenous unit as far as policy formulations are concerned, in view of the wide diversity of the constituent units in terms of their geographical, climatic, social and cultural factors. Each state in the region is characterised by their own peculiar problems so that a common and uniform policy for poverty alleviation may not bear any fruitful result. The state of Assam stands out as the state most adversely striken by poverty, followed by Tripura. In both these cases, plan outlay needs to be stepped up immediately without any delay.

As far as the situation in Arunachal Pradesh is concerned the study reveals that the scenario of poverty is a little complicated. The highest per capita expenditure in the State Plan and also by way of Central assistance notwithstanding, the condition of the people of the state is rather miserable in terms of most of the indicators of poverty measurement discussed above. Per capita expenditure on health services is one of the lowest in the state due to which the state is confronted with the highest death rate and one of the highest growth rate of population in the region. This again may be accentuated by the lowest rate of literacy in the region witnessed by the state. The situation, therefore, calls for a policy consideration which would differ substantially from the policy to be applied to Assam and Tripura. Emphasis should be laid on immediately restraining the population growth and taking steps to invest more in education and step up the literacy rate.

As far as the other hill states of the region are concerned, the position of Meghalaya and Manipur seems to be highly disturbing. In Mizoram and Nagaland, the level of poverty may increase in the future if the growth rate of population is left uncontrolled, though at present the level of poverty may not give us reasons for any grave concern.

In conclusion it may be stated that taking the North Eastern region as a whole, whatever be the policies adapted for poverty alleviation, emphasis should be laid to achieve development from below. All developmental policies should focuss attention to the development of the people and policies should be so geared, so as to benefit the poor directly. In a region characterised by a vast population where the number of poverty striken people are increasing at such a tremendous rate, to expect the fruits of development to percolate down to the poor is a long term expectation, which may take several decades to materialise. It is, therefore, imperative that any attempt at poverty alleviation calls for investment not only in the various sectors of the economy, but also equally important is that investment should be stepped up in the various social sectors too.

22

SOME INDICES OF URBAN POVERTY IN NORTH EAST INDIA
An Overview

S. MUKHERJEE and M. BANERJEE

Introduction

Over the last decade and particularly duııng the last couple of years, estimation of poverty has been a fashionable exercise for economists and social scientists all over the world. The concept of conceptualization and measurement of poverty is too complex a phenomenon cutting across myriad of economic, social, cultural, political and psychological factors (Sharma, 1990). Poverty as a concept is closely related to income inequality. Given the average income with level, a higher level of inequality will tend to be associated with a higher level of poverty (Sen, 1990). Poverty has also been identified with deficiency in the total level of living which includes not only food for energy requirements but also balanced diet needed for health and other components of basic needs, essential for human existence at the tolerable level (Rao, 1977). Sukhatme (1977) a well known physical anthropologist pointed out that "A person who cannot afford a diet which meets his minimum energy needs for healthy and active life is poor and under-nourished as well".

Many of the poverty measurements are based on minimal levels, that directly or indirectly take note of the prevailing social ideas on the subject of poverty. Ojha (1970), Dandekar and Rath (1971), Bardhan (1970), have used specific nutritional standards to measure poverty. The simplest method of determining the poverty level is to ascertain a particular level of either income or expenditure required to meet the minimum needs of life. In practice it is more logical and easier to assess the extent and proportion of expenditure made on the three basic consumer categories, i.e. food, clothing and shelter in order of priority. Thus, Rao has proposed four criteria essential to define poverty line: (i) the proportion of expenditure incurred on the specified essential item e.g., food (ii) calorific value of food, (iii) cost of a balanced diet, and (iv) cost of essentials related to tolerable level of human existence.

On the other hand, criteria for determining nutritional requirements like calories and other essential nutrients do not itself have an unambiguous connotation in quantitative terms. Study of per capita requirement of nutrients depends upon certain diverse factors of the consuming unit e.g. age, sex, body weight, stature, occupation and above all the environment itself. The people living under hot-humid condition of plain land certainly need different levels of calorie than the dwellers of temperate mountain regions. Government of India has recommended a requirement of 2400 calories per person per day for rural and 2100 calories for urban area. Acharya places the per capita level of required calorie at 2,124 per day. Sukhatme (1977) has suggested the cut-off points of 2,200 calorie per day per head for Indian population. The Research and Planning Division of ECAFE Secretariat assumes that for Indians the minimum need for calorie intake is 2500. Hence, though there is a lot of short comings in the concept, the incidence of mal-nutrition constitute the core poverty.

The Present Study and the Data-base

Within the perimeter of this chapter we have attempted to evaluate the urban poverty situation in all the seven states of North East India. For this purpose we have utilized the statewise quantitative information published by the National Sample Survey Organisations and other published materials. The N.S.S.O. report on consumer expenditure is based on the 43rd round survey during June, 1987 to July 1989. To assess the level of consumer expenditure N.S.S. has tabulated their report giving 12 per capita expenditure classes from less than 90 to more than 700 in rupees, spent during the 30 days of survey. This consumer expenditure measurement in three different seasons and then consumption of different food and non-food items are calculated for each expenditure class. For urban areas of each state sampling is done from selected blocks, visiting selected households.

For the purpose of the present work and simplification of the methodology we have equally divided those, 12, Monthly Per Capita Expenditure (MPE) Classes into three. So, we get *Low* MPE Class (less than 160), *Middle*, MPE Class (160-310) and *High*, MPE Class (Above 310). These three factors have been taken up as direct or indirect indices of economic status of poverty, for example (i) proportion of population among three expenditure classes; (ii) proportion of expenditure on food and non-food categories within and among seven North Eastern States, and (iii) variations in calorie consumption among MPE Class in each state and between North Eastern States. The calorific values have been obtained by converting weight of each food items into calorie content level as per I.C.M.R. standard chart.

The tables thus prepared are again plotted as different comparative diagram using simple cartographic techniques.

Interpretations and Findings

A. Percentage of population in each MPE Class for individual states of N.E. India is shown through a comparative bar diagram (Fig. 22.1). In short the following points are revealed from the diagram:

(i) In the states like Assam, Tripura and Arunachal Pradesh there are distinct dominance of the low expenditure class followed by middle and high classes (Table 22.1).

(ii) Manipur and Meghalaya show a dominance of middle class expenditure group followed by low and high MPE classes.

(iii) The low MPE Class is totally absent in Nagaland and Mizoram, where middle class dominates markedly.

(iv) On the other hand share of highest class is almost equal

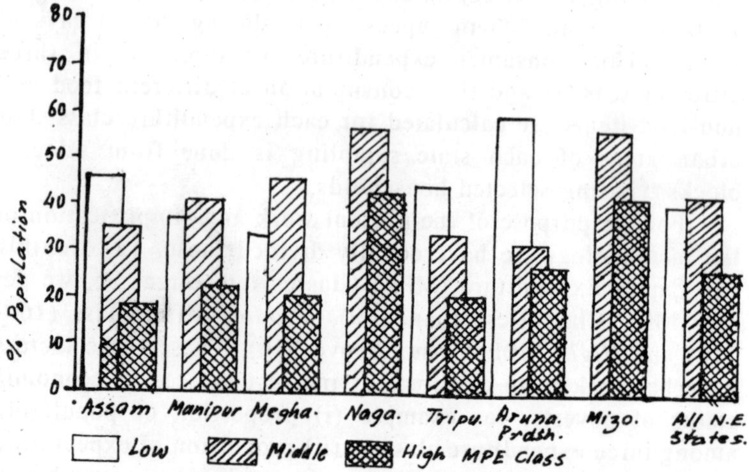

FIG. 22.1: Percentage Population in Each Expenditure Class (Statewise)

and around 20 per cent among four states e.g. Assam (18.79%), Meghalaya (20.65%), Tripura (29.96%) and Manipur (22.62%), and

(v) Interesting to note that the share of high MPE class is over 40 per cent in Nagaland and Mizoram.

B. The diagram on proportionate share in food and non-food categories (Fig. 22.2) helps us to look into another aspect of the urban poverty conditions in this region.

(i) In general, expenditure on food is dominant among all states (61%) which is an indication towards dominance of low MPE class population having very low surplus over expenditure on food.

(ii) Again Assam, Manipur, Tripura and Arunachal Pradesh can be grouped together showing non-food expenditure sharply reduced from high to low MPE class—expressing high income disparity. This can be further varified from the very high coefficient of variability in these two heads of expenditure among three classes (Fig. 22.3).

(iii) The states of Meghalaya, Nagaland and Mizoram show some similar character of low to moderate disparity

TABLE 22.1: **Percentage Distribution of Population Expenditure Classes (Statewise)**

Expen-diture	Assam	Manipur	Meghalaya	Nagaland	Tripura	Arunachal Pradesh	Mizoram	$\overline{X}$	%
< 160	46.14	39.92	33.60	—	45.04	45.68	—	40.48	4.75
160-310	55.07	40.47	45.75	57.02	34.00	32.24	57.29	43.12	9.81
310	18.79	22.62	20.65	42.99	20.96	29.10	42.71	27.97	9.70
Total Population Sample	51,048	61,032	56,030	25,841	55,971	55,456	32,357		

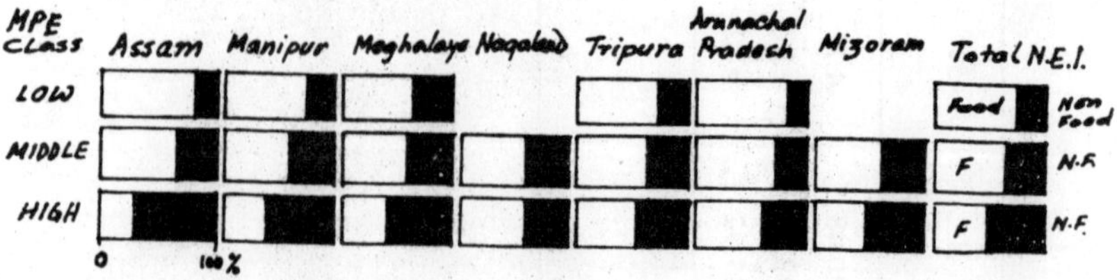

FIG. 22.2: Percentage Expenditure on Food and Non-food in Each MPE Class (Statewise)

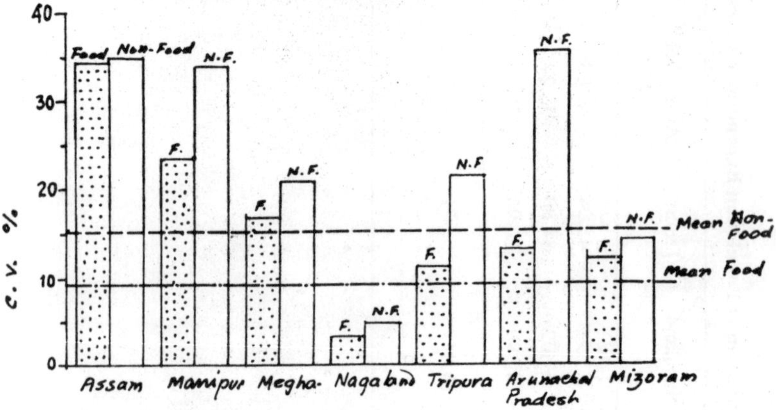

FIG. 22.3: Percentage Variability in Food and Non-food Expenditure (Statewise)

among three MPE classes. But the low variables in Nagaland and Mizoram are due to absence of low class there.

(iv) The C.V. of non-food expenditure, which can be taken as a clear index of economic stature as well as purchasing capacity, is always higher than that of food (Fig. 22.3).

(v) Only in the Nagaland and Mizoram the variability of non-food expenditure remain below the mean variability of the North Eastern States (15-30%).

(vi) The variability of food and non-food expenditure in each

TABLE 22.2: **Percentage Variation of Expenditure in Food and Non-Food among Expenditure Classes (Statewise)**

Expenditure Classes	Assam	Manipur	Meghalaya	Nagaland	Tripura	Arunachal Pradesh	Mizoram
				C. V. %			
Food	34.16	23.11	17.18	3.02	11.32	13.64	12.42
Non-Food	35.64	33.66	21.84	5.12	21.68	35.71	14.52

MPE class in seven states as a whole shows (Fig. 22.4) lowest P.C. in the middle income group and highest P.C. in non-food items of low MPE class. This is again an indication of higher incidence of poverty in the region (Table 22.2).

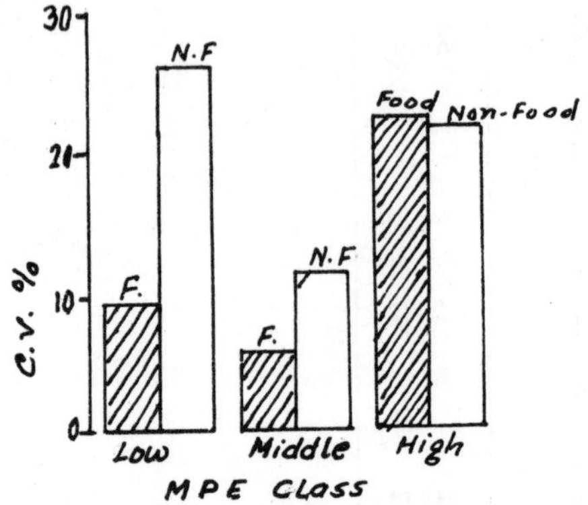

Fig. 22.4: Percentage Variability in Food and Non-food Expenditure (MPE classwise) (All Seven States)

C. In the third phase we have attempted to analyse variations in calorie consumption among three MPE classes and among seven states as well. At a first glance at the composite bar diagram (Fig. 22.5) it is evident that the level of calories consumption in any of the states is nowhere near 2000 Keal/d/unit. This can be explained by the fact that: (a) N.S.S.O. has not considered sex and age-wise variation and the total head count is taken as total consumption unit. Thus the lower rate of consumption of female and child members are reflected in the much lower (mean) consumption, (b) Food items like most of the vegetables and other ready made food products consumed by urban people have also been exempted. Hence we would only consider the variations at inter-class and inter-states level to assess the relative poverty situations in North East India (Table 22.3).

(i) Arunachal Pradesh scores highest in total calorie consumption (620) and leads the group comprised of Manipur (682), Tripura (661) and Assam (625). These states are in general have higher average share of food

TABLE 22.3: **Variation of Calorie Consumption among Three Classes (Statewise)**

	Assam	Manipur	Meghalaya	Nagaland	Tripura	Arunachal Pradesh	Mizoram
Total Expenditure	625.07	682.1	476.89	393.13	661.88	820.34	401.55
Mean $\overline{X}$	208.36	227.36	158.96	196.56	220.62	273.45	240.78
C.V.%	18.08	28.13	29.05	27.15	22.75	27.88	24.00

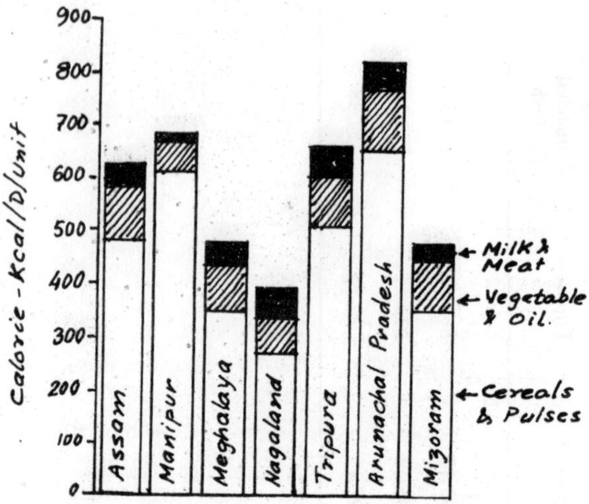

FIG. 22.5: Calorie Consumption (Statewise)

over non-food, of which Arunachal Pradesh has the highest expenditure value on food (72.37%).

(ii) Other three states, Nagaland (393), Meghalaya (477) and Mizoram (481) are in the low calorie consumption group. But these states are showing less incidence of poverty indices, e.g., higher share of non-food expenditure, very less or non-existence of low MPE Class etc. Further, the share of cereals and pulses in their food is less compared to other North Eastern states as a whole (Table 22.4). This can perhaps be correlated with some urban characters available and these states find variety of ready food and also they are getting calories from some other food items which are not taken into account in this study.

(iii) But the proportion of milk and meat is higher among those getting less calorie. It also indicates towards food habit and higher purchasing capacity of those urban population.

TABLE 22.4: **Comparative Calories Consumption in Each Food Categories (Statewise)**

Food Categories	Assam	Manipur	Meghalaya	Nagaland	Tripura	Arunachal Pradesh	Mizoram	C.V.%
1. Total	485.76	612.07	350.40	273.33	512.26	656.26	357.95	28.48
%	77.71	89.73	73.48	69.52	77.4	80.00	74.83	
2. Total	97.31	55.00	82.26	60.74	91.34	104.43	82.73	20.70
%	15.58	8.07	17.24	15.5	13.80	13.34	16.76	
3. Total	47.00	14.96	44.23	59.01	55.25	54.65	42.89	31.11
%	6.72	2.19	9.27	15.00	8.87	6.66	8.91	

Concluding Remarks

Within the limit of this brief overview we can point out a broad grouping of these seven North Eastern States depending upon their location among the three parameters e.g. (a) share of population among three expenditure classes, (b) proportion of expenditure on food and non-food items and (c) comparative calorie consumption levels.

1. Comparatively lower incidence of poverty is found among urban population of the states of Nagaland, Mizoram and Meghalaya. But interestingly these states are consuming relatively lower calorie from most common food items.
2. Relatively higher poverty conditions prevail among Arunachal Pradesh, Assam, Manipur and Tripura. These states are, in contrast getting higher calorie, mostly from cereals and pulses.

Considering whole of North Eastern India it can easily be pointed out that the general standard of living of urban people is not higher sides.

But to find a concrete answer to any question of poverty evaluation in this region any body has to consider a number of complex-interrelated indices or variables from Anthropometric, physiological, occupational, socio-cultural and environmental aspects.

For standard indices of poverty evaluation like poverty line, minimum nutritional requirements, and even the actual nutrient values of some important indigenous food items etc. are required to be calculated separately for North East Indian states.

Finally, we should consider all probable factors, regional or local, while evaluating poverty at macro and micro level so as to provide a comprehensive data base to be utilized for any poverty alleviation programmes in India.

REFERENCES

Bardhan, P.K. (1970), 'On the Minimum Level of Living and Rural Poor', *Indian Economic Review*, April.

Dandakar, V.M.M. and N. Rath (1970), "Poverty in India—Dimensions and Trends", *Economic and Political Weekly*, Jan. 2.

Ojha, P.D. (1970), 'A Configuration of Indian Poverty', *Reserve Bank of India Bulletin*, January.

Rao, V.K.R.V. (1977), 'Nutritions' Norms by Calorie Intake and Measurement of Poverty': *Bulletin of the International Statistical Institute*, Proceedings of the 41st. Session Vol. XIVII, Book I, Invited Papers, pp. 645-54.

Sen, Amatya (1970), "Poverty Inequality and Unemployment: Some Conceptual Issues in Measurement", in K.S. Krishnaswamy (ed.), *Poverty and Income Distribution*, Sampeksha Trust, Oxford University Press, Bombay, pp. 45-60.

Sharma, A. (1970), *Concept and Measurement of Poverty*, Anndl Publications, New Delhi.

Sukhatme, P.V. (1977), Measurement of Poverty based on Nutritional Needs, *Bulletin of the International Statistical Institute*, Vol. XVIII, Book 4, pp. 553-56.

23

IF THE CHILDREN ARE NOT COMING TO SCHOOL, CAN WE REACH THEM?

NEELAM SINHA

With the technological advancement in radio and TV it is virtually possible to go to their huts. A genuine effort is required to provide access to educational opportunities virtually at the paddy field, while planting, tending to cows or goats at the farm house and village gathering place. These places may constitute a place of learning, where father-and-sons, mother-and-daughter or other family members may work together.

Since 1988, Vocationalisation of Higher Secondary Education was introduced with the objective of enhancing individual employability, reduce the mismatch between demand and supply of skilled manpower. But due to various drawback, 150 vocational courses could not attract much students in the formal system.

A number of schemes like Jana Shiksha Nilayams, Shramik Vidyapeeths, Community Polytechnics, Krishi Vigyan Kendras are operating without coordination. Such uncoordinated programmes in the rural areas often confuse the beneficiaries and are wasteful of human and financial resources. Consequently, they fail to produce any impact and make people lose faith in them.

Open learning with the help of radio and television allows learners to continue with their lessons without disruption at their day to day work. Additional support is provided through other educational support facilities like printed instructional materials, lecture or practical demonstration at site. This will not only motivate and develop enthusiasm among learners but lead them towards self-reliant.

Unlike conventional system where teachers and teaching have been given undue advantage, in open learning the focus of attention is the learner. Here he has command over his wishes or interest; which subject to opt for, where to study whether at home, farm, village, factory, school, office or study-centre, when to study and when to appear for examination or whether he may need to appear for any examination. Knowledge or information are gained only from a learner's own conviction—a realisation that the best teacher is really oneself and personal efforts ultimately are the most important. This self reliance or self determination may best by inculcated through open learning.

It is time now to re-examine the conventional school system and encourage flexible alternatives to utilise the modern technologies to bring a larger segment of our deprived groups in the fold of a learning society. While presenting my paper at the conference held at NIEPA (Reforming School Education, Feb. 1996), I have reiterated the need for a cohesive policy approach formal, non-formal and dual mode of integrated approach to fulfil our objectives. Open learning has its potential to extend a wider access of learning experiences and making it a life long process to actively participate in the social reconstruction. This may be used to encompass variety of topics including a number of vocational courses...; including community mobilisation, rural leadership training, small scale home industries, food processing, environmental protection and conservation, population and health education, at the local level with the help of local resources.

Target Clients

I. In spite of substantial expansion of educational opportunities India has about 19 to 24 million children in the age group 6 to 14 years out of school of whom about 60 per cent are girls and about 110.9 million are adult illiterates in the age groups 19 to 35. Programmes are needed for the group of young people after completion of Secondary courses. Ranging between fifteen to eighteen years of age group youth will require knowledge, skill and attitude which will enable him to enter an occupation.

II. Dropout children from formal schools and adult who missed their education and one either unemployed or engaged in part time occupations will require similar treatment.

III. Neo literates from adult and continuing centres who are well motivated and have acquired functional literacy will require different vocational programmes like health and nutrition programme, carpentry, etc.

IV. A number of adult already engaged in their vocations will like to upgrade their skill through modern technological media to increase their output. Farmers, tea planters, electricians, carpenters and technicians may require such courses.

Requisites

1. Before 'Learning to do', a vocational survey is required to assess the availability of human, material and natural resources and then selecting programmes to be introduced in a particular locality/village.
2. It should be functional, integrated and designed to meet each individual's specific needs and learning requirements. Programme is to be the need based aiming at skill formation/skill upgradation leading to horizontal/vertical socio-economic mobility with due emphasis on illiterate workers.
3. In remote, hilly and tribal areas, it is important to identify local leaders/educated persons, available in the community to be resource persons for the community centre. Academically qualified local youth, retired persons, educated farmers and artisans have to come out to help the out of school children.

Due to these factors, there are about 1,14,105 children (I-V) still out of school. The state of drop out children is indicated to be only 32.06 at the primary stage but goes upto 67.42 at the secondary stage. Because of shifting cultivation, most of the children move from one place to other and are unable to furnish the school authorities with a residential address. Generally schools have a fixed age range for admission in a class which cannot accommodate the adults. The extreme poverty of the child acts as a serious deterrent, parents cannot provide the child with books and stationeries essential to carry on his study and children are pushed to work and earn for their sustenance. These child labourers are generally part time wage earners and are unskilled workers. They grow uneducated, untrained and completely alien to social and cultural miller.

National Open School has developed a whole range of open Vocational Courses for different categories of children and youth:

(a) *Package for Vocational Courses*

In this category a candidate may select three vocational courses along with a language course and may qualify for secondary and senior secondary certification. Typewriting, Stenography and Secretariat Services come under this category.

(b) 'Stand alone' is for learning enhancement. A candidate may select out of 40 Vocational Courses to enrich his/her skill upgradation. Dropout children and working youth may go for such courses for theoretical inputs which may help enhancing their understanding in the scientific and technological advancements and increasing their productive output. Course like Plant protection, Water management, Oyster Mushroom Production Technology, Food Processing, Beauty Culture, Baking and Confectionery, T.V. Repairing, Plumbing etc. have already been developed. A certificate is provided at the completion of a course.

Procedure for Implementation

To conduct our practicals, recognised Vocational Institutions, Polytechnics, Shramik Vidyapeeth and Voluntary Organisations (NGOs) are given accreditation as Vocation Study Centres which are also called Accreditated Vocational

Institutions (AVIs).

Interested candidates take their admission through these Study Centres in the month of May/June and October/ November.

Rural Socio-Economic Condition of Meghalaya

Meghalaya is predominantly rural, 81.3 per cent of the State's population resides in rural areas in 1991. Being an agrarian society, agriculture sector contributes nearly one third of the State Domestic Product of the State (30.8% on the State income). Last two rounds of NSS (32nd and 38th round) indicated drastic come down from 48.03 to 28 per cent between 1977-78 and 1983-84 as against 48.13 to 37.4 per cent at the All India level (Table 23.1).

TABLE 23.1: **Comparison of Socio-Economic Condition**

(Percentages)

Area	Meghalaya		All India	
	1977-78 (32nd round NSS)	1983-84 (38th round NSS)	1977-78 (32nd round NSS)	1983-84 (38th round NSS)
Rural	53.87	33.7	50.82	40.4
Urban	18.16	4.0	38.19	28.1
Combined	40.03	28.0	48.13	37.4

In other words 33.7 per cent of rural population of Meghalaya is below the poverty line as against All India figure of 40.4 per cent (rural). As a result per capita income lags far behind the All India average. (Rs. 3251 at current prices and Rs. 1515 at constant) (1980-81).

In this economic background, the pace of growth of schools to cope up with the demand for schooling is rather slow.

Other reasons being:

1. Management of primary schools with the District Councils.
2. Shifting cultivation.

3. Small habitations (65-45% villages with less than 200 population).
4. Illiterate, poor parents.
5. Difficult terrain or climatic conditions.
6. Insufficient educational infrastructure.

TABLE 23.2: **Tution Fees Structure for Vocational Courses**

1.	Integrated Courses	Secondary	Senior Secondary
	Rs. 650.00	Rs. 650.00	Rs. 775.00
2.	Stand Alone Courses	Secondary	Senior Secondary
	Rs. 150.00	Rs. 100.00	Rs. 125.00

Studies are evaluated in a pre-fixed evaluation centres which is practical based and conducted by external examiners. Examinations are held twice in a year, usually in April/May and November.

It is seem that students opting for Vocational Courses are keen to upgrade their scale. They may not be interested in appearing at the examination. Firstly because certificates may not be recognised anywhere but if a candidate is trained in technical field as Electrician or Mechanical personnel, they are highly in demand.

At present there are about 71 such open Vocational Courses have already been developed. Programme is to construct curriculum for at least 150 such Vocational Courses in future and develop audio-video input for greater impact on illiterate learners.

Community Workshop

NOS norms has been to accredit the established institutions as Study-Centres for practical demonstration. But what about those rural areas where schooling facilities, polytechniques, ITIs or Krishi Vigyan Kendras are not there?

In the present context, children of farmers, farm labourers, rural craftsman, who are to be inducted into open vocational courses in the areas where schooling facility is not adequate, the concept of 'Community Workshop' may be developed and established. By grouping the need for 3 to 4 villages, Community Workshop Centre as a resource cum production centre may be opened in the remote and deprived areas. Interested candidates will not only register themselves for a vocational course through the advanced technologies used for the upgradation of a skill or technique. Audio-video cassettes may be exposed to the learners for the training purposes in the presence of the trainees. Such Community Workshops will be in a position to undertake construction, repair and maintenance service jobs with the help of trainees under the supervision of the community leadership. Workshop would act as apprenticeship for the candidates for vocational entrepreneurship in a given area.

Based on the survey of available resources and the requirements of the area, the programmes may be grouped under the following heads:

(i) Agriculture related vocations.
(ii) Horticulture related vocations.
(iii) Animal Husbandry related vocations.
(iv) Civil and Construction related vocations.
(v) Electro-mechanical related vocations.
(vi) Home Science and Food Processing related vocations, and
(vii) Rural art and crafts related vocations.

It has to be borne in mind that one vocational course may suit or not will depend on the resources available and need for such technicians in that particular area.

Infrastructure and Financial Inputs

Community Workshop envisaged may have infrastructure given in Table 23.3.

This infrastructure may accommodate 100 persons for training at each Community Workshop. The Unit cost of vocational education is estimated to be Rs. 2000 only which may decline with the passage of time.

Presently at all-India level, only five Community Workshops will be taken up as on experiment basis. One NGO

TABLE 23.3: **Basic Needs of a Community Workshop**

Infrastructure		Financial inputs
1. 3000 sq. ft or available areas	Rs. 150.00	Rs. 4.50 lakhs
2. Staff members	5 crore professionals Rs. 60,000 per year	Rs. 5.00 lakhs
3. Equipments and raw-materials		Rs. 5.00 lakhs
4. Miscellaneous		Rs. 0.50 lakhs
		Total Rs. 15.00 lakhs

(Talent's Club, Shillong) has proposed such Community Workshop to be opened for the tribal children and youth of Meghalaya.

REFERENCES

Eighth Five Year Plan, Annual Plan 1992-93, *Draft Proposal,* Volume I, Planning Deptt., Govt. of Meghalaya, p. 14.

Manual of Vocational Courses Developed by Sh. S.S. Sangal, Joint Director, Vocational Education, National Open School, New Delhi.

Towards meeting a commitment, status paper on Achievement on Education for All, Department of Education, Ministry of Human Resource Development, Government of India, February, 1995.

24

POVERTY AND HOMELESSNESS

S.K. AGNIHOTRI

In order to consider the major problems faced by the victims of poverty and homelessness, it is necessary to follow the "basic and minimum needs approach" followed by the President of the World Bank, Robert McNamara in 1970s. The five basic and minimum needs are: (a) primary education, (b) primary health, (c) supply of potable water, (d) basic sanitation, and (e) shelter. To this may be added, the presence of a well performing system of law and justice which is primarily a regulatory function of the state. In the last fifty years we have failed miserably on all six counts. Even the World Bank has realised this lapse and is placing more emphasis on social and urban infrastructure development under its "new development paradigm". The Bank proposes to target really disadvantaged and focus more on the relatively neglected problem of urban poverty.

The investment required for meeting above mentioned basic needs is vast and beyond the scope of government if its functioning does not change. The government can find funds either to help the disadvantaged or to provide budget support to loss making Public Sector Undertaking and to maintain a fat administraion. The only way to find funds to meet the above mentioned basic needs is to create an environment of rapid growth. Action is required on behalf of the Government on the following points. It should:

(a) systematically exit from all activities which can be fostered and maintained by market forces;

(b) simultaneously focus hard on the six areas where state intervention is a must; and

(c) transparently encourage domestic and foreign investment in different sectors particularly those which favour disadvantaged.

II

Food Security

The world now produces enough food to feed its population. However, the problem relates to access to food supplies, of distribution and of entitlement particularly to the poor in the urban areas. We, in India, have bumper food stocks but malnutrition and hunger among the poor. Small and marginal farmers in developing countries have been selling their land to big farmers and large agriculture-business corporations due to liberalisation and globalisation. These interests have either converted the land to growing cash crops or growing food for the market. This has resulted in poor finding it difficult to purchase food from the market particularly during the lean season when employment is hard to come by having lost the security provided by production of food for self-consumption.

There has also been a change in what is being produced. The trend is to produce high values rice and wheat and leave low value coarse cereals, largely consumed by the poor. This is due to onslaught of new technologies for agricultural production and commercialisation of agriculture. Even among rice and wheat, the local varieties are fast disappearing as the high yielding varieties are being promoted aggressively by the fertiliser and pesticide lobbies. Thus the culture specificity of food, an important attribute of food security, is getting undermined at a rapid pace. The switch to input intensive agriculture is leading to greater indebtedness among marginal farmers thereby further undermining household food security.

Neither in India nor in any international forum there is any focus on personal/household food security. For example the policy statement of the Food Summit being organised by the Food and Agriculture Organisation at Rome from November 13-17, 1996 pledges that every man, woman and child has the right to be free from hunger and malnutrition. However, both the policy statement and the plan of action talk of food security on a global scale or at best on a national scale. What is required for the poor and the homeless is a food security plan to cover personal food security and not just national or international food security. The Food Summit should be rightly renamed as World Summit on Hunger.

III

Urbanisation

The growth of cities in developing countries like India is one of the main reasons of homelessness of the poor. The reason while cities are pulling in migrants from the countryside is the rural unemployment caused by improvements in agricultural productivity. The migrants would rather have a chance of a job in the city than the uncertainty of unemployment in the countryside. In the villages, peasants already have huts to live in, and wells for water. When they come to cities, they need brick houses, piped water supply, sewers and roads. The rural migrants are unable to afford these due to poverty. Thus Paul Bairoch, a professor of economics at Geneva University argues that "The city is a serious handicap (to development), and agriculture is just about the only solution". A study undertaken by the United Nations in 1979 showed that half the countries in Asia considered their pattern of urbanisation "highly unacceptable".

According to one view, cities are growing too fast and further investment in them should be discouraged for five main reasons:

(1) *Cities have been boosted artificially.* Many developing countries have spent an undue proportion of their scarce resources on providing their cities with cheap food and expensive infrastructure projects. For example, India has concentrated much of its industrialisation effort on building state-run intensive manufacturing plants in the cities.

(2) *Cities are too expensive.* Urbanisation calls for lots of investment in infrastructure that is not strictly necessary because migrants are abandoning perfectly good houses in their villages. According to one estimate, amount required just to build the houses and infrastructure for migrants to Asia's cities expected in the period 1980-2000 will take all of Asia's domestic savings.

(3) *Cities increase unemployment.* There are only two types of labour market in a big city; well paid jobs in the civil services; banking or industry for a privileged few, and hod-carrying or often nothing at all for millions living in slums or shanty towns. The enormous numbers of squatters account for over half the population of some of the cities. The immigrant problem has been especially acute in developing countries with interventionist government.

(4) *Cities breed crime.* Unlike villages and towns where populations are stable enough for newcomers to become known, cities are full of strangers. In such a case, safety of the neighbourhood is largely in the hands of police which is often inadequate.

(5) *Cities waste resources.* People in villages can walk to work, those in towns may have to take a short ride by car, bus or bicycle. Further, in a city the concentration of people causes congestion and raises the cost of travel. The extra time and fuel involved are wasted. As cities expand, the cause of providing basic services often rise exponentially, In addition, there are environmental problems.

Of course some of the disadvantages mentioned above may be considered as exaggerated. City growth need not always be harmful. The cities are expensive to build. New infrastructure in the cities costs more than building anything in the countryside. Many governments in the developing countries have lowered the standards required for new housing. Some of these infrastructure projects are also useful. For example in the late 1980s, 73 per cent of Indian city dwellers had access to safe water, compared with only 56 per cent of the residents in the countryside. Similarly, 1/3 of the city population had good sanitation as compared with almost no one in the villages. This was the main reason why infant and child mortality in the cities were roughly 1/2 of its level in the countryside. It would have been much more expensive to achieve these health benefits by providing safe water and sanitation in rural areas. The city jobs are also more productive as compared to a new job in the countryside even enough, creating a job in the city takes a larger investment. Further, in the developing countries, the rural migrants just do not make for the cities without any clear ideas as to how to proceed. They wait until they see a chance of finding work, often with the help of family or friends who are already in the city. Generally new arrivals establish themselves quickly and move up. The worst-off seem to be poor who were born in the city. It is a fact that subsidised food and subsidised investment do encourage extra people to move to the cities. However, attempts to suppress the growth of cities have failed in China and in Combodia. The other two arguments against the growth of cities namely, their high crime rates and their environmental problems are difficult to refute.

IV

Urban Waste

Poverty and homelessness lead to the disadvantaged coming in immediate contact with waste in urban areas due to inadequacy of shelter and necessity to earn livelihood. The disadvantaged in urban areas, per force, have to deal with such waste. In India we have not yet developed any system of such waste management appropriate to our culture. Discarded waste management technology from the developed world is finding its way to this country. In this connection two issues are of importance as these affect the health and well-being of poor in the urban areas who do not have any shelter—incincration and pelletisation.

Incineration spreads unburnt and newly formed toxins into the atmosphere and into the lungs. Air borne toxic chemicals travel long distances and invariably land up in food and drink. The pollution control filters and toxic ash are landfilled.

Contaminated liquid from scrubbing is released into water ways. Similarly, pelletisation results in spreading toxins to homes and directly into lungs. Pumping and dumping waste into rivers, seas and sewage systems only poison the environment. As for landfills there are none that are completely leakproof. Most of the slums in the cities are on the landfills which are a health hazard for the poor.

V

Possible Solutions for Shelter

The main scheme of urban renewal should include a slum rehabilitation programme within a given time frame. It should acknowledge the right (a) to adequate housing of the urban poor; (b) to rehabilitate them in their current place of residence; and (c) to accept the principle that inevitable displacing in public interest would be up to a maximum distance of 5 kms. from the old site to protect employment opportunities. However, it may be difficult to implement the project due to three major economic inconsistencies: (1) exhorbitant cost of land in the area; (2) the price of redeveloped property will be many times the lifetime income of its residents; and (3) the amount of funds required for rehabilitation may not be readily available.

The possible solution could be full political mobilisation to ensure that the real estate market behaves; to seek cooperation from the non-government organisations and developers in the project development; and to take up the programme in phases.

25

POVERTY AND HOMELESSNESS
Ethical Considerations

THOMAS PULLOPPILLIL

Introduction

Poverty had been understood differently by different people in different times. According to Random House Dictionary, poverty is "the state or condition of having little or no money, goods or means of support; condition of being poor, lack of something specified, deficiency of desirable ingredients, qualities; scantiness and insufficiency. In ordinary parlance, it is equated with squalor, misery and destitution.

1. Levels of Poverty

1.1. *Rich and Poor Countries*

Years of colonisation and the ongoing globalisation has produced two types of countries—poor and rich. The misery and destitution that was the result of years of colonisation and subsequent looting by the western countries, has not diminished over the years but new structures are brought in to give further legitimacy to the existing inequalities. The international debt problem and the new international trade agreement have to be seen in this light.

1.2. *Poor People in Rich and Poor Countries*

Poverty is a malady that has affected a section of the people even in rich countries. The difference may be in this that the welfare system in those countries might take care of food and medicine, whereas homelessness is a major problem that many rich countries have to face. In poor countries on the other hand, basic need of food and medicine is not assured to the poor. In India, the people below the poverty line increased from 35 per cent in 1993-94 to 38 per cent in 1995-96.[1]

2. Causes of Poverty

The causes of poverty is understood differently by different people. We can distinguish three main such misunderstandings.[2]

2.1 *Poverty as the Result of Fate*

According to this understanding poverty is considered as being predetermined, as being the result of forces beyond the control of man. Poverty and the poor will always be with us. It is understood as a punishment by the poor themselves. In this perspective, the remedy to poverty will be charity and relief work to alleviate the sufferings caused by poverty. While charity is needed, it does not answer the real problem. Little effort is made to identify and tackle the root cause of the problem.

2.2. *Poverty as the Result of Backwardness*

According to this view, people are poor because the country is 150 years behind Europe and the USA. They lack technology, they lack education. The remedy is to modernise; modernise education, modernise industry and agriculture. Development is conceived as catching up with the West; Out of the modernising process, something will progressively trickle down to the poor.

2.3 *Poverty as a Result of Injustice and an Unjust Social Order*

A third understanding of poverty considers the root cause of poverty and underdevelopment as *injustice, an unjust social order*. It is an historically created condition. It is the making of man and of the institutions created by man in history. (We do not exclude natural poverty, which is rooted in a low level of development of economy-industry, labour and resources and underutilization of science and technology).

We shall discuss briefly the what we mean by *injustice, unjust social order*.

II. Analysis of Injustice, Unjust Social Order

Structural Analysis

Certain power structures or class organisation of society can hamper the growth of people. They could be political structures, economic structures, social structures or cultural structures.

Political structures: Political structures are the way a society distributes the decision making power; Who has the power? In favour of which social group is power generally exercised?

Economic structures: Answers to questions like who owns the means of production, what is being produced, how are the goods produced distributed etc. will give an idea of economic structures.

Social structures: The society may be a feudal (landlords and peasants) or capitalistic (capital owners and labourers) or socialistic one. Each system builds up its own structures.

Cultural structures: Ideology (meaning system) in this context is the main explanation and justification given for the economic, social and political organisation of a given society. It can be a culture, a philosophy, or even a religion.

Historical Analysis

When history is taken seriously, we develop a historical consciousness. This historical consciousness regards the passage of time not simply in terms of natural process such as the seasons of the year or the biological cycles of growth and decay. Rather, time, in this case marks a series of specific events, specific changes in which we are involved and which we can—if we know the historic process—influence through collective action.

III. Toward a Solution

If injustice and unjust social order is the cause of poverty, an inquiry into this virtue and its practical application will lead us to a solution.

The Virtue of Justice

The virtue of justice tells us to give each his due. It is widely acknowledged that the primacy duty of the state is to oversee that justice is done among the citizens, although some capitalistic ideologies would think differently. The Greeks (e.g. Aristotle) understood the virtue of justice as general/legal justice or particular justice. The latter was subdivided into commutative justice and distributive justice. Commutative justice which focuses on relations of members of a society to each other, rectifies both voluntary transactions such as contracts and involuntary transactions such as theft or robbery. On the other hand, distributive justice, which considers the whole in relation to its parts, focuses on the community's distribution of benefits, such as honours and wealth, and burdens such as taxation, to individuals and groups. Since 1931, the terms 'social justice'[3] is used to denote the latter and the emphasis is on common good.

Social Justice

An understanding that the world and everything in it belonged to the entire human race is an ancient as man himself and can be found in all religious traditions. *Isavasyam idam sarvam*[4] (Everything belongs to God.) is the motto of Indians since the Upanishadic times. This principle is also found in Christianity (Universal destination of created things)[5]. The *Quran* proclaims preference to the poor and the oppressed (*mustad'ifin*).[6]

The Anglo-Saxon writer John Rawl's book *A theory of justice*[7] is considered to be the standard work on justice in the Western world. Justice according to Rawls is the first virtue of social institutions. Persons participate in political society as free and equal in pursuit of their plans of life. Political and economic institutions should begin from an agreement among persons basing on their life plans to be free and equal. These basic rights of equality and freedom must be guaranteed for any meaningful society which is just. Social and economic inequalities should be allowed only in as far as the least advantageous persons in the society would stand to benefit from it.

This view has to be distinguished from Utilitarianism (the maximum happiness of the maximum number of people) and Capitalism of the libertarian type (which gives priority to the protection of arrangements freely consented to) and Socialism of the Marxian type (which stresses social and material equality through the abolition of private privileges.)

Re-distribution of Wealth

In the first place, ways and means should be devised whereby riches that got accumulated over the years with certain nations should be redistributed so as to eradicate poverty in poor countries. Within a country too redistribution of the wealth that has accumulated in the hands of few can be achieved through taxation, making the right to work as a fundamental right or through establishing a welfare state.[8] At another level, a new system has to be devised to distribute that which the government has taken from the wealthy citizens. For example, about 25 million tonnes of food grains are lying with the government at various warehouses but it is a pity that the poor has to go hungry in our country.

Eradication of Poverty

Some of the immediate steps suggested by the leading Indian economists to eradicate poverty are food for work and cash for work programmes, a primary school with five class rooms in every village, a source of drinking water in every village, well-equipped and functioning community and primary health centres throughout the country, homes for the homeless—both rural and urban. Access to work and education would remove the squalor and misery to which many of our brothers and sisters are subject to. The economists also called for structural changes in the economy and wanted the working and poor people at the centre of the new economic policy. In 1964, President Lyndon Johnson launched a programme known as War on Poverty in the USA which was considered to be a success and brought down the effects of poverty dramatically in that country. We too need to make use all our resources, energy and talent to a similar time bound programme that will wipe out poverty and its causes.

Conclusion

Everyone should receive a share of the world's riches, sufficient for an existence worthy of a human being. There is no reason why a few countries/persons with a large amount of wealth at their disposal should enjoy a privileged use of the wealth of the world. One particular characteristic of our times is that science and technology has proved that eradication of poverty is within the reach of man. The question is whether we really want it or not. Our mastery over nature through science and technology is more often used to exploit other countries, peoples, groups and individuals than for the benefit of all. Globalization and other modern phenomena has led to more division that to unity, alienation than communication, to oppression and domination rather than to greater respect for others. Our aim should be universal brotherhood based on equality and freedom than pursuit of wealth for its own sake. All the poverty is the result of man's selfishness rather than God's weakness.

This selfishness which is in man's innermost being has to be attacked constantly. Right ethical convictions are the urgent need of the hour. We should promote such beliefs and ideologies that stand for the well being of all God's children than those that promote the interests of a section of the population.

NOTES

1. Statement issued jointly by the leading Indian economists, in *Frontline* XIII, (April 20-May 3, 1996), 8 p. 23.
2. Paul de la Gueriviere, "Social Analysis", in J. Murickan, (ed.), *Poverty in India, Challenges and Responses*, Trivandrum, A Xavier Board Publication, 1988, p. 89-114 (109).
3. The first author to use the term 'Social Justice' was the Sicilian priest Taparelli d'Azeglio in his *Theoretical Essay on Natural Right Based on Facts* (1840). Plus XI's *Qudragesimo Anno* popularised the term in the whole of Europe and since then it is used widely. For a critique of social justice from the capitalistic point of view see, Michael Novak, *The Catholic Ethic and the Spırit of Capitalism*, New York, The Free Press, 1993, p. 62 ff.
4. *Isavasa Upanishad.*
5. Pope John Paul II, *Centessiumus Annus*, no. 46.
6. *Quran* 28:45 says, "And we have desired to show favour unto those who were oppressed in the earth, and to make them leaders and make them inheritors."
7. John Rawls, *A Theory of Justice*, Delhi, Oxford University Press, 10th ed., 1990. According to Time survey this is one of the fifty most read books.
8. Welfare system of late has come under criticism of various economists and social scientists.

26

A PROFILE OF POVERTY

B. DATTA RAY

The population of North-East India was estimated at 31,547,314. About 90 per cent of this population live in the rural areas. The main character of the population is the rapid growth of it. Compared to all India growth rate (3.73-2.47 1981). But the density of population is low at a little over 100 per sq. km. as again more than 200 sq. km. found at all India level. But the remarkable feature of the population is that more than 25 per cent of the population of the region are scheduled tribes as shown in Table 26.1, while they form less than 8 per cent of all-India total.

It was estimated in 1981 that approximately 52.63 per cent of the population in rural areas and 33.37 per cent in urban areas in North-East India live below the poverty line. The present day position has not very substantially changed. There might be a marginal decline about the percentage of people both in rural and urban areas living below the poverty line. The poverty line for such examination has been fixed more than two decade back at nutritional requirement of 2400 calories per person per day for rural areas and 2100 calories per person per day for town people. Consumption need like minimum clothing should also be considered in estimating poverty line. Social consumption in education particularly in primary sector, health, sanitation, potable water supply and housing should also be computed in making such estimate. In North-East India, at least 40 per cent of the population is literate, particularly women. Neoliterate go back to illiteracy in

TABLE 26.1: **Statewise Total Scheduled Caste and Scheduled Tribe Population of the North-East India (1991 Census)**

Sl. No.	State	Population		
		Total	Scheduled Caste	Scheduled Tribe
1.	Arunachal Pradesh	864,558	4,052 (0.47)	550,351 (63.66)
2.	Assam	22,414,322	1,659,412 (7.40)	2,874,441 (12.82)
3.	Manipur	1,837,149	37,105 (2.02)	632,173 (34.41)
4.	Meghalaya	1,774,778	9,072 (0.51)	1,517,927 (85.53)
5.	Mizoram	689,756	691 (0.10)	653,565 (94.75)
6.	Nagaland	1,209,546	—	1,060,822 (87.70)
7.	Tripura	2,757,205	451,116 (16.48)	853,345 (30.95)
		31,547,314	2,161,448 (6.85)	8,142,624 (25.81)

the absence of effective follow-up measures. The picture of availability of health services, both preventive and curative is dismal. Potable water supply even in urban areas is most inadequate to meet the minimum needs. The housing is by and large inadequate and unsanitory.

Although in recent years efforts were made in the plain areas of the region to bring self-sufficiency in foodgrains, the gap between production of foodgrains and consumer of it remain big. The Food Corporation of India brings from other regions more than a million tonnes of foodgrains every year.

The nutritional level is extremely low in the region. It has been estimated by the Centre for Inter-disciplinary Studies, Calcutta that in 1987-88, the estimate availability of food grains in rural Assam, where 70 per cent of the population of the region live, was only around 290 grams per capita per day. While in 1961, from her own internal production Assam could provide 376 grams per capita per day.

In 1950-51, per capita income of India at current prices as a whole was Rs. 245.50. The corresponding figure for composite Assam was 299.20 or nearly 22 per cent higher. In 1986-87, per capita income of India and Assam region were respectively Rs. 2,974.20 and Rs. 2,204.30 at current prices. Thus income level in the region is 26 per cent lower than that in India. This rapid relative decline of income is indicative of the extent of poverty in the region.

North-East India is one of the poorer regions in India. D.T. Lakdawala Committee 1979 estimating the number of poor in India has favoured continuation of poverty line approach based on a caloric norm. On the basis of National Sample Survey conducted every quinquinium, the figures of 1986-87 show the percentage of rural poor was 39.06 (230 million) and the urban poor was 40.12 (312 million) taking the total number of poor people in India to a staggering 542 million. North East India's share of the poor people out of the region's total population is also shockingly high. This was anchored in the recommendation per capita daily intake of 2,400 calories in rural areas and 2,100 calories in urban areas with reference to consumption patterns as in 1973-74.

The aggregate number of poor people, below the poverty line is placed at 352.7 million against 237 million of earlier official estimates. The percentage of people below the poverty line has gone up from earlier 29.9 to 39.34 per cent.

The cereals are the main source of calories, providing on the average 70 per cent of the total calories consumed for the different expenditure groups. As the capacity to spend money increases, the proportion of total expenditure spent on foodgrains decreases. Pulses consumed, the poor man's only source of protein, are inadequate in North-East India (percentage share is 3.21, all India average is 4.31). The consumption of milk, milk products, fruits, nuts and meat, fish and egg is by and large beyond the purchasing power of the destitutes and very poor section of the people in the region. They form 25 per cent of the people of the region. Poor people who consume on the average 2100 calories may indulge in fish, meat, egg etc. on rate occasions. Cereals are the main sources of calories in North-East India because of low purchasing power of the people as indicated below. The overall average is 70 per cent. It is higher in poorer groups and lower for the relative richer groups.

It has been estimated by agencies like National Nutrition Monitoring Board, Indian Council for Medical Research, and National Institute of Public Cooperation and Child Development that 250 million people in India suffer from varying degrees of malnutrition. As a result, out of every 100 deaths in rural India, 58 are of children, 7 million children are affected by blindness because of vitamin A deficiency, of them 60,000 go blind, 90 per cent of babies below 2 kg dies and half of the expectant mothers are anaemic because of iron deficiency.

Health picture of the country is dismal. India spends a meagre 6 per cent of the per capita Gross Domestic Product on health care, with public and private sector's share being 1.3 per cent and 4.7 per cent . The North-East picture is more bleak.

A staggering 70 million children under the age of five year are malnourished in India. About 130 million people have no access to any kind of health services and 645 million are deprived of the minimum sanitation facilities. Social issues in North-East India get low priority because of general poverty and inhospitable terrain. The slogan of 'Health for All' by the Year 2000 will remain a dream for another 50 years.

Of the total population of 31,547,314 (1991 Census), the Scheduled Castes and Scheduled Tribes forming 6.85 and 25.81 per cent of the people are mostly victims of poverty along with other backward communities. In other words, at least one out of three persons in North-East India suffer from poverty related issues.

There may be a changing pattern of total consumption expenditure in North-East India in recent years. Consumption of cereals is going down over the years for the bottom 60 per cent (poor) as well as for the top 40 per cent (non-poor). A food surplus will be shown eventually. This surplus with full

TABLE 26.2: **Net State Domestic Product at Constant (1980-81) Prices**

(Rs. in Crores)

State	1980-81	1981-82	1982-83	1983-84	1984-85	1985-86	1986-87	1987-88	1988-89 (P)	1989-90 (Q)
Arunachal Pradesh	97	112	115	123	134	150	160	168	180	180
Assam	2,356	2,640	2,831	2,914	3,155	3,282	3,336	3,519	3,590	3,996
Manipur	201	215	220	240	251	266	267	285	301	300
Meghalaya	185	187	196	195	205	214	218	237	249	257
Nagaland	105	122	134	147	162	172	183	203	222	—
Tripura	238	274	309	299	307	312	326	353	375	403
All India	1,10,340	1,17,101	1,20,320	1,30,396	1,35,021	1,40,260	1,45,418	1,51,746	1,68,382	1,76,980

P: Provisional : Q: Quick Estimate, Not available.

Source: *Central Statistical Organisation*.

TABLE 26.3: **Per Capita Net State Domestic Product at Constant (1980-81) Prices**

State	1980-81	1981-82	1982-83	1983-84	1984-85	1985-86	1986-87	1987-88	1988-89 (P)	1989-90 (Q)
Arunachal Pradesh	1561	1747	1744	1804	1908	2074	2139	2184	2260	2199
Assam	1200	1307	1367	1375	1457	1483	1474	1521	1516	1650
Manipur	1430	1488	1485	1578	1607	1661	1630	1693	1748	1702
Meghalaya	1331	1379	1361	1354	1385	1412	1397	1485	1514	1515
Nagaland	1383	1539	1616	1700	1806	1844	1889	2016	2123	—
Tripura	1323	1312	1443	1361	1363	1356	1385	1470	1532	1611
All India	1625	1687	1697	1801	1827	1858	1889	1933	2105	2169

P: Provisional : Q: Quick Estimate, Not available.

Source: *Central Statistical Organisation*.

of cereals stocks in the warehouses may be the result of decreasing purchasing capacity of the 60 per cent people in the countryside in the face of ever-rising price line of the cereals.

This grim situation is the result of persistent growing of poverty engendered by the present unequal socio-economic and political forces. The land-relations in the countryside in chaotic. There is an expanding landless army even in the tiny state like Meghalaya. We are to create condition for the use of labour intensive technology in every field of production to make use of the vast army of unutilised labour power throughout the year. The controversy between labour intensive versus capital intensive technology is irrelevant in the present day ground realities of economc stagnation. Towns in North-East give us a misleading picture. They are the fortress of wealth surrounded by hungry victims of poverty. This rural poverty is due to low land-man ratio, dependence of the poor people on wage income and their inability to find wage employment through out the year. Even the statutory minimum wages are very often denied to them.

REFERENCES

Basic Statistics of North Eastern Region, 1992 (NEC).

Brief Review of Economy of Assam, 1988-89, Directorate of Economics and Statistics, Assam.

Census of India, 1991.

Eighth Five Year Plan Document, Govt. of India.

Health Expenditure in India—VHAI.

National Sample Survey, 42nd Round, 1986-87—Report No. 361, March, 1989.

Statistical Hand Books, Assam and Meghalaya.

27

DEVELOPMENT STRATEGY AND POVERTY ALLEVIATION PROGRAMME
A Case Study of Mizoram

S.N. GUHA THAKURTA

If the objective of development strategy is to have any impact on the reduction of the poverty level, two apparently different approaches between the percolating (or "trickling down" effect and direct attack on poverty do not seem to be as contradictory as they might appear initially. For, in any case, growth in state's productive capacity is required to be augmented to enable its economy to raise more value-added commodity and services. In the process community's traditional institutions such as communal land ownership, common property resources (CPRs) and exchange labour system might undergo modification or ultimately be supplanted by newer ones. But ultimately, whether or not any change will auger well for the state's economy from the point of poverty alleviation is to be judged from the point of sustainability of employment and income in the commodity producing or real sector.

Land Utilisation and Population Pressure

Of the total area in the state of Mizoram, about one-tenth is not available for cultivation. The proportion, compared to all north eastern states (21%) and all-India (13%), seems to be good. The cultivable waste land is about 3.5 per cent of the total reported area, and the ratio corresponds to the one for the aggregate of north eastern states but less than all-India ratio. However, the potential for extending cultivation may be guessed from the availability of vast tract of land, the so-called cultivable waste land, which may be used for raising crops—agricultural or horticultural. In Mizoram more than 90 per cent of cultivable land is cultivable waste. The ratio is significantly higher (91.3%). Multiple cropping area or area sown more than once is again much less (4.6%) than in any other state of the region (the region's average percentage (28.9) or the country as a whole (24.7%). Out of the state's 65,000 ha. net cropped area, only 3000 ha: are double/multiple cropped area.[1] Rice yield in Mizoram is poorest and the growth rate during the '80s is negligible compared to both the north-eastern states and as well as all-India level (percentage change in 1987-88 over 1980-81 for Mizoram, all north-eastern states and all-India was respectively 3.9, 5.0 and 10.2). One reason for low productivity is low input of fertilizer, besides the nature of terrain.

Growth of population in the state has since 1951 almost been consistently higher than the all-India rate. In the last two decades the change has been significant—48.55 per cent and 38.98 per cent as against all-India growth rate of 25 per cent and 23.5 per cent in the seventies and eighties respectively. The growth of urban to total population has doubled in every decade since the sixties. In 1961, 1971, 1981 and 1991 the percentage growth of urban to total population was respectively 5.34, 11.36, 24.67 and 46.20. Among the urban areas which are not many, Aizawl town seems to have borne the brunt of population pressure. In the last two decades of '60s and '70s, the population in this town has gone up by about 123 and 135 per cent respectively. On the contrary, the rural population growth has been moderate. In the last decade there has been in fact a negative growth in rural areas. One apparent reason for such abnormal growth of population in some urban areas seems to be the availability of government jobs in which one in every 20 persons in Mizoram is engaged. This ratio is much ahead of all-India figure in the same year (1:113) or in the neighbouring state of Assam (1:101).[2]

In the post-statehood era of seventies and eighties, Mizoram (along with other states of the north-east) having been declared "a special category state" receives adequate subsidy in the form of grants-in-aid etc. to cover its excess non-developmental expenditure on revenue account over revenue income. In the absence of central subsidy and grants-in-aid agriculture continues to be the main source of income. Increase of government jobs notwithstanding (much of which is due to liberal central assistance), productivity in agriculture has to be the main determinant of state income.

There is much pressure on land, and the pressure seems to drive the agricultural population towards extensive cultivation. Area available for rice cultivation in the state was 29 thousand hectares in 1980-81 whereas in 1987-88, it was increased to 48.5 thousand ha. The yield (kg/ha) has only marginally increased, which implies that there has been hardly any improvement in the technique of cultivation or in capital and fertilizer input. Nor there has been any substantial reduction in the traditional or shifting cultivation. Very little land is subjected to double or multiple cultivation.

The land-man ratio in the state, like other hilly areas of the region, is relatively favourable, and this is observable despite a high growth rate of population. But unlike areas in the plains, the hilly areas of the region is characterised by very low yield per unit of land as well as of labour.

Food Production and Consumption

Mizoram is chronically a food deficit area. And going by the latest data it appears that the deficit is on the increase. The state has to import more than half of its requirement from outside the state. Demographic pressure has added to the problem. It will be seen from the following Tables (Tables 27.1 and 27.2) that the state's import of food cereals has been rising quite fast. The principal cereal is rice. In 1985 the state had to import more than 59 thousand MT while in the next three years the imported quantity of rice increased to about 75,000 and 79,000 and 81,000 M.T. Table 27.2 gives a crude estimate of deficit. It appears that in 1990 the state could produce only 45 per cent of its food requirement and remains deficit to the extent of 55 per cent. This of course does not take into account the part of production that does not reach the consumer.

During the '80s although there has been substantial increase in the gross cropped area for rice cultivation—the increase was 77 per cent yield (kg/ha) has increased by only 27 per cent. Low productivity on the one hand and demographic pressure on the other has put the state in a very vulnerable position. A rising consumerism and overstretching service sector resulting in a flow of money income much ahead of the state's absorbing capacity due to a constrained commodity production sector has added to the state's problem.[3] Fortunately, the state has not faced any major food crisis after the one in the '60s following which insurgency broke out in the state—thanks to India's creditable handling of food management.

TABLE 27.1: **Quantity of Essential Commodities Procured from Outside Mizoram: 1985-88**

Year	Quantity Procured in '000MT	
	Rice	Wheat
1985	59.16	0.64
1986	74.76	0.66
1987	78.63	0.76
1988	81.46	0.76
1989 (up to October)	73.54	0.70

Source: *Statistical Hand Book,* Mizoram, 1989.

TABLE 27.2: **Net Availability of Foodgrains, 1990-91**

1.	Population in 1991('000)	686
2.	Requirement of foodgrains (Rice/Wheat) @ 500 gm. per capita per day (MT)	343
3.	Yearly foodgrains requirement ('000 MT)	125.19
4.	Add requirement for seed and wastage @ 12.5% of consumption ('000 MT)	15.65
5.	Total requirement (3+4) ('000 MT)	140.84
6.	Estimated production ('000 MT) Rice	63.80
7.	Deficit (–)/Excess (+) (5–6)	(–)77.04

There are about 800 fair price shops in Mizoram;[4] about 69 per cent of which are in Aizawl district alone. This suggests disproportional flow of subsidised food in the urban areas, which thereby gain an advantage over rural areas.[5]

Food Habits and Preferences

People of Mizoram in general take two principal meals a day, one in the morning and the other in the evening. In between they take light refreshment, tea and/or a working lunch. Staple food is rice with boiled and leafy vegetables. Mizos have a liking for fermented foods (Soyabean, Pork, Fish etc.). Dried or smoked fish, meat (pork, beef, a chicken) constitute the main protein items. The milk intake is very low among all the age groups except the group belonging to the group 1-2. The Mizos like other tribals in the north-eastern region has a special liking for pork in particular: next in preference comes beef. In villages (and among in not so affluent section) even dog meat is also consumed. Chicken being costlier than pork is also consumed, but not so much in the villages as in urban areas.

Menifestation of Poverty

There are various manifestation of poverty with varying degrees of intensity. Availability of and accessibility to food stock at affordable exchange rate are important issues. The latter will depend on the household's ability to buy. The other aspect relevant on the measurement (head count) or poverty is the nutritional value of food consumed. A few studies in India (including a part of the present one relating to Meghalaya)[5a] have been made on the basis of calorie intake. In case of Mizoram the absence of reliable expenditure data did not enable us to arrive at any reasonable estimate of poverty on the basis of calorie intake. However, poverty is not uni-dimensional, but multi-dimensional, although some aspects of it may be more critical than others at different points of time and do influence or are influenced by some of them (Table 27.3).

Apart from availability of and accessibility to food, factors that either influence or are influenced by poverty are: illiteracy, unemployment, low income, accessibility to Public Distribution System (PDS), gender bias in food intake and public distribution of health and welfare, crude birth rate, life expectancy, child mortality rate, etc. Mizoram is fortunate in some aspects, viz., its literacy rate is high (total 67 per cent, male 70 per cent, female 64 per cent, Rural Total 58 per cent and Urban Total 78 per cent). The state is also having highest percentage of trained teachers in the region at high school (76.72%) and at middle school levels (68.27%). At the primary level the percentage is 49.31—higher than in Meghalaya and Tripura. There is one teacher for every 18 high schooi, 14 middle school and 28 primary school students. The respective ratios for Assam are: 25, 30 and 40. Per capita, the state spends highest Budget resource (Rs. 401 in 1987-88 and Rs. 466 in 1989-90) in its revenue account.[6] But, as we have seen, notwithstanding a high literacy rate, the state's demographic pressure (3.89% growth per annum during '80s and 4.85 per cent during the '70s) continued unabated. One should note here that unlike some of its neighbouring state viz., Tripura and Assam, Mizoram's growth of population is almost entirely endogenous that is, due to excess of birth over death rate.

Accessibility to Public Health

In terms of doctor population ratio Mizoram is yet to make significant advance. Its relative position is lower than Arunachal Pradesh (1:3536), Manipur (1:2629) and Tripura (1:3822), but much better than more populous state like Assam (1:8750). However, in terms of PHC and sub-centres, it appears that the Health Centre—rural population ratio stands at 1447 (255 centres against 3,69,000 rural population) in Mizoram as against the corresponding ratio of one health centre/sub-centre for every 3400, 2706, 4295 and 4276 in Meghalaya, Manipur, Nagaland and Tripura respectively. So far as the ratio is concerned, it thus stands in a much better relative position *vis-a-vis* other north-eastern hill states. But accessibility does not get reflected merely by the number of Health Centres. It is reflected by the *availability* of doctor, medicine and treatment and care. Even Government Statistics tell a distressing tale. During 1985-87, as against 85 doctors and 164 nurses available for Aizawl district, the respective numbers for Lunglei and Chhimtuipui districts were 16 and 46 and 6 and 18 only. The availability of other medical personnel during 1985-87 in the districts is shown in Table 27.4.

TABLE 27.3: **Some Indices of Public Health Accessibility to Mizoram 1990-91**

	Index	Mizoram	All-India
1.	Doctor-Population ratio as on Dec. 1990	1:5123	—
2.	No. of PHC as on March 1991	35	21,641
3.	Ditto Sub-centre of Public Health	220	130,960
4.	Population per Hospital Bed as on January 1990	613	1347
5.	Per capita State Govt. expenditure on Health (Rs.)	434	—

Source: Basic Statistics of North Eastern Region, 1992.

TABLE 27.4: **Districtwise Availability of Medical Staff in Mizoram during 1985-87**

District	Doctor	Nurse	Mid-wife	Pharmacists	Matron/ Sister
Aizawl	85	164	215	56	20
Lunglei	16	46	60	13	5
Chhimtuipui	6	18	63	6	3

Source: *Statistical Hand Book, Mizoram*, 1987.

The urban bias in the availability of health care and medical facilities may be seen from the response we received from our field investigation (Table 27.5). As against only about 3 per cent and 4.5 per cent reported about non-availability of medicine and doctor respectively in Aizawl district, the respective percentages in Lunglei are 20.1 and 16.8 and in Chhimtuipui 23.5 and 25.7. The data relate to the year 1988.

Accessibility to Safe Water

The state receives rainfall during the monsoon season which begins in the first part of May and continues till mid-October. It receives good amount of rainfall (about 2000 mm on an average). Yet, like 'poverty in plenty' the rural population in

TABLE 27.5: **Response from Households about Non-availability of Public Health Facilities in Mizoram during 1988**

Non-availability of	Districts	% of Households reporting	
	Aizawl	Lunglei	Chhimtuipui
1. Medicine	2.8	20.1	28.6
2. Doctor	4.5	16.8	23.5
3. Diagnostic equipment	3.4	18.4	25.7

Source: Field investigation.

particular do not receive adequate quantity of safe drinking water from any reservoir during the dry season (Oct.-April). During the monsoon the rain water serves the purpose of drinking water besides other uses. The villagers store rain water in a big drum made out of tin-sheets through a pipe attached to the roof tops of their dwelling houses. A cloth is spread over the drum to eliminate pollution. In a relatively populous villages reservoirs which are fed by hill streams/falls through a bamboo pipe store the water for distribution from its tap. The village elders or *chowkidar* oversees the distribution. In winter and summer dry months water is distributed through ration cards. Water really becomes an economic (scarce) commodity not only in urban areas when a bucket of water is sold at Rs. 5 or even more, but also in village areas where it has to be fetched from a distant area with ups and down involving considerable personal hardship. Villages by the side of main highways have adopted a unique indegenous system of transporting water from the river bed or road-side taps whose numbers are not many. It is about a 3 ft wooden flat trolly fitted with three small metallic wheel—one in the front trolly and two in the rear. Two to three kerosene tin full of water can be transported through metallic road in each trip.

Nutritional Status

The infant mortality rate (per 1000 live births) and maternal mortality rate (per 1000) have been estimated at 46 and 2.7

respectively.[7] By all accounts the rates seem to be very moderate. In some LDCs, the mortality rate is as high as 40 per cent.[8] Although some study indicates that protein deficiency, anemia and vitamin A deficiency are "more or less prevalent in the entire state particularly in the rural areas of Mizoram".[9] We are sceptic about this. Although we are not in a position to provide a good statistical profile on this because most of the responses are multiple responses and therefore could not be additive nor could they be fitted into specific category—yet, our association and close observation of the investigation show that both meat and vegetable intake per household is not on a very low scale as to warrant such pessimism.[10]

The NRTC (Calcutta, 1988) study also shows that on the basis of Rao's ratio of weight-height, 26-28 per cent of boys and girls in the age-group 1-5 years are having protein-energy malnutrition, while for the 72-74 per cent the nutritional status is normal.[11] However, one noteworthy feature of the Calcutta study is that it shows an element of male bias in the matter of food intake. For example, upto three years age the percentage of girls in the below normal category exceeds that of boys in the same age and category.

An extreme form of malnutrition is Oedema. Among the children in the age group 0-14 years, about 1 per cent in Aizawl and a little more than 1 per cent in Chhimtuipui district were suffering from Oedema. The nutritional status in case of about 75 per cent has been found to be normal or above normal. The rest could not be determined. Vitamin 'A' deficiency in eyes was observed in a little over 8 per cent children in the state, with Aizawl district recording a little more (11% children) and the other two districts much less (around 4%).[12] The Central Goitre Survey Team in 1978 carried out a survey on the prevalence of Goitre and found Mizoram as "Goitre endemic area".[13]

On the whole, the calorie and protein deficiency on an average seems to be much less, at least in urban areas, as Table 27.6 and 27.7.

Urbanisation and Breaking-up of Age-ole Institutions

In Mizoram the so-called service and non-commodity

TABLE 27.6: **Dietary Survey Findings in Aizawl Town**

Age Group	Cereals gms	Pulses gms	Fruits gms	Vegetables gms	Roots & Tubers gms	Milk gms	Meat gms	Sugar & Jaggery gms	Fats & Oils gms	Nuts & Oilseeds gms
Adult Male (20 yrs. above)	489	47	62	374	71	105	140	37	26	13
Adult Female (20 yrs. above)	435	42	55	336	63	95	126	33	23	11
Adolescent (13 to 19 yrs.)	440	47	62	374	71	105	140	37	26	13
Child I (9-12 yrs.)	351	37	49	299	56	143	112	29	20	10
Child II (7-8 yrs.)	307	32	43	261	49	90	98	25	18	9
Child III (5-6 yrs.)	263	28	37	224	42	85	84	22	15	7
Child IV (3-4 yrs.)	219	23	31	187	35	110	70	18	13	6
Child V (1-2 yrs.)	175	18	24	149	28	400	56	14	10	5

Note: Results in gms per consumption unit per day.

Source: Survey Report of Zirtiri Women's College, Mizoram.

TABLE 27.7: **Percentage Fulfilment of the Recommended Dietary Allowances**

Age Group	Cereals %	Pulses %	Fruits %	Vegetables %	Roots & Tubers %	Milk %	Meat %	Sugar & Jaggery %	Fats & Oils %
Adult Male (20 yrs. above)	106	118	206	374	142	70	466	123	58
Adult Female (20 yrs. above)	106	105	183	240	126	63	420	165	92
Adolescent (13 to 19 yrs.)	102	94	206	166	95	70	233	123	65
Child I (9-12 yrs.)	81.6	82	98	299	197	57	373	64	44
Child II (7-8 yrs.)	123	53	86	240	—	45	327	98	60
Child III (5-6 yrs.)	97	80	68	280	210	84	280	55	60
Child IV (3-4 yrs.)	81	66	62	234	175	44	233	45	52
Child V (1-2 yrs.)	100	51	80	248	280	133	137	47	67

Source: Survey Report of Zirtiri Women's College, Mizoram.

producing sector has been growing at a faster rate than the commodity producing sector. One element of service is the transport cost that is increasing year after year due to the administered pricing of petroleum goods. But apart from this, a large chunk of expenditure on revenue account is spent to meet the "organs of state" and administrative expenditure. Apart from specific plan allocation and grant from NEC, the state's total receipt from revenue and capital account stands at about Rs. 375 crores. The per capita plan outlay of the state during the Seventh Five Year Plan was Rs. 5200—one of the highest in the country. The question that arises how much of development expenditure is truely trickled down to the poor? On the surface, a visit to any urban centre of the state will show noticeable change in the life style of the people and in their consumption pattern. This seems to have brought institutional change as well. One such change relevant for our study is the privatization of landed property, partly substituting CPR.

Technically, land under the ownership of an individual within the framework of his or her legal rights and obligations recognised by the state is called private land. Such land can be used for three specific purposes: (a) for building houses, shops, stall sites etc., (b) wet rice cultivation (WRC), and (c) for garden.[14] The positive aspect of privatization is that it has reinforced government's policy to restrict *jhuming* and encourage WRC. Besides, it may also encourage a sort of (capitalistic) acquisitiveness which may give rise to enterprise and drive for individual prosperity, albeit some time at the expense of community.

Obviously with increasing urbanisation and growth of service sector rising faster than the commodity producing sector and thereby facilitating the speedy emergence of a middle class with conspicuous consumption in their life style, the casualty in the process would be the CPR. Historically CPRs included community forests, common grazing grounds, river beds and banks, etc.[15] These resources have contributed much to village economy of Mizoram, of which mention may be made of maintaining an ecological balance through a longer duration of *jhuming* cycle, checking deforestation and thereby siltation and soil erosion, and above all an egalitarian distribution of land based on family needs, of fodder, fuel wood, manure, fruits and medicinal herbs etc. It is true that for various reasons—demographic pressure in particular—the longer cycle of *jhuming* is being gradually shortened and thereby some of the evil effects of CPR has been highlighted. The poor land productivity has been one important reason for encouraging WRC. And there is no doubt that Mizoram needs all incentives and encouragement for boosting agricultural production. But it does not follow necessarily that for boosting agricultural production individual proprietorship only will guarantee WRC. Further, to the extent land re-distribution is taking place at the cost of CPR, the rural economy, particularly the economy of the rural poor is likely to be subjected to severe hardship.

Another institution that is being gradually eroded is the exchange labour system which is being replaced by wage labour system. Our field investigation suggests that the latter system has not improved the accessibility to higher employment in man days terms although it has increased income. But the point is sustainability of employment and income in rural areas so that their successive generation over period of time is ensured. Reduction in CPRs through privatisation has various dimensions. One is curtailment of *jhuming*, which under the present demographic pressure may be welcome. The other dimension is WRC which also seems to be necessity. Logically, however, it does not follow that this requires a degradation or marginalisation of CPR. The moot point is that when the CPRs are redistributed and allowed to be privatised in a regime of somewhat distorted semi-capitalistic phase of trade economy (rather than commodity production economy), all the erstwhile beneficiaries of CPRs may not gain. A number of them will be losers in the trade-off. Some of the rural poor may be beneficiary out of the new land policy, but many of the urban rich and emerging middle class is likely to encroach on the rural poor's accessibility to the usefulness and beneficiary aspects of the CPRs.

In a recent article Professor Hanumantha Rao has aptly said that it is necessary to integrate the major poverty alleviation programmes with the overall development objectives.[16] Given the objectives as sustainability of employment and income growth on a long-term basis, and given the fact that agriculture and its allied activities should be the main plank of sustained growth in the state; not merely rice cultivation but also the development of horticulture—fruits, orchids, plantation of tea/coffee and rubber—should be in the 'agenda' of development. And for this CPR may be a good base which may reduce income disparity. At present except ginger there is hardly any commodity that is exported outside the state. In the New Economic Policy, we are talking about exporting value-added items in agricultural sector. The emphasis on the development priority should be on specialization, and not on diversification in every field where the state cannot take advantage on competitive basis.

The state needs significant breakthrough in developing infrastructural base through building roads, communication net-work, water supply, public distribution of food and health care, soil conservation and drainage. To the extent CPRs are capable of efficient allocation of rural resources including intangible ones and to the extent such mechanism and institutions are environment friendly and not anti-poor and to the extent a change in institution of land ownership may have negative external effects, a compromise between raising land productivity on the one hand and environment friendly land distribution on the other has to be evolved to avoid any mismatch.

A point on demographic pressure. In spite of a high literacy and considerably low mortality rate among children, the population growth rate is well above the all-India rate. In the absence of any in-migration in the last two decades, a high growth rate seems a bit surprising, for low mortality rate should act as an incentive for limiting family size. That the land is no longer a "free" good should also act a constraint. The Non-Government Organisations should play an effective role in mobilising public opinion in this regard. In a society of considerable literacy it should not be difficult to bring home the point that the impact which limitation of a family can make on nutritional status in particular and general well being of the family is considerable.

Finally, a point on the scope of non-traditional employment in a rural backward economy. With respect to employment prospects, two significant characteristics of the economy as we could find from our field investigation is that (a) absorbing capacity of the state's agriculture has been declining, and (b) the overall growth in the economy has not been compatible with that of employment.

Concluding Observation

If, as has been the case so far, population growth is taken as an exogenous variable,. the scope of creating additional employment in the economy seems to be very limited. The one alternative that is usually suggested is the expansion of employment prospect in the non-farm activities in the rural areas. But what are the activities that may absorb the additional labour force in the rural economy? And, precisely, what could be the source of growth of such activities?

The source of non-farm employment in rural areas can emerge from growth in agriculture. The hypothesis of agriculture led growth in non-farm employment presupposes growth in the land and labour productivity in agriculture. In areas where agriculture itself is constrained due to primitive way of cultivation such as *jhuming* and/or peculiar topography of the area settled cultivation (or wet rice cultivation) may be one alternative.

An impetus to the growth of cottage and village industry may, it is argued, lead to some initial shift in the demand for labour in non-farm employment, but it may be argued that once the demand for such products catches up substantially, a labour-displacement technology may usurp the employment benefit. Further demonstration effect of manufacturing articles coming from industrial regions may also nullify the non-farm employment shift in the rural areas.

In areas such as north-eastern hilly region where landman ratio is still relatively favourable and where jhuming does much harm to the ecology as well as the economy, plantation of commercial crop like tea, coffee, rubber, etc. may, it is suggested, offer a viable alternative route to win over the existing jhumias from *jhumming* as well as to absorb the additional working force.

NOTES AND REFERENCES

(This is an abridged version of a part of an ICSSR Project on Poverty, Unemployment and Development Policy in North-eastern region carried out under the Directorship of the present author. This chapter is based on a study relating to Mizoram where the field survey was carried out at two points of time during April-July 1987 and August-November 1988 for which two independent multi-stage random stratified samples were drawn from among 722 villages (390 in Aizawl District, 162 in Lunglei and 170 Chhimtuipui District).

1. The data relate to the year 1980 (*Source*: *Basic Statistics of N.E. Region*, 1985).
2. NC, *Basic Statistics of NE Region*, 1990.
3. For relatively detailed account, see S.N. Guha Thakurta, "Emergence of a New Working Class in Mizoram: A Marxist Note" in V.S. Mahajan, (ed.) *Emerging Pattern of North Eastern Economy* (Deep & Deep Publications, New Delhi, 1987).
4. The figure available till 1st August 1989 is as follows: Aizawl district 542; Lunglei district 144 and in Chhimtuipui district 107.
5. A study made by Stephen Houes and Shikha Jha shows that an average urban dweller gains more than an average rural dweller. Article by S. Houes & S. Jha "Urban Bias in Indian Public Distribution System" in *Economic and Political Weekly*, May 9, 1992, pp. 1022-30.

5a. For major findings, see S.K. Ghosh and S.N. Guha Thakurta "Poverty Level in Meghalaya" in *Assam Economic Journal*, March 1992.

6. The figures for other state of the north-east are as follows:

	Per-capita Budget Expr. on Rev. A/C in 1989-90 (Rs.)	% of Budgeted Expr. on education to total Rev. expr. in 1989-90
Assam	148.10	20.36
Arunachal Pradesh	438.04	15.35
Manipur	318.18	21.41
Meghalaya	316.77	19.35
Nagaland	375.18	13.39
Tripura	371.00	22.12
All-India	145.95	19.94

7. See, *Nutritional Profile for the State of Mizoram*, p. 14. Nutrition Research & Training Centre, ICMR All-India Instt. of Hygiene and Public Health, Calcutta, April, 1988.
8. S.G. Shrikantla, Social Costs of Malnutrition in Poverty, *An Inter-*

disciplinary Approach, by B. Sarveswara Rao & V.N. Deshpande, (eds.), MIDS, Madras, 1982.

9. *Ibid.*
10. Our suspicion seems to have been confirmed by the same study, see, *Nutritional Profile, op.cit.*, p. 20. "All age groups consumed excess of meat which often lead to health complications like atherosclerosis and bone disorders.
11. *Ibid.*
12. *Ibid.*
13. National Goitre Control Programme, Mizoram Survey Report, 1978, as quoted in *Nutritional Profile for Mizoram, op.cit.*
14. In 1963 permanent settlement system was introduced in the capital town of Aizawl for houses, stalls and shops. Subsequently the scheme has been extended to Champhai, Serchip, Kolasib and Saitual towns. There is no ceiling on holding under this system. The number of certification, the area as well as average size of holding are all on the increase year after year.

    The land ownership system under WRC and garden is governed by the Mizo District (Agricultural Land) Act, 1963 and the Mizo District (Agricultural Land) Rules, 1971. Like the permanent settlement system, the number of certificates issued till 1987-88 has been on the rise resulting an increase in the area of land under WRC from about 6 ha. to 487 ha. From 1977-78 to 1987-88, the no. of certificates issued for these purposes has gone up from a mere or 2 to 275.
15. N.S. Jodha, "Common Property Resources and Rural Poor in Dry Regions in India" in *Economic and Political Weekly*. No. 27, (July 1986).
16. C.H. Hanumantha Rao, "Integrating Poverty Alleviation Programmes with Development Strategies—Indian Experience" in *Economic and Political Weekly*, November 28, 1992.

28

LITERACY AND THE POOR
A Study of Selected Slums of Shillong

A.C. MOHAPATRA and NAZARENE V. MARBANIANG

Introduction

India with her 900 million people is still struggling, with the menace of illiteracy and low level of human development; her world ranking being 135, behind most of the neighbouring countries, if not all (UNDP : HDR 1994). With a (crude) literacy of 43 per cent (1991) and perhaps effective literacy of around 50 per cent, India holds the largest segment of the world's illiterate population and perhaps would continue to do so for sometime (despite varied successes of NLM and TLC). However, the problem of literacy (or illiteracy) has substantial regional differences, with Kerala achieving full literacy in 1992 and the performance of many smaller and larger states being commendable. The bulk of the illiterate population is still concentrated in the four populous states of Bihar, U.P., Madhya Pradesh and Rajasthan (euphemistically called the BIMARU states; the sick ones).

Nearer home, the performance of Meghalaya (with total population of 17.7 lakhs, 1991) has been far from satisfactory, i.e. having kept pace with the national literacy rate for decades, it has fallen behind during the decade of 1981-91 with the CLR of 39 per cent compared to the national average of 43 per cent. This, despite a long history of education brought initially by the missionaries, but subsequently supported by the State Government, which would mean that there is substantial rural and urban differential in the literacy situation in the state.

However, the present chapter aims at studying a very small facet of the problem of literacy in the state, in the urban sector and then confined to the urban poor segment (in Shillong). Essentially it is accepted that the poor have little incentive or motivation for education. Moreover, in a growing privatised education, they may not have access to education. Concurrently even if the children are enrolled, they may not perform well and drop-out of formal education process. This needs some detailed looks at what is happening on the ground. The study is based wholly on a bench mark survey carried out in mid-1993 in selected poor localities of Shillong under support from Meghalaya Urban Development Agency (MUDA). The survey covered a census of all households of Upper Lumparing, Lower Lumparing (predominantly S.T. localities) and Barapathar (with a large component of non-Scheduled Tribe population) with a total households numbering about 1500 and population of about 9000. The present study uses only part of the information relating to education and income. The study aims to highlight the differences between the S.T. and non-S.T. population (represented by Upper Lumparing and Barapathar), the various income classes and their response to educational services and the various age groups and their literacy/educational situation.

Methodology

Methodologically the entire population has been classified into five income classes on the basis of their annual household income in current prices. The Planning Commission had set the urban poverty line at Rs. 11,850 per family (of five) at prices of 1990-91. Since, there has been some price changes due to inflation between 1990-91 and 1993-94, approximately Rs. 12000 has been taken as the PL. The below PL population has been classed into, those who are extremely poor (below Rs. 6000 hh income per year) and those (between Rs. 6000 and the PL). The population above the PL is classed into three groups, the population falling between Rs. 12,001 and Rs. 18,000 (on the margin), those between Rs. 18,001 and Rs. 36,000 and those above annual income above Rs. 36,001. In reality the family size often would determine the actual situation, because a hh with 10 members and annual income of Rs. 25,000 would equate, with a family of 4 members and Rs. 10,000 income, the latter falling below the poverty line. This moderation however could not be incorporated at this stage.

The second way of classification of the population is into age classes, pre-school stage (below 6 years), primary stage 6-11 years, Middle school, between 12-15 years, the main labour stream stage, 15-35 years, 35-65 years and those above 65 years. While the age classes upto 14 years is important from formal education point of view, those in 15-35 years are important for non-formal or adult literacy point of view, the 35 and above group being in a second priority. Since the senior citizens are not directly involved in the economic activities, this group is not successfully a target in literacy and HRD efforts, from policy perspective.

Analysis

Table 28.1 provides the household annual income distribution for the two predominantly low income localities, Upper Lumparing and Barapathar. The Table 28.1 indicates that the households below the poverty line are only around 20 per cent in both the localities (Barapathar, 21.47 per cent and Upper Lumparing, 21.98 per cent) with no significant differences between the localities. However, within the ST and non-ST segments, the distribution are quite different. For example, while among the ST the percentage below the PL is 16.67 per cent in Barapathar, it is 21.62 per cent in the non-ST and in Lumparing among the ST the BPL constitute 25 per cent while among the non-ST the percentage is only 14.81 per cent. This indicates that where one segment is dominant in the overall population, its poverty constituents are also higher and *vice-versa*.

On the other hand, if one takes the income class just above the PL (upto household income of Rs. 20,001) the total composition upto that class limit is marginally higher in Upper Lumparing compared to Barapathar (64.84% and 61.26% respectively). The proportion of higher income class constitute (Rs. 34,000 and above) 7.27 per cent in Barapathar and

TABLE 28.1: **Distribution of Approximate Annual Income**

	Rs. 6000 & below		Rs. 6001-12000		Rs. 12001-18000		Rs. 18001-36000		Rs. 36000 & above		% of hh		Total
	ST	Others	ST	Others	ST	Others	ST	Others	ST	Others	ST	Others	
BARAPATHAR		2.62	0.52	18.33	1.05	19.37	1.05	39.79	0.52	16.75	3.14	96.86	100
% OF HH		2.70	16.67	18.92	33.33	20.00	33.33	41.08	16.67	17.30	100	100	
U. LUMPARING	3.30		14.28	4.40	20.88	4.40	26.37	13.19	5.49	7.69	70.32	29.68	100
% OF HH	4.69		20.31	14.81	29.69	14.81	37.50	44.45	7.81	25.93	100	100	

TABLE 28.2: **Literacy in Barapathar and Upper Lumparing**

Locality	Male	Female	Total
Barapathar	57.76	42.24	79.19
U.Lumparing	50.93	49.07	81.06

13.18 per cent in Lumparing, not a significant difference between the two localities.

Table 28.2 shows the situation of literacy by distribution of males and females in the two localities. The overall literacy situation in the two localities appear to be high, 79.19 per cent in case of Barapathar and 81.06 per cent in case of Upper Lumparing. However, though there is no significant difference between male and female literacy in Upper Lumparing, there is a 15 per cent difference between male and female literacy in Barapathar which has predominantly non-S.T. population. The lower female literacy by and large accounts for the 7 per cent lower overall literacy figure.

TABLE 28.3: **Distribution of Literates by Sex and Income Classes**

Income Class/area	M/F	Rs. 6000 & below	6001-12000	12001-18000	18001-36000	36001 & above	Total
% of literates in Barapathar	M	1.92	13.82	16.70	42.61	24.95	100
	F	1.57	13.39	18.37	42.52	24.15	100
% effective literates in Barapathar	M	1.92	13.24	16.12	40.12	23.80	95.20
	F	1.57	12.34	16.01	41.21	23.36	94.49
% of literates in U.Lumparing	M	1.83	11.01	24.77	44.04	18.35	100
	F	1.90	16.67	20.00	43.81	17.62	100
% effective literates in U.Lumparing	M	1.83	8.72	22.02	40.83	17.89	91.29
	F	1.90	14.76	17.62	40.00	16.67	90.95

The income classwise distribution of literates (Table 28.3) indicates that in Barapathar 15.74 per cent of males and 14.96 per cent of the females belong to the below poverty line class. Another 16.70 per cent (males) and 18.37 per cent (females) are in the marginal above poverty line class. Similarly in Upper Lumparing 20 per cent (females) belong to the marginally above poverty line class. Therefore, the bulk of the literates belong to the relatively higher income classes. This is to be seen in light of the fact that approximately 40 per cent of the population in both these areas belong to either the below PL group or marginally above the PL.

TABLE 28.4: **Distribution of Effective Literacy among the S.T. and other categories in each Income-Group**

Income Group	ST/ Others	Rs. 6000 & below	6001-12000	12001-18000	18001-36000	36001 & above	Total
% of literates in Barapathar	ST		18.52	18.52	25.93	37.03	100
	Others	1.83	13.49	17.37	43.09	24.22	100
% effective literates in Barapathar	ST		18.52	18.52	25.93	37.03	100
	Others	1.83	12.69	16.00	41.03	23.20	94.74
% of literates in U.Lumparing	ST	2.59	15.86	25.24	43.69	12.62	100
	Others		8.40	15.13	44.54	31.93	100
% effective literates in U.Lumparing	ST	2.59	13.27	22.01	39.48	12.62	89.97
	Others		7.56	14.29	42.86	29.41	94.12

Table 28.4 indicates the distribution of literates by income classes as well as their belonging to either ST or non-ST population in both the areas. In Barapathar, though the bulk of the population in non-ST, only 15.32 per cent of the literates fall within the BPL category, where as 18.52 per cent of the ST literates fall in this category.

Educational Situation

A look at the situation of the pre-school education of the children in the two localities (Table 28.5), shows that about 48.97 per cent of boys and 51.28 per cent of girls in the age group of 2-5 years are attending some pre-school facility in

TABLE 28.5: **Status of Pre-primary Education**

	Barapathar			Upper Lumparing		
	Male	Female	Total	Male	Female	Total
% of children 2-5 yrs. age group	45.71	54.29	100.00	47.30	52.70	100.00
% of attending children pre-primary school	52.08	36.84	43.81	48 57	51.28	—
% of children not enrolled in pre-primary school	47.92	63.16	56.19	51.43	48.72	—

Upper Lumparing. On the other hand, 52.05 per cent of boys and 36.84 per cent of girls in the same age group in Barapathar are in pre-school facilities. Though in Lumparing the gender bias in not significant, it appears that in Barapathar there is a pronounced bias against the girl child so far their enrolment in pre-school education is concerned. The general enrolment level in Upper Lumparing also appears to be higher than Barapathar.

In the primary school going group (6-11 years) the overall non-enrolment level is 6 per cent and those of the dropouts is another six per cent, with no pronounced difference between the boys and the girls (BMS, Shillong Report, 1994). Table 28.6 indicates that the level of enrolment is high, 94.51 per cent and 92.86 per cent boys and girls respectively in Barapathar and 97.92 per cent and 95.24 per cent respectively in Upper Lumparing. There are no unenrolled children in Upper Lumparing, only about 3 per cent dropouts.

In the middle-school group (age 11-14 yrs.) the enrolment situation is 83.33 per cent and 77.19 per cent for boys and girls and in Upper Lumparing the figure is 86.20 per cent and 96.15 per cent respectively. The gender bias is in favour of the girls, significantly (by about 10%) and about 20 per cent compared to the girls in Barapathar (Table 28.7).

The situation of literacy and level of education is indicated in Table 28.8 for young adults (age 16-35 years). This shows that while in Barapathar the overall illiterates in

TABLE 28.6: **Status of Primary Education**

	Barapathar			Upper Lumparing		
	Male	Female	Total	Male	Female	Total
% of children 6-11 yrs. age group	48.15	51.86	100.00	53.33	46.67	100.00
% of attending children primary school	94.51	92.86	93.65	97.92	95.24	96.67
% of dropouts	—	3.06	1.59	2.08	4.76	3.33
% of children not enrolled in primary school	5.49	4.08	4.76	—	—	—

this age group for males and females for 7.84 per cent and 20.20 per cent respectively, the figures for Upper Lumparing is 5.20 per cent and 13.08 per cent i.e. not only the overall illiteracy is less, but the sex specific illiteracy favours the adult female population. The share of women graduates and post-graduates in Upper Lumparing is also highest 6.55 per cent compared to only 3.04 per cent in Barapathar. In the

TABLE 28.7: **Status of Education in age group 12-15 yrs.**

	Barapathar			Upper Lumparing		
	Male	Female	Total	Male	Female	Total
% of children 12-15 yrs. age-group	48.65	51.35	100.00	52.73	47.27	100.00
% of attending children middle school	83.33	77.19	80.18	86.20	96.15	90.91
% of dropouts	14.82	15.79	15.32	6.90	—	3.64
% of children not enrolled in middle school	1.85	7.02	4.50	6.90	3.85	5.45

TABLE 28.8: **Status of Adult Education**

	Barapathar			Upper Lumparing		
	Male	Female	Total	Male	Female	Total
% of adults in 16-35 yrs.	57.73	42.27	100.00	41.85	58.15	100.00
% of illiterate persons	7.84	20.20	13.09	5.20	13.08	9.78
% of literate persons	8.21	10.60	9.23	11.69	14.95	13.59
% of adult having passed class V	25.37	20.70	23.39	18.18	9.35	13.04
% of adult having passed class VIII	30.60	28.79	29.83	36.36	28.97	32.07
% of adult having passed Matric	21.64	16.67	19.53	18.18	27.10	23.37
% of Graduates	6.34	2.53	4.72	7.79	5.61	6.52
% of Post-Graduates	—	.51	.21	2.60	.94	1.63

elderly group (age 36-65 yrs.) the situation (Table 28.9) indicates that both in Upper Lumparing as well as in Barapathar the female illiteracy is considerably higher (30-40%). This bias of the older generation is gradually getting evened out, which is a healthy situation.

The distribution of school dropouts according to income classes (Table 28.10) shows that though the overall dropout situation is not alarming, there are either no dropouts or insignificant dropouts in the higher income class households (Rs. 36,001 +) in both the localities on the other hand, about 14.29 per cent boys and 10 per cent of girls are dropouts in Barapathar belong to the BPL families. In Upper Lumparing there are no dropouts in this class, but all the dropouts belong to the marginally above poverty line class. This could also be due to the fact that the MAPL class has a relatively higher family size, therefore they are effectively no different from the BPL class.

TABLE 28.9: **Status of Adult Education (36 yrs. and above)**

	Barapathar			Upper Lumparing		
	Male	Female	Total	Male	Female	Total
% of adults in 36 yrs. and above	58.33	42.11	100.00	56.57	43.43	100.00
% of illiterate persons	12.69	39.36	23.68	5.36	30.23	16.16
% of literate persons	14.18	18.09	15.79	28.57	20.93	25.25
% of adult having passed class V	17.16	18.09	17.54	10.74	11.63	11.11
% of adult having passed class VIII	26.12	20.20	23.68	26.79	16.28	22.22
% of adult having passed Matric	21.64	2.13	13.60	25.00	9.30	18.18
% of Graduates	8.21	2.13	5.70	3.57	9.30	6.06
% of Post-Graduates	—	—	—	—	2.33	1.01

TABLE 28.10: **Status of Drop-outs in each Income Group**

		Rs. 6000 & below	6001-12000	12001-18000	18001-36000	36001 & above	Total
% of children enrolled in Barapathar	M	0.71	15.83	20.86	46.76	15.83	100.00
	F	0.69	12.41	20.00	50.35	16.55	100.00
% of dropouts in Barapathar	M	14.29	28.57	14.29	42.85		100.00
	F		20.00	10.00	70.00		100.00
% of children enrolled in U.Lumparing	M	4.11	5.48	30.14	53.42	6.85	100.00
	F	1.47	19.12	22.06	47.06	10.29	100.00
% of dropouts in U.Lumparing	M				100		100.00
	F						

Conclusion

Though the study is of exploratory nature and tries to summarise the literacy and educational situation in the two low income localities of Shillong, the following generalisations could be made:

(i) The overall literacy level is fairly high, but there is a marked bias towards female literacy in Barapathar, which is predominantly a non-ST locality. The relatively egalitarian situation in the ST societies contributes both for an overall higher literacy (as seen in Upper Lumpering) as well as a significantly higher female literacy.

(ii) The literacy situation in the older adult generation is not only lower but this is biased against the female literacy (30-40% illiterates in age group of 36 years and above), which indicates that modernization and economic opportunities facilitate a higher literacy.

(iii) The income bias of literacy and education are vindicated, but they are not as pronounced between the income classes as normally they are portrayed to be. This indicate that given enough motivation and supportive action from Govt. and non-Govt. agencies, even the poorest of the poor could improve their literacy status, education and overall developmental situation.

29

SHELTER FOR URBAN POOR

H.K. MAZHARI

The past decades have witnessed phenominal growth of Urban Areas and exodus of population from the Rural Areas in search of employment and better quality of life. The Urban Population since Independence has shown upward trend. This is mainly attributed to the process of development and growth in the economy and modernisation of agriculture activities; the farm labourer having to face unemployment due to change in the agriculture practices due to utilisation of machineries and farm equipment. Due to this change and adoption of new farm technology, the agriculture labour market got affected which led to out migration from Rural Areas.

With Green Revolution and higher productivity, the labour per unit of agriculture land also got reduced. The marginal farmers could not switch over to the new farming technology and other agriculture input were beyond their reach in spite of the Governmental efforts in this direction. This also led to marginal farmers abandoning their agriculture land, selling off and moving out to new areas unknown to them and trying to get a foothold in urban centres.

The rural population generally find extremely difficult to adjust in a new urban environment and to get reasonable means of income for their survival; they do not have the skill to find better jobs. With their income, they cannot afford to have a reasonable shelter and avail of social services as these are invariably beyond their paying capacity. In order to survive they get themselves engaged as domestic help, unskilled construction labour and such other occupation which do not require any specialised skill and where income is very low. Their skill in agriculture and farming have no relevance in the changed surroundings. Since their income is low they cannot affort shelter and have to leave the family behind supporting financially their family back in the village. The pavements, abandoned public buildings, the hume pipes and the ramshackle structure in the slum areas serve as their shelter. Slumming of cities and growth of rundown area is increasing at a much faster pace leading to over crowding, congestion, insanitation, strain on the civic services and degradation of Urban Environment. These areas are the ones which absorbed the poor either migrating from the rural areas or from the smaller towns. In the coming decade face of poverty will become increasingly urban because of the large influx. The urbanisation of poverty will acentuate the demand for shelter and others basic infrastructure. Our failure to meet this demand will have dire political and social consequences.

The urban population in the country was 217.61 million in 1991 and expected to reach 300 million by the year 2001 AD. If 30 per cent of the urban population is taken as living below the poverty line, there will be nearly 100 million urban poor by 2001 AD in the country.

In Meghalaya there are 7 Urban Centres in the State and the urban population is 3,30,047 persons. Though in term of absolute numbers, it may not be a cause of concern but in term of percentage (18.60%) it does pose a serious problem. Urban poverty in Meghalaya being in the range of 40 per cent, the urban poor are nearly 1.30 lakhs.

Climatic conditions in most of the urban centres in the State have prevented pavement dwellers, squatters but slums have come up even in smaller towns. Most of the Local Government/Public Agencies have either made little attempts or have limited their efforts in construction of new tenement far away from the places of work which are invariably not occupied and sold to others who are economically better off. The urban poor have to depend largely on his own resources to provide a shelter, they make their own houses, own public convenience using land which the city planners in their Master-Plan zealously provide as green area, the breathing space, the lungs of the city. These houses are made by them in any vacant land provided near to their place of work, community every day is not acceptable and severe strain on their income.

As stated above the places most sought after by them are non-buildable land like area subject to flooding, swampy area and Government land as they are not in a position to build house in any other city area. This is how Shanty Towns are developed much to the annoyance of the city administrator. Their shelter remain devoid of basic services like water, drainage, sanitation and electricity. The administrators and the city planners get busy to find out the ways of removing the infrastructure built with the genius of the user. The city authorities have miserably failed in their efforts to provide the bare minimum facilities like shelter and try their best to enforce and implement recommendations of the Master-Plan to erase such eye sore. What moral right they have to destroy whatever has been built with self help by the beneficiaries using their own resources. It is appalling to see city authorities after city authorities trying to demolish structure in the name of city beautification or Master-Plan enforcement. They come up with solution of construction of multi-storeyed building not favoured by urban poor. Why not capitalize on the genius of the urban poor and use their resources for providing shelter which is more affordable, viable and acceptable to them.

An Approach to Shelter for Urban Poor

Shelter for urban poor needs to be dealt in a proper perspective. The Urban poor are largely migrant who come to the cities in search of employment and move to the growing Urban Centres as well as in areas where new development is taking place such as extension of the city area or development of new cities. Housing the urban poor in existing town and cities and the new settlment has to be based on different approaches.

While planning new settlements the city planners are expected to earmark certain areas preferably near the proposed work centres as reception centres having bare minimum civic infrastructure like sanitation, power and water supply. The migrants are likely to flock to those areas in search of employment and may find these centres very convenient. Such centres should invariably have proper pavement, drainage, power-lines, public water taps, bathing and sanitation units. The useable area may also be paved; demarcation of each plot may be made so that the urban poor on his own, erect his own shelter as he does on pavement, open spaces and Government land. These plots should be made available to them only on rental basis and the payment should be made every day to the caretaker of the centre. The caretaker should remain at the site to ensure cleanliness of the area with the help of the Local Municipal Authority. Such centres may be dispersed throughout the city, close to their work places and may be fenced out completely to avoid any extension and encroachment on neighbouring sites.

It is expected that with the increase of the income level and having gained some financial stability, the urban poor and his family members may start looking for better accommodation and may move on to such areas where Local Authority can provide a developed site or a skeleton house, or just plinth made with a sanitary unit. These developed site should have all the necessary infrastructure and community facilities, like school and health etc., such developed site may be made available either on long term lease or out right sale. With further increase in income the family may be in a position to move into better housing, a regular house meant for economically weaker section of the society or the houses meant for low income group. Such schemes are already under implementation in almost all the cities in the country except that there is no provision made for shelter of new comers to the city. Hence, the proposal to have a reception centre meant exclusively for the urban poor. The above may be workable in new towns it may be difficult to locate new reception centres within congested cities. Hence, improvement of shelter in existent towns are to be taken up only as an *In situ* exercise. Some of these schemes which are in operation or which have been tried in the part are indicated below.

Immediately after Independence of the country, the planners took up the programmes of new houses in various cities and made large number of units for the urban poor. These schemes could not be sustained for long and had to be abandoned in view of the financial constraint. After gaining experience of partial utilisation of new houses made for urban poor, the policy of providing individual housing unit to each family got shifted to providing civic amenities to a group of people living in slum and run down area.

This was the approach introduced in the Fifth Five Year Plan (1974-79) and was the beginning of the environmental improvement of urban slum scheme. This scheme concentrates on provision of basic amenities, water supply, sewerage, storm water drain, community bath, community latrines, widening and paving of existing lane, street light and community facilities. This schemes was introduced with a view to improve living conditions of the urban poor and slum dwellers who have no access to such public amenities. In this scheme only the physical manifestation of urban poverty was dealt. The scheme was modified from time to time and ceiling expenditure of Rs. 100 per capita in Fifth plan is now raised to Rs. 800 in May, 1995. Also a new item of construction of community creche and community centres was introduced in this scheme. It is now realised that slums are here to stay and that the best appraoch to deal with slum is through improvement programme.

In Meghalaya our experience of implementing this programme is quite satisfactory. We have been able to cover, 1,10,289 slum population up to 1995-96, with the total expenditure of Rs. 378.68 lakhs. The scheme has been implemented in all the Urban Centre in the State. Implementation of the scheme have to be viewed in context of no homeless population. There are as many as 44 slum areas. These areas are deficit in the basic civic infrastructure and the State Government have declared such areas as slum areas.

In the above schemes, the individual houses and their housing needs have not been given proper focus and the need for improvement of the individual houses was not given due priority. Various ongoing scheme in the Government of India, largely supported by finances from HUDCO dealt merely on construction of new units. It was in 1991 that Government of India as a part of urban poverty alleviation programme introduced Shelter Housing Upgradation Scheme (SHASU). This scheme was for urban poor having a maximum income of Rs. 11,850 per year each family. The scheme provides subsidy of Rs. 1000 and Rs. 3000 loan at the interest 6 per cent payable within a period of 20 years. In spite of the best efforts made by the State Govt. and by implementing agency, the achievement is far from satisfactory. The main reasons appears to be the following:

1. The Urban Poor mostly are tenants and have no land of their own.
2. Being encroaching on Govt./Private land are constantly under threat and liable for legal actions.
3. In absence of the legal right on the land they occupy, subsidy and loan cannot be sanctioned.
4. The land owners are not interested in availing the above loan assistance as they do not expect any increase in the rental.

It is not only in Meghalaya but throughout the country this scheme has not taken off probably for the reasons stated above. In the mean time some State Govt. like, Maharashtra have gone back to the same approach initiated in fifties and they are planning to make individual houses for the slum dwellers. With the only change that these new houses are to be constructed within the existing slum areas involving the private sector and making such scheme commercially viable. It is too early to make any comments at this juncture as the scheme has just started. Construction of multi-storeyed tenements on the existing slums was also taken up by Tamilnadu in seventies with some degree of success.

There cannot be a single solution to this complex problems. The right approach will be try all the three depending on the local conditions. SHASU can be successfully implemented if loan ceiling of Rs. 3000 is increased and loan sanctioned to the tenants. Recently Govt. of India has raised the limit to Rs. 9950 additional loan from HUDCO can also be secured upto the limit of Rs. 195,000 under economically weaker section. This may bring the desired result if the land is allotted to the urban poor or the land owner may also be persuaded to avail loan assistance and may be allowed enhanced rentals.

30

STATUS OF AIR POLLUTION IN MEGHALAYA

S.C. KATIYAR

Introduction

The term Air Pollution may be defined as the situation in which the ambient atmosphere contains materials in concentrations which are harmful to man and his environment. The composition of ambient air changes continuously due to the emissions of natural and man made pollutants. The air pollutants emitted from natural processes include vegetational decay, forest fires, volcanic erruptions and bacterial activities. The anthropogenic or man made activities which mainly contribute towards air pollution problems include emissions from industrial processes, urbanisation, automobiles, solid waste disposal etc. With increasing population, expansion in industry and growth in agriculture the problem of air pollution is also increasing with an alarming pace. Green House Effect and Ozone Layer Depletion are a few well known examples of air pollution problems.

Meghalaya is situated in the North-Eastern Region of the country and lies between the latitude 25°N and 26°N and longitude 90°E and 92°E. The state covers an area of 22,429 sq.km. with total population of 17,74,778 as per the 1991 Census. Though the state is having tremendous potential for industrialisation but the pace of the same has been slow in the past due to certain bottlenecks. With the implementation of new industrial policy in the country it is expected that the state shall also pick up the momentum and more industries would come up in near future. At present, there are about 1100 industries operating in the state. Most of these industries are small scale industries and are non-polluting category of industries. Out of these, only a few fall under the category of large and medium scale category of industries. Cement industries and Lime-kilns are the main sources of industrial air pollution. Mining activities have also started in the state in early eighties to exploit the mineral resources like coal, lime stone, granite etc. Mostly these mining activities are carried out in an unplanned and unscientific manner which is resulting in serious environmental problems. Jhum cultivation is another such practice which apart from creating massive deforestation problems also contributing quite significantly towards air pollution. Vehicular exhaust emissions are the main source of air pollution in urban areas of the state. The problem of vehicular pollution is further magnified due to absence of alternative transportation facilities.

Status of Ambient Air Quality

The Carbon-mono-oxide (CO), sulpher-di-oxide (SO_2), oxides of nitrogen (NOX) and suspended particulate matter (SPM) are a few primary pollutant which together contribute more that 90 per cent of total air pollution. The main sources of these pollutants and its major health and other impacts are summarised in (Annexure-I).

The Meghalaya Pollution Control Board has started monitoring of ambient air quality from the 2 Nos. stations located at the State Central Library and in the Board's Office premises at Lumpyngngad, Shillong. These stations which are in operation since the year 1989, are established under National Ambient Air Quality Monitoring (NAAQM) programme and is sponsored by Central Pollution Control Board (CPCB), Delhi. The Board collects air samples twice in a week from these stations. These air samples are then analysed for Sulpher-dioxide, oxides of Nitrogen and suspended particulate matter in Board's Central Laboratory. Some meteorological parameters like humidity, ambient air temperature, rainfall etc. are also monitored simultaneously at the time of air sampling as the climate conditions play vital role in transportation of pollutants from one place to other place. The results of the ambient air quality conducted during the year 1993-94 are given in Table 30.1 and 30.2.

TABLE 30.1: **Status of Ambient Air Quality at State Central Library, Shillong**

Sl. No.	Seasons	SPM (μg/nm³)		SO_2 (μg/nm³)		Nox (μg/nm³)	
		Min.	Max.	Min.	Max.	Min.	Max.
1.	Spring	25.3	38.2	BDL	—	BDL	2.9
2.	Monsoon	21.1	39.2	BDL	2.6	BDL	9.4
3.	Autumn	24.0	38.6	BDL	—	3.1	5.5
4.	Winter	37.0	55.6	BDL	3.6	BDL	6.5

TABLE 30.2: **Status of Ambient Air Quality at Lumpyngngad, Shillong**

Sl. No.	Seasons	SPM (μg/nm³)		SO_2 (μg/nm³)		Nox (μg/nm³)	
		Min.	Max.	Min.	Max.	Min.	Max.
1.	Spring	27.4	46.7	BDL	3.2	6.4	19.6
2.	Monsoon	21.1	28.9	BDL	8.2	4.0	145.6
3.	Autumn	20.4	22.6	BDL	3.2	BDL	8.9
4.	Winter	29.6	52.1	BDL	3.0	BDL	8.0

The Central Pollution Control Board, (CPCB) Delhi has laid down air quality standards in 1982. For the purpose the Geographical areas were categorised into three classes viz. industrial and mixed use (I), Residential and Rural (R) and Sensitive (S) which includes hill stations, national parks and monuments. The said standard are given in Table 30.3.

As per the ambient air quality standards (Table 30.3) Shillong falls under the category of sensitive areas as it is a hill station. If we compare the ambient air quality results of Shillong (Table 30.2) with the CPCB standards, it is

TABLE 30.3: **Ambient Air Quality Standards**

Sl. No.	Category	SPM	SO_2	CO	NO_2
		(All concentrations in $\mu g/nm^3$)			
1.	Industrial and Mixed area	500	120	5000	120
2.	Residential and Rural (commercial)	200	80	2000	80
3.	Sensitive	100	30	1000	30

evident that only the oxides of nitrogen (Nox) from the NAAQM station situated at Lumpyngngad has violated the standard concentration in Monsoon season. Rest of the results are well within the ambient air quality standards.

The Board has also made surveys to assess the ambient air quality of the district headquarters of the state in order to have first hand data on the status of the ambient air quality of these places. The air sampling from these district headquarters was conducted in the dry season of the year and central places of the towns of Nongstoin, Nongpoh, Jowai, Tura and Williamnagar were selected for the purpose. The results of this survey are given in Table 30.4.

TABLE 30.4: **Status of Ambient Air Quality at Various District Head Quarters of the State**

Sl.No.	Stations	SPM ($\mu g/nm^3$)	SO_2 ($\mu g/nm^3$)	Nox ($\mu g/nm^3$)
1.	Nongstoin	120.0	8.2	37.3
2.	Jowai	236.3	BDL	37.9
3.	Nongpoh	211.8	BDL	30.0
4.	Tura	130.8	BDL	25.0
5.	Williamnagar	162.7	BDL	32.0

As per the ambient air quality standards (Table 30.3) all the towns where air sampling was conducted fall under the category of Residential and Rural (Commercial) and as such the maximum limit for suspended particulate matter is 200 μg/

nm^3. From the results obtained from the survey it may be observed that at Jowai and Nongpoh the limits of suspended particulate matter are violated. The violation of the standard limits may be attributed to the reason that the sampling was conducted during dry weather conditions and the stations were located at the central places where maximum activities take place.

Status of Vehicular Pollution

Vehicular emissions have become the most significant and critical air pollutants because of the unprecedented increase in vehicular population in Urban Areas. Pollutants loads released from vehicles depended not only on the number and type of vehicles but also on the extent they are used and also the various operational conditions. The air pollutants which are emitted from vehicular exhaust emissions mainly comprises of hydrocarbons (HC), Carbon mono-oxide (CO), oxides of nitrogen (Nox), particulate matter, oxides of sulpher (Sox), Lead (pH), odour and carcinogenic compounds like polynuclear aromatic Hydro carbons (PAH), benzopyrene and benzathracine etc. Emission factor of major vehicular pollutants (Lbs/1000 gallons of fuel, consumed) is given in Table 30.5.

TABLE 30.5: **Exhaust Emission Factors**

Sl.No.	Pollutant	Emission factor lbs/1000 gallon	
		Petrol Engine	Diesel Engine
1.	Carbon mono-oxide	2300	60
2.	Hydrocarbons	200	136
3.	Oxides of nitrogen	133	222
4.	Oxides of sulpher	9	40
5.	Particulate matter	11	110
6.	Aldehydes	4	10
7.	Organic Acids	4	31

The Government of India has notified the guidelines under the Central Motor Vehicle Act, 1988 and the Central Motor Vehicle Rules, 1989 to the manufacturers of the vehicles to control the problem of vehicular pollution from the grassroot levels. Vehicular exhaust emission standard for various petrol and diesel driven vehicles were also notified which are summarised in Table 30.6.1 and 30.6.2.

TABLE 30.6.1: **Vehicular Exhaust Emission Standards for Petrol Driven Vehicles**

Sl.No.	Type of Vehicle	% Co v/v
1.	Four wheeled	3.0
2.	Two and Three wheeled	4.5

TABLE 30.6.2: **Vehicular Exhaust Emission Standards for Diesel Driven Vehicles**

Sl.No.	Method of Test	Maximum Smoke Density		
		Light Absorption coefficient	Bosch units	Hafridge smoke unit
1.	Full load at a speed of 60 per cent to 70 per cent of maximum engine rated speed declared by the manufacturer	3.1	5.2	75
2.	Free acceleration	2.3	—	65

As the vehicular exhaust emissions are the main source of air pollution in the state the Meghalaya Pollution Control Board made a survey about the status of exhaust emissions of petrol driven vehicles. A total of about 1228 petrol driven vehicles were tested for the purpose. It was found that about 40 per cent of four wheeled vehicles were emitting exhaust gases more than the prescribed standards. Similar survey was conducted for the diesel driven vehicles and about 1709 diesel driven vehicles were tested for the purpose. It was observed that about 62 per cent of these vehicles were emitting smoke more than the prescribed standards.

Conclusion

At present, the ambient air quality of the state generally meet the prescribed standards. But there is no place for complacency as the number of vehicles in the urban centres of the state is rising by leaps and bounds and it is also expected that the pace of industrialisation shall also take a big step forward due to economic liberalisation and implementation of new industrial policy. The need of hour is to adopt sustainable development programmes for the state and take concrete steps to abate and control the problem of vehicular pollution so that the quality of ambient air may not deteriorate further and the coming generation may inherit a pollution free environment.

ANNEXURE-1

Health and Other Impacts of Major Air Pollutants

Sl.No.	Pollutant	Sources	Health Impacts	Other Impacts
1	2	3	4	5
(01)	Carbon mono-oxide CO	— Automobiles (About 90% of Total) — Industrial sources	— Reduces blood's ability to absorb oxygen — Can cause heart and brain damage. — dizziness, fatigue, headache — can aggravate heart disease.	— Have produced cancer in animals — Plant damage
(02)	Sulpher-di-oxide SO_2	— Burning fossil fuels — Industrial Sources	— Impairs breathing — Causes eye, throat and lung irritation.	— One cause of acid rain. — Corrodes iron, steel, nickel, aluminium. — Weakens building materials — Deteriorates fibres.
(03)	Oxides of Nitrogen Nox	— Automobiles — Refineries	— Respiratory infections — Causes eye, noise, throat irritation.	— One cause of acid rain — Corrosion of metal.

(Contd.)

ANNEXURE-I *(Contd.)*

1	2	3	4	5
—		Power Plants	— Can damage lung tissue	— Deterioration of rubber and fabric.
		— Chemical Plants	— Can contribute to emphysema	— Dangerous to animals.
				— Can damage vegetation.
(04)	Hydrocarbons HC	— Automobiles	— Carcinogenic	— Produce smog when combined with nitrogen oxides+sunlight.
				— Have produced cancer in animals.
				— Plant.
(05)	Suspended particulate matter SPM	— Industry — Automobiles	- Disrupts normal self cleaning of lungs, affects respiratory system.	— Reduces sunlight causes haze.
		— Incinerators		— Can damage or corrode buildings.
		— Burning fossil fuels		— Soils clothes, buildings.

31

SAFE WATER TO THE URBAN DWELLERS

S.P. BHATTACHARYYA

As far back as historical records, go, patterns of community organisation have varied, but the house has been essentially the same throughout the centuries. Health is probably the most personal factor in human living. The individual should look to the house first for health. The home needs help from outside its own resources and, therefore, the family group has a right and an obligation to look to the community for such health safeguards as cannot be provided by the home unaided, such as a safe water supply and sewage disposal.

The present trend of migration of rural population to urban areas, because of employment opportunities, attraction of better living condition is a recent phenomenon in most of the developing countries in general and India in particular. The size of urban population in India has increased from 10.8 per cent in 1901 to 20 per cent in 1971 and 23.3 per cent in 1981. The urban population in India is 217.61 million in 1991 compared to 159.5 millions in 1981 and 78.9 million in 1961. By the year 2000 this figure is expected to rise to 367 millions (Table 31.1). India has the third larget urban population in the world. The continuous migration of people from rural to urban areas constitutes a social crisis, the ramification of which may eventually impair the quality of life.

No country was ever more blessed with an abundant supply of clear, sparkling streams, lakes, rivers. Yet as we have become more urbanized and industrialized, we have seen

TABLE 31.1: **Population Trends in North Eastern Region**

Census Year	Arunachal Pradesh	Assam	Manipur	Meghalaya	Mizoram	Nagaland	Tripura	All India
1901	—	3290	284	341	82	102	173	2,38,396
1951	—	8029	578	606	196	213	639	3,61,088
1961	337	10,837	780	769	266	369	1142	4,39.235
1971	468	14,625	1073	1012	332	516	1556	5.48.160
1981	632	18,041	1421	1336	494	775	2053	6,83.229
1991	865	22,414	1837	1775	690	1210	2757	8,46,303

Source: Census of India 1991 Series 1, page-2 of 1992, Final Population Totals.

one after another of these beautiful resources polluted by the byproduct of urban civilization. Of the total population nearly half have only contaminated water to drink. In the developing countries, the panorama of infections is dominated by diarrhoeal diseases. Millions of cases of Gastroenteritis occur each year mostly amongst children and also among adults. Lakhs of children die annually of malnutrition and water borne infection.

Inadequate of non-existent public health with poor hygiene and limited availability of potable water, increase the spread and persistence of infections in over populated urban dwellings and urban communities. The deterioration results from years of abuse in which natural waterways were inundated with quantities of raw sewage, waste products of industrial and chemical plants and slaughter houses, petroleum residues, poisonous herbicides and insecticides the list is almost endless, but our water supply is not improved.

The analysis of various issues related to environmental hygiene, it is important to look into some basic datas relevant to the subject.

TABLE 31.2: **Distribution of Population by Area-1991**

State	Total	Rural	Urban	Percentage of Urban Population
Arunachal Pradesh	864,558	753,930	110,628	12.80
Assam	22,414,322	19,926,527	2,487,795	11.10
Manipur	1,837,149	1,331,504	505,645	27.52
Meghalaya	1,774,778	1,444,731	330,047	18.60
Mizoram	689,756	371,810	317,946	46.10
Nagaland	1,209,546	1,001,323	208,223	17.21
Tripura	2,757,205	2,335,484	421,721	15.30
All India	846,302,688	628,691,676	217,611,012	26.13

TABLE 31.3: **Per cent Decadal Variation of Population 1901-11 to 1981-91**

State	Total (T) Rural (R) Urban (U)	1901 to 1911	1951 to 1961	1971 to 1981	1981 to 1991
Arunachal	T	—	—	+ 35.5	+ 36.83
Pradesh	R	—	—	+ 31.14	+ 27.20
	U	—	—	+ 139.63	+ 167.04
Assam	T	+ 16.99	+ 34.98	+ 36.05	+ 24.24
	R	+ 16.91	+ 30.98	+ 33.85	+ 22.56
	U	+ 20.55	+ 126.57	+ 58.79	+ 39.58
Manipur	T	+ 21.21	+ 35.04	+ 32.46	+ 29.29
	R	+ 27.96	+ 23.93	+ 12.27	+ 27.36
	U	+ 3.34	+2,226.07	+ 165.36	+ 34.67
Meghalaya	T	+ 15.71	+ 27.03	+ 32.04	+ 32.86
	R	+ 14.95	+ 19.14	+ 26.60	+ 32.00
	U	+ 41.76	+ 100.78	+ 63.98	+ 36.76
Mizoram	T	+ 10.64	+ 35.61	+ 48.55	+ 39.70
	R	+ 10.64	+ 33.05	+ 26.24	+ -0.04
	U	+ —	+ 105.14	+ 222.61	+ 161.01
Nagaland	T	+ 46.76	+ 14.07	+ 50.05	+ 56.08
	R	+ 48.91	+ 6.91	+ 40.78	+ 52.94
	U	– 21.66	+ 364.41	+ 133.95	+ 73.18
Tripura	T	+ 32.48	+ 78.71	+ 31.92	+ 34.30
	R	+ 33.47	+ 74.20	+ 31.10	+ 27.80
	U	+ 6.48	+ 141.81	+ 38.93	+ 86.69
All India	T	+ 5.75	+ 21.51	+ 24.66	+ 23.85
	R	+ 6.40	+ 20.49	+ 19.32	+ 20.01
	U	+ 0.35	+ 26.41	+ 46.14	+ 36.47

+ Increase, (–) Decrease.

Source: Census of India 1991, Series I, Paper-2 of 1992.

TABLE 31.4: **Pattern of Investment in Water Supply and Sanitation in different Plan Periods in Public Sector, Centre, States & Union Territories**

	Period	Rs. in crores
1.	Ist Plan 1951-56	11.0
2.	Second Plan 1956-61	74.0
3.	Third Plan 1961-66	105.7
4.	Annual Plan 1966-69	102.7
5.	Fourth Plan 1969-74	458.9
6.	Fifth Plan 1974-79*	1091.6
7.	Sixth Plan 1980-85	3977.6
8.	Seventh Plan 1985-90	7122.7
*9.	1979-80 Annual Plan	387.6
10.	1990-91 Annual Plan	1912.8

TABLE 31.5: **Total and Per Capita State Govt. Expenditure on Health**

(Rs. in Crores)

	1980-81	1985-86	1986-87	1987-88	1988-89	1989-90
Arunachal	—	—	19	25	26	26
Pradesh			(271)	(357)	(325)	(327)
Assam	40	71	100	167	179	172
	(22)	(32)	(44)	(71)	(75)	(70)
Manipur	14	12	35	30	35	37
	(93)	(75)	(219)	(176)	(205)	(219)
Meghalaya	16	15	27	32	38	47
	(120)	(100)	(169)	(200)	(236)	(277)
Mizoram	—	9	3	29	29	30
		(150)	(50)	(483)	(416)	(434)

(Contd.)

TABLE 31.5 *(Contd.)*

	1980-81	1985-86	1986-87	1987-88	1988-89	1989-90
Nagaland	16	32	39	49	49	63
	(197)	(355)	(433)	(490)	(497)	(594)
Tripura	6	13	23	29	35	40
	(31)	(57)	(96)	(121)	(140)	(161)

Includes medical, family planning, public health, sanitation and water supply.

Note: Figures in brackets denote the per capita expenditure.

Source: Centre for Monitoring Indian Economy, Bombay.

There is no data available for urban areas regarding availability of potable drinking water in N.E. Region. The data available for the rural areas is good in papers but is at much variance with the ground reality. The annual death from Gastroenteritis, cholera/water borne diseases in thousand does not show any sign of abating.

Regarding urban areas—Shillong the prestigious hill station and capital of Meghalaya—where safe water samples examined sometime back and was found to be unfit for human consumption for all the water sources and were found contaminated with faecal matter.

The demographic growth and fast urbanisation all over the world are bringing profound social and environmental changes. India is still lagging behind many countries in the field of environmental health and there can be no state of positive community health and well-being without safe water supply. The basic problems of safe water supply and sanitary disposal of human excreta are yet to be solved. In Uttar Pradesh after water works sanitation, the cholera death rate decreased by 74.1 per cent, typhoid fever death rate by 63.3 per cent, the dysentery death rate by 23.1 per cent and the rate of diarrhoeal diseases by 42.7 per cent (W.H.O. 1964). These figures indicate the great importance of safe water supply.

A survey conducted by W.H.O. about two decades back revealed that in India 80 per cent of the urban population had

TABLE 31.6: **Details of Inland Water Resources of Various Types**

State	River & Canals (Length in km)	Reservoirs	Lakhs in Hectares	
			Tanks & Ponds	Beels, Lakes & Derehit Water
1	2	3	4	5
Arunachal Pradesh	2000	—	0.01	0.03
Assam	4820	0.55	0.20	1.10
Manipur	3360	Neg.	0.30	0.29
Meghalaya	1000	0.01	0.02	Neg.
Mizoram	1748	—	0.02	—
Nagaland	1600	0.27	0.50	Neg.
Tripura	1200	0.06	0.07	0.07
All India	1,64,121	19.73	22.12	12.96

Neg. — Negligible.

Source: *Hand Book of Fisheries Statistics*, 1991.

TABLE 31.7: **Coverage of Number of Problem Villages in N.E.R. with Supply of Drinking Water and Annual Requirement of Water for Domestic Purposes (As on 31.12.91)**

State	Problem Villages as on 1-4-1985	Coverage of Problem Villages During		Water Requirement (in Cubic km) During	
		1985-90	1900-91	1991	2001
Arunachal Pradesh	391	391	—	0.024	0.029
Assam	9,570	9,126	356	0.632	0.883
Manipur	862	862	—	0.060	0.074
Meghalaya	3,658	2,237	406	0.053	0.072
Mizoram	596	527	68	0.025	0.035
Nagaland	623	597	7	0.036	0.052
Tripura	2,893	2,763	120	0.080	0.088
All India	1,61,722	1,53,357	3032	27.111	35.521

Source: Water & Related Statistics, Central Water Commission, 1992.

access to community water supplies, but only 18 per cent of rural population had access to safe water. Meanwhile the scenario has changed with mass pollution of all kinds of water resources and also increase in population. The magnitude of health hazard in the country due to unsafe water can be guazed from the epidemic of cholera in the slums of Delhi, a few years back and the Country's Public Headquarter in the capital city remaining a helpless mute spectator is tragic tale of event, which only shows how vulnerable are we even today only 4 years away from 2000 AD.

A daily equirement of 150 to 200 litres (35-40 gallons) per head is considered an adequate allowance. The selection of source requires expert advice.

The upland surface water of the N.E.R. derives its impurities from the catchment area, the sources being human habitation, and animal keeping or grazing. The general belief that mountain streams are very pure water is often untrue.

River water contains dissolved and suspended impurities of all kinds. Rivers are described as a direct connection between the alimentary canal of the people living upstream and the mouths of those below.

The usual ground water sources are wells and springs. The shallow wells are often grossly contaminated.

Ingestion of contaminated water and its use for purpose of personal hygiene may affect the health of people. The hazards of two broad groups (1) Biological (2) Chemical.

The National Water Supply and Sanitation Programme was launched in 1954 by the Government of India as a part of health plan to assist the States to provide adequate water supply and sanitation facilities in the entire country. Provision has been made in each successive Five Year Plans to improve the water supply. People must recognize safe water as a 'felt' health need and give up their old unhygienic habits of polluting water resources.

We are finally beginning to realize the seriousness of the problem and to make efforts to prevent further pollution and abating insofar as possible that which now exists. To be successful, these efforts must have the whole hearted support of every citizen. Support that is not only vocal, but is also backed up by a willingness to spend money to build the treatment facilities need to correct or prevent pollution.

No advanced medical measures are required to improve dramatically public health in developing countries but adequate economic resources would be needed to solve the problems. The public should examine how public resources are presently being allocated.

32

THE URBAN POOR AND CIVIC SERVICES
A Case Study of Shillong

GEETA SARIN

Urban poverty is far more complex and baffling than rural poverty. In recent decades the urban populations of third World countries have experienced unprecedented growth. There will be around 4 billion people in urban areas by the year 2020. One of the consequences of high rate of urban population growth has been a rapid increase in the total number of the urban poor.

Since urbanisation in most developing countries, India, being one of them, is accompanied by lower level of economic growth, industrialisation and employment, it inevitably results in a great pressure on the existing civic services leading to a poor quality of life. The urbanisation of poverty leads to slumming of cities and growth of rundown areas resulting in overcrowding, congestion, insanitation and ultimately degradation of the urban environment.

According to the U.N. Commission's Report (1994) by 2030, urban populations will be twice the size of rural populations. Primarily due to a decaying urban environment at least 600 million people in the world already live in life threatening situations. Upto one third more live in substandard housing. At least 250 million urban residents have no easy access to safe piped water and 400 million lack sanitation.

Some 14 million children under the age of five in developing nations die every year of lack of safe drinking water, poor sanitation and common diseases and some 3 million are disabled. Diarrhoea alone is responsible for 4 million deaths annually.

The poor are in fact, the least served in the urban areas. The elite of the urban areas can acquire the civic services with money and can also improve the quality by various means but the urban poor are unable to privately acquire access to these facilities. They are totally dependent on social services and so they are the ones who suffer most from lack of environmental hygiene and appalling living conditions. Also they have the least economic and political muscle providing them basic services of high quality at a cost assumes great significance.

How is the presence of poor perceived in Urban Areas? Those who believe in the concept of 'city beautiful' feel that the poor negatively affect the aesthetics of city, while those who fight for the poor, feel that it is due to lack of cooperation from the authorities and the residents that the poor live under such inhuman conditions. It is not the fault of the poor entirely that the cities look filthy. The elite, municipal bodies are doing nothing for them. The poor do have a positive contribution to make in cities and do not play only a negative role. For example the rag pickers in Delhi clear 4000 to 5000 tonnes of garbage that is nearly 15 per cent of the squalor is cleaned by them.

Since doctors are paid highly for providing the public's health care, should not trash collections receive similar compensation because they too contribute to the fight against disease by keeping the environment free of garbage. Number of other positive functions are performed by the urban poor. The poor guarantee that the daily menial job get done. Moreover, poverty creates a variety of jobs for the non-poor, from social workers to pawnbrokers. They do from an indispensable part of city system and should be catered at least in terms of basic services. That is why this issue assumes significance today.

The social realities in the North-Eastern Region are closely related to its poor economic condition. The level of urbanisation is low in these states—14 per cent as compared to the national average of 27 per cent. But since 1961, the large cities of the region are growing at a very fast rate resulting in a high urban growth, causing an increase in the number of urban poor and in straining the existing civic infrastructure. In Meghalaya, particularly the level of urbanisation is far less stable than the rest of the north-east as the whole urbanisation scene is dominated by a single urban agglomeration in Shillong city region. Urban poverty is in the range of 40 per cent the urban poor account for 1.3 lac. The urbanisation process is very rapid in Shillong (Urban agglomeration) as it provides certain unique characteristics due to its typical socio-cultural and environmental settings. It is a typical case of urbanisation mushrooming even with low level of development, harsh life of the surrounding rural areas and the vicious cycle of abject poverty and under-development. The inevitable consequence of this pseudo-urbanisation is the emergence of nearly 32 slum area as the city was planned originally for a population of 20,000 people. The growth rate during the past one decade is 41 per cent within the Shillong urban agglomeration which includes Shillong Municipality, Shillong Cantonment, Mawlai, Nongthymmai, Madarting and Pynthorumkhrah. The slums are distributed in all the municipal wards except European and Jaiaw wards (Fig. 32.1).

The study has been carried out in the slum areas of Shillong to determine the status of the existing civic infrastructure and overall living conditions of the poor taking into consideration the ethnic composition of the slum areas dominated by tribal (5.44%) as well as non-tribals (48.50%) including Nepali, Biharis, Bengalis and Punjabis and the differences in the living standards of the tribes and non-tribes.

The main findings of the study are outlined below:

1. The poverty scenario in the city is relatively different from cities in other areas as it is relative deprivation which appears to be more significant because in most slum areas of Shillong the harrowing existence of life with widespread hunger and malnutrition is far lower compared to slum dwellers of other cities.
2. 93.44 per cent of the tribes have ration card and are using it compared to 66 per cent of non-tribes who have ration card and 56 per cent are using it.
3. Level of income is low as 70 per cent of the households

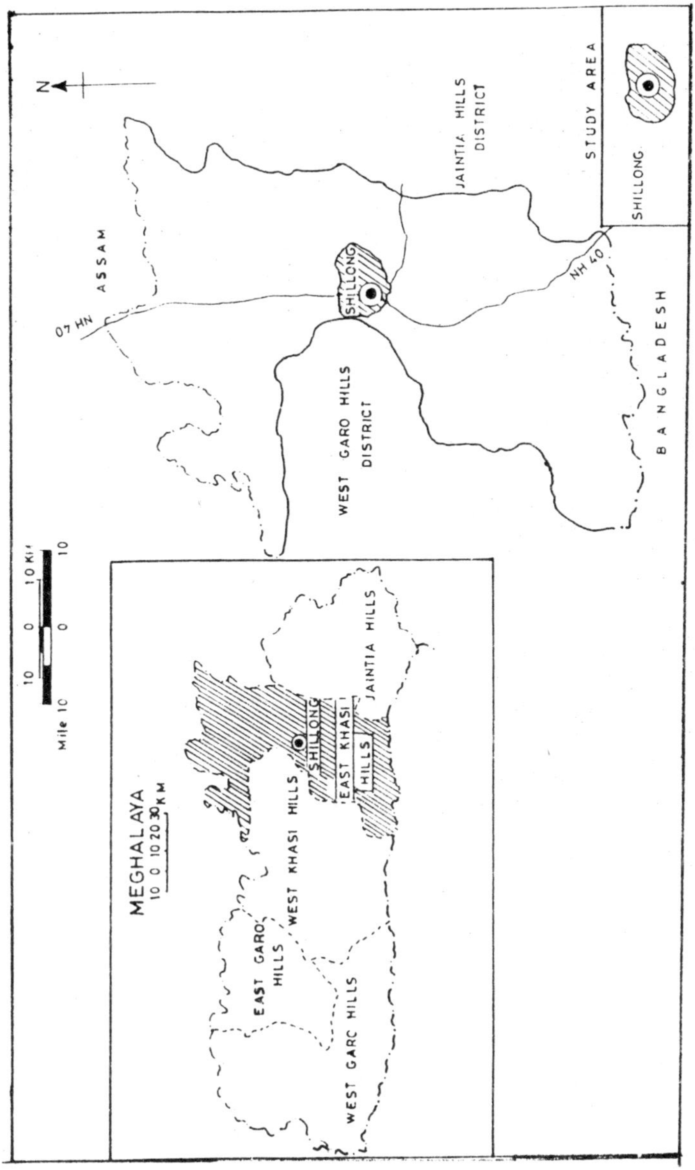

FIG. 32.1: East Khasi Hills: Location of Study Area

had an income level of below 1500 per month.

4. *Access to Electricity:* Nearly 70 per cent of the households have access to electric supply and only 10 per cent to street lamps.
5. *Availability of Roads*: 3/4th of the slum areas are approachable by only kutcha roads or steps. There are no paved roads leading to most of slum areas.
6. *Water Supply*: The access to safe water supply is very crucial to health. In the surveyed slum areas, not only is there a scarcity of good quality drinking water but also profusion of a occurrence of gastro-interstinal disorders. It is estimated that 76.45 per cent of the tribal and 50 per cent of the non-tribal people are dependent on outside sources of water like community taps and have to stand in long queues to get water. Nearly 75 per cent of the people draw water from community taps and only 20 per cent had individual taps in the houses and 5 per cent obtained water from individual handpumps as is clear from Fig. 32.2. Ninty per cent of the households even after standing in the line got only 4-5 buckets of water for their needs have to buy water also. This indicates the deplorable condition of water supply in the area.
7. *Housing Conditions*: As far as quality of housing is concerned, study reveals that nearly 30 per cent of the slum dwellers live in pucca houses compared to 70 per cent staying in semi-pucca and kutcha houses as showing in Fig. 32.3. Nearly 56 per cent of the non-tribes are staying in kutcha houses compared to none of the tribal population.

   The availability of physical infrastructure shows an interesting profile. Fig. 32.3 reveals that only 28 per cent of the non-tribes have their own houses compared 67.65 per cent of the tribes. On the whole, 65 per cent of the surveyed slum population are staying in rented house which are semi-pucca. Majority are staying in two room houses having no facility of drinking water and toilets.
8. *Status of Sanitation*: Sanitary means of excreta disposal

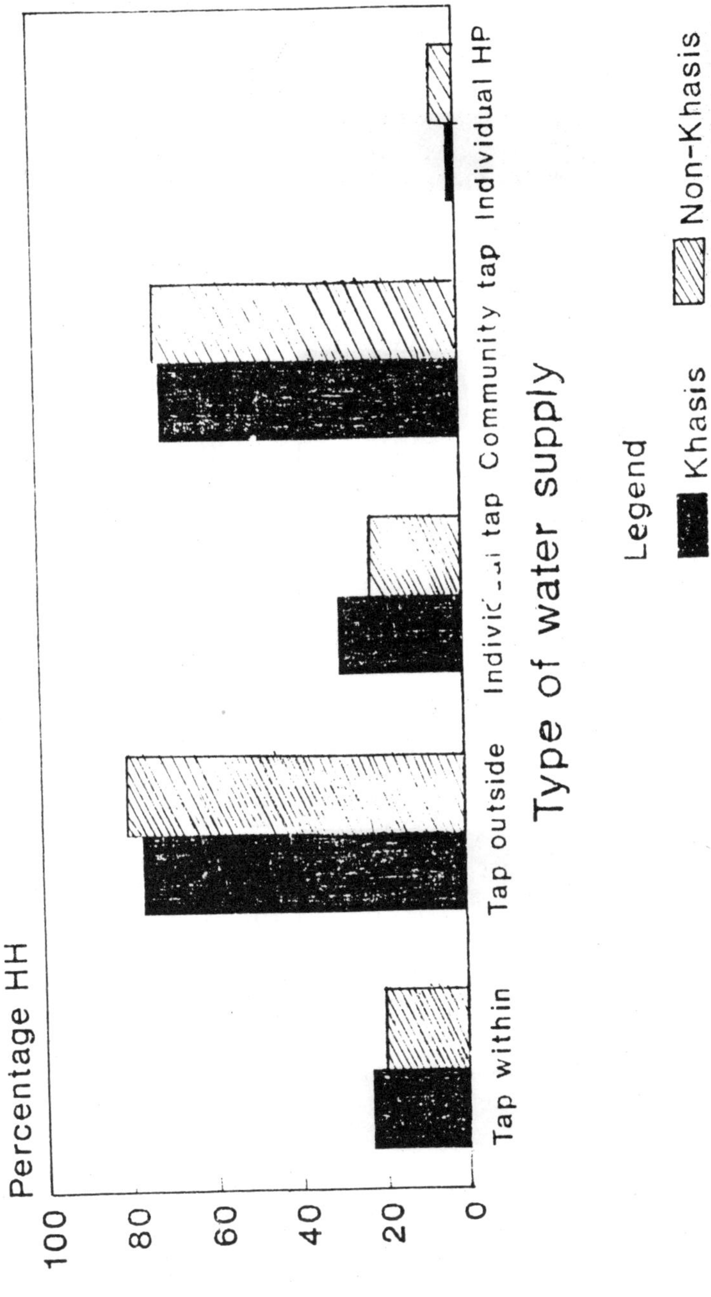

FIG. 32.2: Slums of Shillong: Status of Water Supply

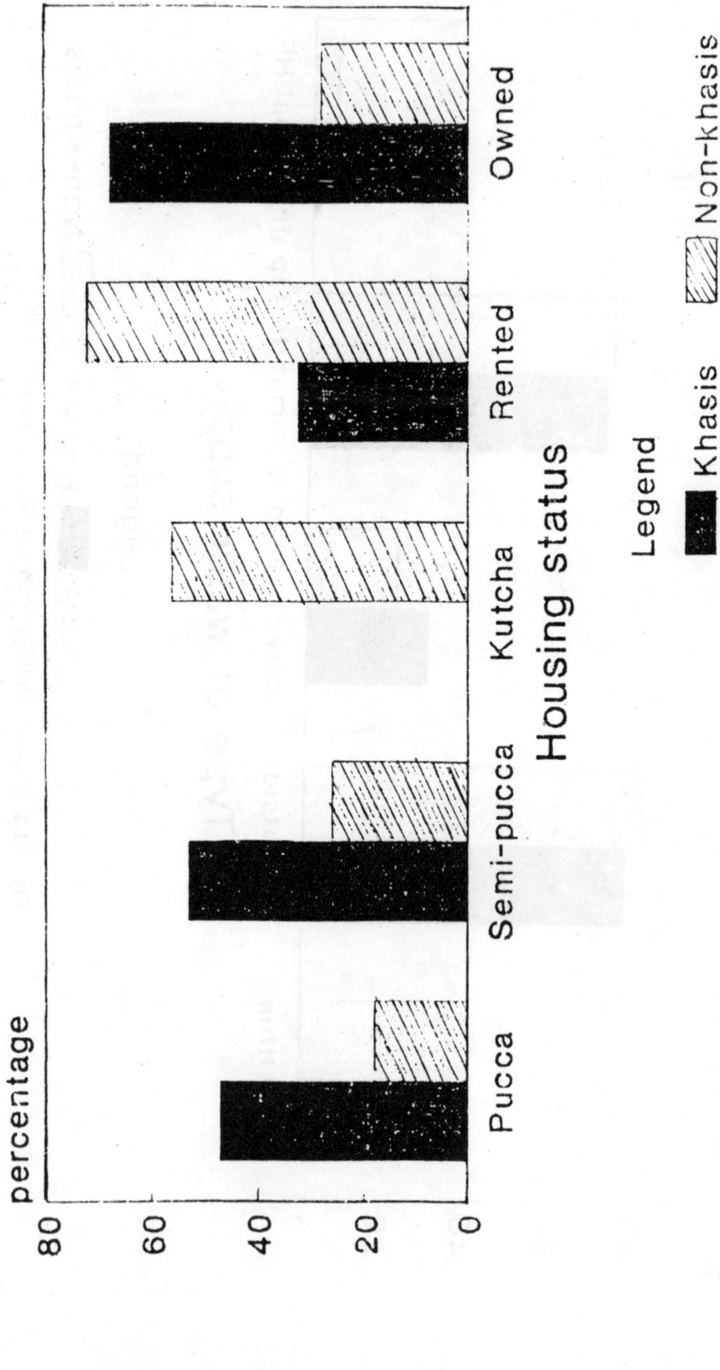

FIG. 32.3: Slums of Shillong: Housing Condition

are available only in a few households. A great majority of the households have to go out to use tiolet facility and only 21.42 per cent have access to private tiolet facility as shown in Fig. 32.4. 28.23 per cent of tribes have access within the house compared to 10 per cent of the non-tribes. Eighty-eight per cent of the non-tribes have to go out of the house for using tiolet facility. This infrastructure is poorly developed and there is a need for better sanitation facilities to improve the environment of the slums.

Fig. 32.4 reveals that nearly 72 per cent of the poor people use community dry/community pourflush of toilets. Only 17.85 per cent use individual dry type of toilets and 9.72 per cent are using individual pourflush toilets. Thus half the population are using community dry type of toilets for excreta disposal which leads to poor sanitation of the area and raises the question about the cleaning of these toilets.

9. *Garbage Disposal:* There are no garbage bins to put away the rubbish and no municipality vans come to clear the garbage. So 80 per cent of the slum dwellers deposit rubbish on the streets drains and 20 per cent out side the houses.

The study highlights acute deprivation of the urban poor of basic services. Safe drinking water is not available in 75 per cent of the surveyed slums. Moreover, facilities are over-crowded, this indicates that the services are generally underprovided.

There is a high incidence of diseases like diarrhoeal disorders, viral infections etc. in these slums which is the results of environmental hazards such as contaminated water, unhygienic disposal of human waste, lack of facilities for disposal of garbage and poor personal hygiene. The crux of the problem is that city authorities have not been able to extend basic services, such as piped water, community toilets and organised collection and disposal of the household wastes to the already underprovided, lower income urban population. Municipal bodies are non-functional in Shillong. Then how can

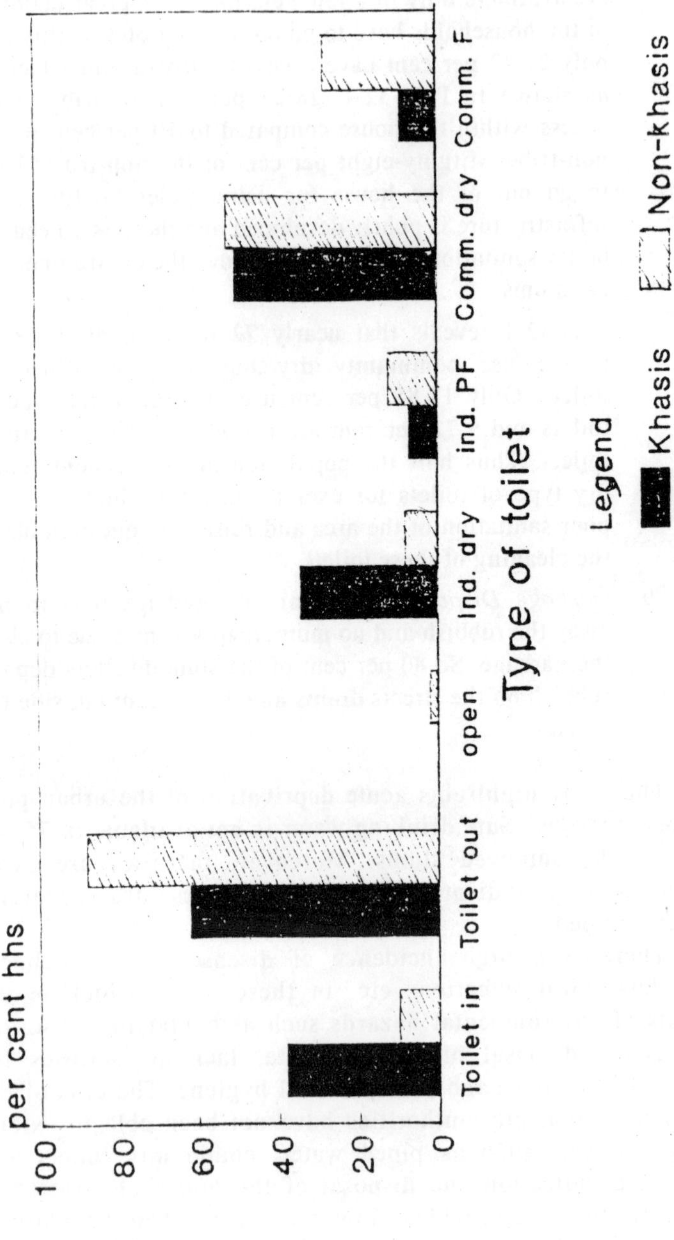

FIG. 32.4: Slums of Shillong: Status of Sanitation

the elite blame the poor for the environmental hygiene problems and the breakdown of the inbuilt environmental defence mechanisms. The poor, trapped in web of poverty, are forced to live in slum like conditions as the society has failed to provide the right social environmental for them.

Taking care of the needs of the poor will save us a lot of effort in terms of money as epidemics spread from these slum areas and lead to a poor quality of life. The recent outbreak of plague in some areas of country manifests the need to clear garbage. The environmental improvement of these slum will help ameliorate and improve the environment of the city and make it a more healthy place to live in.

Social dimensions of urban planning remains unacceptably week causing poor environment. This suggests that urban planning should no longer be confined only to land use and build environment but also include plans for socio-economic development and poverty alleviation. The urban poor need to become the focus of a city plan. The city administrations bear an urgent responsibility to improve access to basic services and facilities for the urban poor. This goal can be achieved through the process of community organisation. A firmer partnership between a strengthened local government and organized community is called for. The community based approach to basic services for the urban poor, which can thrive only in an informal and flexible environment seems to be the answer in retrieving the urban balance.

33

THE QUALITY OF LIFE OF THE URBAN POOR

SUSMITA DAS

Poverty has emerged as one of the most formidable challenges being faced by the country. At present nearly 30 to 35 per cent of the country's urban population are living below the poverty line (i.e. the household whose annual income is less than Rs. 11,850 as per 1990-91 prices). Although the poverty is the result of many factors, rapid urbanisation and growing inequalities in income in the urban areas are one among the many causes which results in poverty. As such, the quality of life that the urban population leads differs significantly. Although theoretically speaking changes in the quality is viewed as positive and towards a better way of livelihood. But a careful examination of the conditions reveals that such a quality of life is confined to a minority of people, while majority of the urban population experiences a decline in the quality of life. Therefore, an assessment of the quality of life of the urban poor assumes additional significances.

The study has been carried out in four slum localities of Shillong (selected on the basis of dominance of a particular community), under three broad indicators of quality of life i.e. physical, social and economic. The data pertaining to these indicators have been collected and compiled at the household level.

The study area contains around 51.44 per cent tribal population and around 48.56 per cent non-tribal population. Although the sex ratio is in favour of male, at the aggregate level, but it is higher among females when the tribal population are taken into consideration. Of the total population nearly 48.30 per cent belongs to the Khasi community, followed by the Bengalees (33.50%). The other communities together represent around 18.20 per cent to the total population.

The main findings of the study are outlined below:

1. The availability of physical infrastructure shows an interesting profile, while the housing condition reveals that nearly 41 per cent have own houses, but it is not irrespective of localities and communities. As for instance, the tribal and Khasi dominated locality of Lumsohphoh covers 61 per cent of the families with own accommodation, in other localities it is around 30 per cent families who enjoy own houses. Thus a large number of families live in a rented accommodation.

However, if the tribal and non-tribal households are taken exclusively, it is then found that around 45 per cent of the tribal households live in rented accommodation whereas among the non-tribal the percentage is as high as 73 per cent.

As far the quality of housing is concerned it is noticed that both among the tribals and non-tribals, majority of the families live in a semi pucca (51.75%) type of houses or in a kutcha type (26.50%). Primarily it is the non-tribals and those who live in a rented house live in a kutcha type of houses.

Again the infrastructure like water supply and sanitation are found to be poorly developed as 76 per cent of the households do not have an individual water supply facility and around 74 per cent do not have proper sanitation facilities. The condition appears to be the same in all the localities and among the communities.

2. The literacy rate among the poor is significantly high as 89 per cent are found to be literate. As usual the rate is higher among males (93%) and also among the non-tribals (93.3%). In spite of a high literacy rate, the level of education is comparatively low as 70.35 per cent have formal education upto the matriculation level only. A sharp decline is noticed among the non-tribal females after the middle school level, whereas uniformly it declines among the male and female in the tribal population.

Although the percentage of illiterates is quite low, it is

higher among females in general, but higher among males in the tribal population.

The school enrolment is too quite satisfactory since 91.84 per cent are found to be attending. Here the enrolment is higher among female child. However, the female enrolment is higher among the tribals and male among the non-tribals. It has also been observed that at the secondary level of education, a number of child tends to drop out. Moreover, the dropout rate is higher among the tribals and higher among the male child.

3. In the poverty localities it is found that only 33 per cent children below two years of age are fully immunized leaving behind at large as 67 per cent who are either particularly immunized or not immunized. Here too the coverage is better among males (34.48%) and also among the non-tribals (35.14%). Most of the females both among the tribals and non-tribals remain partially or not immunized.

The major cause of child morbidity appears to be cold, cough and fever, as 36 per cent of the child below five years of age are found to be suffering from it in all the localities. Around 20 per cent children suffered from diarrhoeal disorders. The infant and child mortality rate as 22 per thousand child in the study area.

4. The importance of income and employment needs no elaboration. While 41.15 per cent in the age group of 15 to 19 years are found to be working, there is not much of a difference between the tribal and the non-tribal population. However, the percentage is significantly higher among the male population both at the individual locality level as well as among the tribal/non-tribal segment. In all the localities the work participation rate is above 60 per cent among males but is as low as around 15 per cent among the females. Again the female work participation is higher among the tribals (23.77%) as compared to their non-tribal counterpart (10%).

In the study area, the occupation of the people varies from unskilled casual labourer to the professional, technical level. However, a majority of the people in the study area are found to be government employees (nearly 70%). Nearly 12 per cent are employed as unskilled casual labourers and the rest in small business, as domestic servants etc. At the individual locality level it is found that Lumsohphoh with the highest number of illiterates also has a higher percentage of people engaged as unskilled labourers (27%).

At the household level, it is found that approximately 18 per cent of the household annual income is less than Rs. 11,850 (identified as the poverty line income as per GOI classification at 1990-91 price level), and another 18 per cent earns between Rs. 11,850 and Rs. 20,000. Most of these low income household are, however, confined to two localities namely Mynsain (40%) and Lumsohphoh (51%). Another 48 per cent of the household has income between Rs. 20,000 to Rs. 50,000 and 16 per cent of the household has above Rs. 50,000 income per annum. Most of the high income families are located at Jacksontrace. A composite index of quality of life is being made by taking ten variables. Each of the variables were assigned with weightage value. All the households were then given a weightage value under each variables. To arrive at a simple composite index the variables were made scale free by dividing each value of a variable by its mean and then adding them up to give a composite index value at the household level.

The index (quality of life index) reveals that nearly 13 per cent of the households have a very low quality of life both in terms of economic and other social sector components. Another 35.50 per cent has low quality of life while approximately 40 per cent of the household have moderate quality of life, and nearly 12 per cent enjoys a better quality of life.

The situation at the individual locality level reveals that in two localities namely Mynsain and Jacksontrace around 14 and 21 per cent respectively has a very low quality of life. The percentage of houses with high quality of life is just 13 and 1 per cent respectively in these two localities. On the other hand, Shillong and Jacksontrace has 9 and 7 per cent of the household with a very low quality of life and around 18 per cent household in both with a better quality of life. Thus what is common among these four localities is that in all a large number of households has low to moderate quality of life.

Thus it appears that though around 18 per cent of the household has income below the poverty line, but when the social sector components are added to it, the household in poverty or with a low to very low quality of life accounts for roughly around 48 per cent.

34

POVERTY IN RURAL MEGHALAYA

BENAY LAHIRI

Agriculture constitutes the main occupation of 80 per cent of the people of Meghalaya. About 85 per cent of the geographic area of Meghalaya (total area of Meghalaya is 22,429 sq. km.) cannot be used for cultivation. Land is generally owned either by the community or privately owned and subject to annual shifting cultivation in many areas except government owned forests and other small land holding. Actual survey of persons wholly dependent on *Jhumming* has not been carried out so far. However, from a study undertaken by Agrc-Economic Research Centre for N.E. India, Jorhat in 1969, it has been estimated that about 43 per cent of the population of Meghalaya (about 25 per cent in Khasi & Jaintia Hills and 67 per cent of the tribal people in Garo Hills) are dependent on shifting cultivation. About 65,000 families are dependent on shifting cultivation and the area affected are about 400000 hectares. Most of the areas full in the heaviest rainfall belt which causes erosion in the slopes which made bare of the vegitation and covered by shifting cultivation. Due to growth of population and increase of pressure on land near the village, small villages have grown in outlying areas where no facilities for education, medicine, roads etc. exist. Land tenure system in Meghalaya is broadly of two types viz. *Raitwari* and Tribal land system which varies from district to district. *Raitwari* system is prevalent in plain mouzas of Garo Hills and community and private ownership in other parts of Meghalaya. There is no uniform land tenure system in Meghalaya excepting in Jaintia Hills (Raj land) and in the plain mouzas of Garo Hills.

The Report on Rural Economic Survey in Khasi & Jaintia Hills District in 1963 it is seen that the total area covered by land holdings of all sizes in border area, project area and general area are 5266.42, 1892.42 and 613.24 acres respectively. The average size of holding per family are 5.3 acres, 2.9 acres and 3.3 acres respectively and holding per head are 1.48 acres, 0.63 acres, 0.70 acres respectively. Proportion of landless families in Border area, Project area and General area 31 per cent, 29 per cent and 10 per cent respectively. It is seen that out of the families owning land at least 35 per cent in Border area, 14 per cent in Project area and 11 per cent in General area were left fallon due to uneconomic return. In page 62 of the same economic survey of K & J Hills, it is stated that total rented area in Border area, Project area and General area is 675.52 acres, 265.23 acres and 49.36 acres respectively and similarly lands based out are respectively 25.41 acres, 91.56 acres and 16.75 acres goes to show that the owners of such land live outside the village. Absentee landlordism which was uncommon in tribal society has developed. Tribal social customary practices are being replaced by feudal practices.

Land in K & J Hills and in the hill mouzas of Garo Hills have not been cadestrally surveyed nor any record of right for each class of land has been prepared. Due to mass pressure organised by the Communist Party of India, the then APHLC government in 1976 had set up a Land Reform Commission (1) to enquire into and examine the various land systems and subsequent changes that have taken place. (2) To study the difficulties caused by lack of cadestral map and records of right and to examine the desirability of undertaking cadestral survey and preparation of records as well as to recommend appropriate measure. Subsequently, the recommendations were submitted to the Government and State Assembly passed law accordingly in 1980.

Entire Sixth Five Year Plan programme on land reforms in Meghalaya is based by and large on the Cadestral Survey Scheme as well as other land reforms measure thereafter. It was planned to cover the entire state within a period of 10-15 years. In a year 450 villages were expected to be covered. During the Sixth Five Year Plan it was proposed to cover 2300 villages but only 117 villages cadestrally surveyed and these were not mapped out even upto the end of Sixth Five Year Plan. For this, dismal result, the Government Department in charge of this programme put forward the argument for the inadequate provision of funds by the Government. But on further enquiry it is revealed that the proposal for fund was initiated only in the last part of 1985. It is also noteworthy that whatever fund was available was squandered away for unproductive things e.g. purchase of 2 printing machines, theodolites-47 numbers, huge quantity of cartridge paper-1584 reams, scholar paper-567 reams, tents-321 numbers, Tarpaulines-300 numbers. It is stated by the Deptt. that failure is due to opposition in East & West Khasi Hills but is silent about Jaintia & East and West Garo Hills. The plan outlay and target was fixed on the basis of functional capacity of the unsophisticated instruments and the staff for implementation was sanctioned accordingly.

Due to Abysmal failure of the government to prepare the right of records on the basis of cadestral survey, the bulk of the peasants of Meghalaya cannot avail the facility of cheap loan offered by the nationalised bank. Generally, the rich peasants with political backing get the bank loan which in turn is lent out at higher rate of interest to the share-croppers and poor peasants. The peasants generally borrow from money-lenders of local origin at 200-300 per cent for a period of 4-5 months, either in cash or kind. If one fails to return the loan during the stipulated period, the interest is added with the principal to become new principal. This system is prevalent throughout Meghalaya and most of War areas.

There is no up-to-date State Government record available to show the extent of rural indebtedness and its impact on the economy. But from the report of Rural Economic Surveys carried out in 1963 of Khasi & Jaintia Hills (page 62) it is seen that 62 per cent of the families in Border areas, 50 per cent in the Project area and 28 per cent in General area are heavily indebted. The same report says that it is the agriculturists and labouring families who constitute the list of indebted families. Although there is 'The Meghalaya Rural Indebtedness Relief Act, 1975' but the State Government did not take any action to popularise this Act amongst the rural population to enable them to take the help of this Act in case of necessity. Only in 1976, some peasants in 'Umroi' (Ri-Bhoi District) area got some relief through this Act, due to the timely intervention of Communist Party. The process of alienation of land is growing very fast throughout Meghalaya and rural indebtedness is also growing unabeted.

The Census report of 1951 records the existence of 906 non-cultivating owners of land and agricultural rent receivers in K & J Hills district. Similarly, it is seen from the Census report of 1951 and 1971 concerning the areas comprising the state of Meghalaya there has been phenomenal growth of agricultural labourer.

TABLE 34.1: **Growth of Agricultural Labourer**

	1951	1971
U.K. & J Hills	28994	33000
Garo Hills	—	10000

This is due to changes in socio-economic structure of tribal society resulting in concentration of land in the hands of few. The average size of operational holding in 1976-77 agricultural Census was 1.20 hectares in Meghalaya as against All India average of 2 hectares. On an analysis on industrial classification of 1961, 1971 and 1981 it will be seen that the proportion of cultivators to workers has fallen in Meghalaya. On the other hand, the proportion of agricultural labourers to working class has risen. The percentage of female agricultural labourers has increased at a rapid rate in Meghalaya vide Table 34.2.

TABLE 34.2: **Percentage Distribution of Main Workers by Cultivators, Agricultural Labourers and other Workers in Meghalaya**

	Cultivators			Agricultural labourers			Other workers		
	1961	1971	1981	1961	1971	1981	1961	1971	1981
P.	73.28	69.15	63.56	4.26	9.88	9.92	22.46	20.97	26.52
M.	66.61	63.35	59.08	4.00	9.34	9.20	29.39	27.11	31.72
F.	82.34	78.30	70.67	4.61	10.75	11.05	13.05	10.95	18.28

Source: Census of India, 1981, Paper-3, pp. 50-53.

P : Persons, M : Male, F : Female.

The Table 34.2 points out the fact that the percentage of female workers has increased at a rapid rate in Meghalaya, proportion of cultivators to total main workers has come down. At the same time the percentage of agricultural labourers has gone up. The condition of agricultural workers is worst. Govt. of Meghalaya have fixed the minimum wage Rs. 35 per day in 1994 but due to the absence of the enforcing authority, the benefit is not enjoyed by the workers in most cases. Even some state Govt. departments violate this provision.

In Meghalaya there are large number of share-cropper or Adhiars. Exact number is not known as no census has been undertaken. In 1974, when the land reform commission's report for Khasi and Jantia Hills was finalised it was observed that many land owners took back the land from Adhiars and got it cultivated through labourers, to prove that they were the owner cultivators. Uptill now there is no law to protect the rights of peasants. There is also no statutory recognised uniform pattern of sharing the crops between the landlord and the Adhiars. At present 2 systems viz. sharing the crop on 50:50 basis or on cash contract. In the 1st case the owner supplies the land and seed and the rest viz. tilling, harvesting, mowing and carrying the crop to the owner's house is Adhiar's duty. For supplying of bullock for cultivation, the Adhiar has to pay rent in kind and the rate varies from place to place. In case of loss of bullock the Adhiar has to pay compensation fixed by the owner. Cattle lifting is a big menace in the border areas and many peasants due to loss of bullocks have become agricultural workers. Since 1977, the landowners under Shela Wadedarship in East Khasi Hills, have introduced the system of paying *Selami* or popularly known as *Nazrana*. The rate of *Nazrana* is dependent on the quality of the land over and above *Tanka* for each harvest. In War area of Khasi Hills, it is also noticed that for getting land for sharecropping, one must agree to borrow money from the land-owner. It is also noted that the fertility of the land is constantly falling as neither the owner nor the share-cropper take any interest to improve the fertility of land and the share-cropper is not sure whether the same plot of land will be given to him for cultivation next year.

Process of concentration of land in the hands of few have

already started. Most of them do not cultivate themselves. There is no law in Meghalaya prohibiting eviction of peasants from land. Eviction of peasants is going unabated throughout Meghalaya society in Syiemship of Mawing, Mahajam, Bhawal, Malai and Sardarship of Duara, Mawlong, and Shella Wadedarship in Khasi Hills. The reasons for such eviction are generally the inability to return the loan in time extension of irrigation facilities, disposal of land to avoid future ceiling law etc. various harrassing methods are also adopted e.g. increase of house tax, on agricultural land tax on cattle head etc. As per 6th Schedule land is under District Council and no other authority can impose any tax on land or cattle heads etc. These were brought to the notice of the Government of Meghalaya and Khasi Hills District Council but of no avail. I am giving one example to show how tribal customary law is being voilated by richer section of the tribal people. Mynsoin village is in Ri Bhoi district of Meghalaya. In this village out of 90 families only 6 have land for cultivation. But the major portion of paddy growing lands are in the hands of persons not residing in Mynsain village. These lands are 'Raj land' and as per Khasi customary law, cannot be settled with any non-resident. The present owner of the land in question acquired from other non-resident owner under the system known by 'Luksan' which means that the former owner is supposed to have invested some money for reclamation of that land. Thus he incurred some loss in the scope and the present owner paid compensation to the former to acquire the land. But Khasi customary law prohibits sale/transfer of 'Raj land' to non-resident of the village. Generally, it is to be surrendered to the village Durbar which in turn shall distribute it amongst the landless residents of the village. Slowly feudalism is growing in the tribal land system.

From a study of main agricultural production viz. rice, jute, mesta, wheat and cotton *vis-a-vis* acreage under cultivation from 1978-83 it is found that rice production rate per hectare is constantly falling due to failure to procure improved variety of seed, absence of irrigation facilities and dependence on nature etc.

Similarly in case of jute and mesta, production is good but acreage under cultivation constantly falling because of failure to get remunerative price *vis-a-vis* the high cost of production.

Cotton production increased per hectare and area under cultivation also increased. But do not get the remunerative price. No Government initiative to market the produce. Middle man rules the root. Same is the case with cash crop growers whole production also increased but due to absence of any Government machinery to market the produce the growers are compelled to sell at unremunerative price causing the farmers to sell their produce at the middleman dictated price.

That is why the number of people in Meghalaya below poverty line has increased to 64 per cent from 50 per cent in 1971.

35

VICTIMS OF POVERTY
A Case Study of the Scheduled Castes of Assam

R.P. ATHPARIA and D.N. PANDEY

Introduction

According to the Scheduled Castes and Scheduled Tribes orders (Amendment) Act, 1976 there are sixteen Scheduled Castes communities in Assam. These are: Bansphor, Bhuimali/ Mali, Brittal Banka/Bania, Dhupi/Dhobi, Hira, Jalkeot, Jhalo/ Malo/Jhalo-Malo, Kaibartha/Jaliya, Lalbegi, Mahara, Mehtor/ Bhangi, Muchi/Rishi, Namasudra, Patni and Sutradhar.

As per 1991 Census, the total Scheduled Castes population in Assam is 16,59,412 persons according to 7.4 per cent of the total population of the state. The highest concentration is found in Nowgaon district (1,89,693 persons) followed by Cachar district (1,78,624 persons), Kamrup district (1,50,743 persons) and Karimganj district (1,20,602 persons). Tinsukia district shows the lowest concentration with 25,137 persons while North Cachar district has 3,198 persons and Karbi Anglong with 27,991 persons. The 1991 Census also shows that the Scheduled Castes population is 13.82 per cent in the urban areas as compared to 11.11 per cent for the State as a whole.

Out of the sixteen Scheduled Castes, some are indigenous and they are distinguished as Assamese Scheduled Castes. Others are non-Assamese. The Assamese Scheduled Castes are: Brittal Banka/Bania, Dhopi/Dhobi, Dugla/Dholi, Hira, Jalkeot,

TABLE 35.1: **Statewise Total, Scheduled Caste and Scheduled Tribe Population of the North Eastern India (1991 Census)**

Sl.No.	State	Population		
		Total	SC	ST
1.	Arunachal Pradesh	864,558	4,052	550,351
			(0.47)	(63.66)
2.	Assam	22,414,322	1,659,412	2,874,441
			(7.40)	(12.82)
3.	Manipur	1,837,149	37,105	632,173
			(2.02)	(34.41)
4.	Meghalaya	1,774,778	9,072	1,517,927
			(0.51)	(85.53)
5.	Mizoram	689,756	691	653,565
			(0.10)	(94.75)
6.	Nagaland	1,209,546	—	1,060,822
				(87.70)
7.	Tripura	2,757,205	451,116	853,345
			(16.48)	(30.95)
		31,547,314	2,161,448	8,142,624
			(6.85)	(25.81)

Kaibartha and Mali. The Bansphor, Lalbegi, Mahara, Mehtor/ Bhangi are non-indigenous Scheduled Castes of Assam. They are non-agriculturists group and have no scope for acquiring any land for agriculture. They are generally under the employ of Municipal bodies of different towns. The Muchis/Rishis are also not indigenous Scheduled Castes. They are mostly from Bihar and engage themselves in leather-work. They move from place to place and do their daily business on leather-made things like shoe repairing and manufacturing at certain convenient places of urban and semi-urban areas. They do not possess any permanent land for residential purposes. They live in the hired residential houses. Though the Bhuimali is listed as Scheduled Caste in Assam but there is no record of such community in Assam. The Namasudra Patni, Sutradhar and Jhalo-Malo, who are included in the list of Scheduled Caste of

Assam, are Bengali speaking communities and mostly concentrated in the Barak Valley districts.

In this chapter an attempt has been made to discuss some problems which are considered to be the core problems of poverty, unemployment and homelessness.

Land Holding

Land is the basic item of the rural folk. Its ownership, size and use determines the economy of a household. Therefore, umemployment and poverty tend to vary with the size of the land holding. As per 1985-96 agricultural census, Assam has 24,19,200 number of operational holdings belonging to all social groups of the people with a total area under operational holdings of 31,61,500 hectares. Out of the total land holdings, 1,14,500 (i.e. 4.73%) only belong to Scheduled Castes which is much lower than the population percentage. Only 4.08 per cent area is operated by the Scheduled Castes. It is also noted in the same Census that the average size of operational holding is 1.31 hectares for all social groups. It is only 1.13 hectares for the Scheduled Castes (C.E. Neog 1995:3). The said Census also shows that most of the Scheduled Caste are marginal farmers (60.3%) operating only 26.3 per cent of the land. The marginal and small farmers of the Scheduled Castes together account to 84.7 per cent operating 56.6 per cent of the agricultural land. Neog (1995:4) states that the farms below two hectares of land are non-viable. Hence, these marginal and the small farmers who possess below two hectares of land suffer from poverty and unemployment specially during the non-agricultural seasons.

Occupation

A number of Scheduled Castes communities of Assam pursue agriculture as their major occupation. They engage themselves in cultivation during the cultivation season keeping other months in other occupations. Bania (1995:21) opines that "many of these people are landless—their holdings are limited to 5 bighas per family—the production of which is not sufficient for maintenance of a family. They are also financially extremely weak. They subsidise their maintenance expenditure out of petty fish business". The Scheduled Castes who fall in this category are: Jalkeot, Kaibartha, Namasudra, Patni and Sutradhar. Some of them have no residential plot even. It is on record that the Government of Assam once decided and promised to allot 40 bighas of land to some of the Scheduled Castes for residential purpose of Guwahati. But it was not materialised so far due to some technical reasons (Bania 1995:21). It is a fact that the production from the limited cultivable land of 5 bighas is not at all sufficient for the Scheduled Castes people to maintain the family. So many of them take to Marakia system of cultivation on half to half harvest share. But this system is also gradually disappearing from the society as the land holders are themselves cultivating their land with the help of improved variety of seeds, fertilizer and loan for plough etc. from the Agriculture Department.

Next to agriculture, fishing is an important occupation of most of the indigenous Scheduled Castes of Assam. It is practised mostly by Kaibartha, Jalia, Namasudra and Jhalo-Malo. Earlier, fish catching and selling was exclusively done by the above communities only. But now, the fishermen from other states have taken over this age-old trade from the indigenous fishermen communities of Assam. Moreover, some affluent persons from the fishermen communities began to patronise this trade. Sharma Thakur (1995:95) states that "even those poor Kaibartas who are clinging to this traditional business in spite of the odds, are suffering from the 60:40 syndrome, i.e. a sizeable share of the catch has to be given to the Mahajans who provide the capital. The Mahajans lend money to the fishermen on that for small catches, the fishermen have to pay 40 per cent to the Mahajans and for bigger catches their percentage is 60. The poor fishermen have no alternative but to agree to the terms of the Mahajans. It is also observed that the fishing sources like rivers, beels etc. are not accessible to the poor fishermen as the same are auctioned to the big traders or Mahajans who generally prefer the fishermen of other states than to the local ones. Consequently, the local fishermen are suffering from the economic hardship.

It is noteworthy to mention here that the local fishermen are exploited by the middle men (*dalals*). For improving the economic status of the fishermen communities, the Assam Government has taken up a number of development schemes, like Fishery Development Corporation, Fish Farming Development Agencies and Fishery Co-operative Societies. Government of Assam has also established a Fishery College at Raha, in Nowgaon district for upgrading and to train the unemployed fishermen and enthusiastic young boys in this profession. In spite of all these attempts, the fishermen are not benefited out of it. They are still in the poverty line.

One more traditional occupation of the Scheduled Caste people of Assam is goldsmithy. It was the chief occupation of the Bania/Brittal Bania since time immemorial. Now, this profession has taken up by other caste groups. It is on record that this noble profession was encouraged by the Ahom Kings and the Banias were allowed to access to the inner apartment of the Ahom Kings and the Queens (C.F. Bania 1995:25). The Banias are not only goldsmith but they are expert in silversmiths also. Before the influx of outsiders on this trade, the Banias were the main source of supply of gold and silver ornaments to the people of Assam. But at present, the Banias have almost left this profession.

Another sadest occupation of the Scheduled Castes of Assam is the pottery industry. This occupation is confined to the Hiras only. They have been carrying this occupation for their livelihood since the past. No alternative source of income was obtained by them as they got a good earning from this occupation. Earlier, they used to produce some particular earthen pots for cooking and other use for the common people, which have been replaced now by the modern metallic utensils and equipments available in the market.

In the past, the Hiras used to exchange their products in terms of food and others in the barter system. As they were happy with the traditional occupation, they did not feel for any other occupation other than the pottery industry. They were even not engaged in cultivation and its related occupation in the past. As such, the Hiras have neither cultivable land nor any other base for engagement. But now the Hiras are facing some problems in collecting the raw materials popularly known as 'Hira Clay'. This clay is found in some specific areas of Goalpara, Kamrup, Darrang and Nowgaon districts. Since

British period the Hiras used to collect the 'Hira Clay' from the specified clay fields or *bathans* at free of cost without any obstruction. Now, there has been a serious problem to the Hiras to collect the clay from the *bathans* as most of the clay areas have been occupied by some occupants who obstruct the potters to collect the clay. Due to non-availability of the 'Hira Clay' the pottery industry has become almost dead. Besides this, there are some other problems of the Hiras like housing, education and unemployment. By and large, the Hiras live below the poverty line.

Conclusion

There is no denying fact that the Scheduled Castes people of Assam are socially and economically very poor. Social backwardness is due to certain socio-cultural factors which make them neglected by others. Economic backwardness is due to the dependence on the indigenous occupations. However, growth of population, sub-division and fragmentation of land holding, pressure of population, tough competition from machine-made goods, lack of technical knowledge of modern system of production, lack of capital money, influx of outsiders on the trade once solely meant for Scheduled Castes are the main causes of poverty, homelessness and unemployment among the Scheduled Castes of Assam.

REFERENCES

Bania, N. 1995: "Identification of existing occupation of S.C. People and problems connected with their improvement and ungradation." In *Core Problems of the Scheduled Castes of Assam.* Edited by Bimal Kumar Hazarika, Guwahati Assam Institute of Research for Tribals and Scheduled Caste.

Neog, A.K. 1995: "Problems of the Scheduled Castes of Assam and Plans for Development". In *Core Problems of the Scheduled Castes of Assam.* Edited by Bimal Kumar Hazarika, Guwahati Assam Institute of Research for Tribals and Scheduled Castes.

Sharma, Thakur G.C. 1995: "An insight into the core problems of the Scheduled Castes of Assam". In *Core Problems of the Scheduled Castes of Assam.* Edited by Bimal Kumar Hazarika, Guwahati Assam Institute of Research for Tribals and Scheduled Castes.

36

LITERACY SCENARIO OF NAGALAND

PREMLATA DEVI

Nagaland is a hilly state of North-East India. It is situated between 25°06' N and 27°04' N latitudes and 93°20' E and 95°15' E longitudes. The state is surrounded by Arunachal Pradesh in the north, Myanmar in the east, Manipur in the south and Assam in the west. It has an area of 16,579 sq. km. supporting a total population of 12,09,546 (1991 Census) with an average density of 73 persons per sq. km. Nagaland comprises of seven districts and has low accessibilities within the districts as well as poor link with other states of North East India.

Various Naga tribes of Nagaland belong to Indo-Mongoloid stock of Tibeto-Burman linguistic group. In Nagaland, there are as many as 25 communities of people staying together out of those communities 14 belong to the Naga constellation of tribes. Besides these there are three other non-Naga inhabitants of Nagaland who are recognised as Scheduled Tribes of the state. They are Kacharis, Garos and Karbis. The rest are migrant communities accounting for a small fraction of Nepali, Bengali, Bihari, Rajasthani and Assamese etc.

The Nagas do not have their own script but use Roman script as their official language. In order to facilitate verbal communication amongst themselves they adopted 'Nagamese' language which is only a broken form of Assamese language. Hence 'Nagamese' becomes a communicative media among the Nagas.

Despite serious language problem, accentuated by

difficult terrain and overwhelmingly rural composition of its population, Nagaland ranks second position in the North-Eastern Region and thirteenth position in the country as a whole as far as the literacy rate is concerned.

The Census of India, 1991, accords literacy status to 'one who could read and write with understanding in any of the languages.' The effective literacy rate have been defined as that population which attains seven years of age and above. Out of the total population (12,09,546) of Nagaland, 10,02,059 persons are in the age group of seven years and above.[1] Within this age groups as many as 6,17,736 persons are literates constituting 61.65 per cent. The decadal increase of literacy rate between the year 1981-1991 is 11.37 per cent against the decadal growth rate of population +56.08 per cent.

Nagaland comprises of seven districts viz., Kohima, Phek, Zunheboto, Wokha, Mokokchung, Tuensang and Mon. Table 36.1 represents districtwise literacy rates of Nagaland (1991 Census) for the persons seven years and above. It indicates that Mokokchung is the most literate district (77.85%) whereas Mon accounts for the lowest proportion of the literates (36.02%; Fig. 36.1). Gender disparity in literacy is quite evident with male literacy being as high as 67.62 per cent against 54.75 per cent female literates (Table 36.1). Urban literacy rate (83.10%) too is much above the rate attained by the rural area which is as low as 57.23 per cent. Though this hilly state is poor in road communication, but three nodal centres like Mokokchung, Wokha and Kohima somewhat have had good linkage with the plains of Assam. This, probably one of the causes of higher literacy rate (Fig. 36.2).

An analysis of individual group of Naga tribes reveals that the Aos are the most literate group among all the Naga tribes (Fig. 36.3). Their literacy rate is 93.52 per cent. On the other hand, the Sangtam tribe has the lowest literate tribes of 67.68 per cent.[2] This indicates that most tribal groups in Nagaland are close to attaining total literacy. Table 36.2 shows that all the tribes of Nagaland will achieve the 85 per cent literacy rate which is considered as total literacy as per the norms set by National Literacy Mission of India. Concerted efforts, however, has to be initiated to check the growth rate of population of Nagaland which is the highest in the century

TABLE 36.1: **Districtwise Literacy Rates of Nagaland**

(in percentage)

State/District	Total	Male	Female	Rural	Urban
1. Kohima	69.16	75.58	61.41	62.68	83.83
2. Phek	62.59	72.28	51.34	60.93	81.62
3. Zunheboto	64.36	70.76	57.63	61.93	83.12
4. Wokha	73.92	81.06	65.99	70.97	88.05
5. Mokokchung	77.85	80.52	74.88	76.07	87.65
6. Tuensang	48.39	53.98	41.98	45.74	76.48
7. Mon	36.02	41.90	29.10	33.39	70.96
8. Nagaland	61.65	67.62	54.75	57.23	83.10
9. India	52.21	64.20	39.19	44.69	73.08

Source: Census of India, 1991, Series-I, Paper 2.

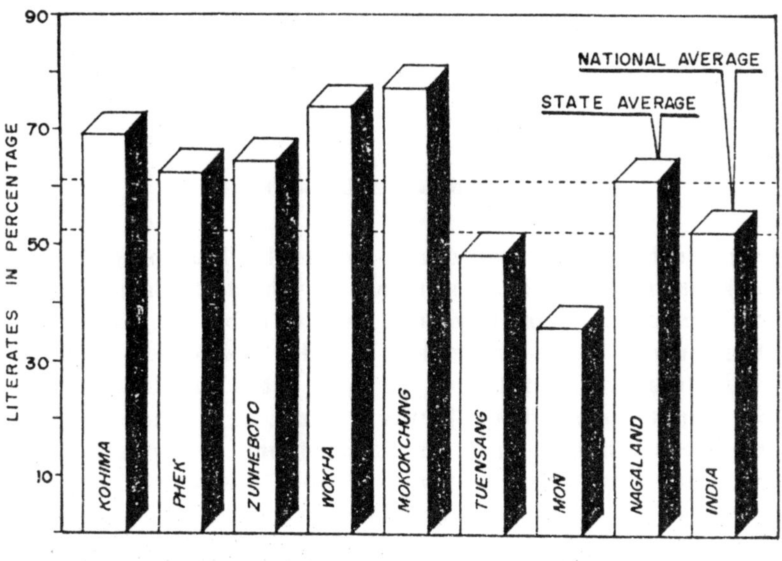

FIG. 36.1: Literacy Rates of Nagaland (Districtwise, 1991)

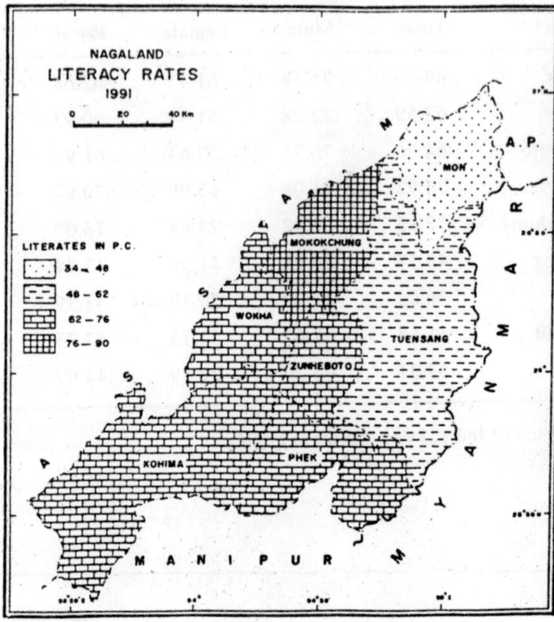

FIG. 36.2: Nagaland—Literacy Rates

registered during the last decade (1981-91).[3] Flow of illiterate migrants from outside the state may have hindered the progress of literacy rate in Nagaland. Noble effort of Christian Missionaries in pre-independent period who extended medical and educational facilities to the Naga tribes was the dynamo for initial literacy drive. It was regarded as 'fashionable' to become a Christian and get educated and westernised.[4] In addition there are as many as 1200 Government Primary Schools at present in Nagaland whose contribution is considered to be impressive in increasing present literacy rate.[5]

A recent endeavour of National Literacy Mission (NLM) of India through active participation of State Resource Centre, North-Eastern Hill University (NEHU) is another milestone

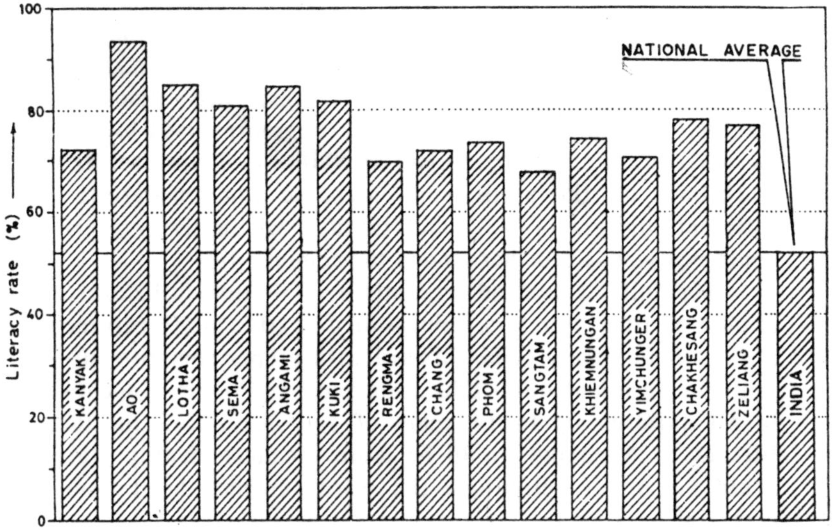

FIG. 36.3: Literacy Rates of Naga Tribes

TABLE 36.2: **Number of Different Tribal Language Speakers, Illiterates, Literates and their Literacy Rates of the Nagaland**

Groups of Tribes Language Speaker	No. of Speakers	No. of Illiterates	No. of Literates	Literacy Rate (%)
1. Kanyak	1,49,649	41,880	1,07,769	72.01
2. Ao	1,58,374	10,250	1,48,124	93.52
3. Lotha	82,612	12,548	70,064	84.81
4. Sema	96,218	18,480	77,738	80.79
5. Angami	98,525	15,420	83,105	84.34
6. Kuki	28,832	5,360	23,472	81.40
7. Rengma	38,512	11,630	26,882	69.80
8. Chang	43,699	12,313	31,386	71.82
9. Phom	49,247	13,074	36,173	73.45
10. Sangtam	52,610	17,003	35,607	67.68
11. Khiemnungan	38,390	9,940	28,450	74.10
12. Yimchunger	42,845	12,560	30,285	70.68
13. Chakhesang	1,02,516	22,845	79,671	77.71
14. Zeliang	60,085	14,110	45,975	76.52
Total	10,42,114	2,17,413	8,24,701	79.14

Source: Directorate of School Education, Kohima, Nagaland, 1993.

towards achieving the target of total literacy. Under the IPCL (Improved Pace and Content of Learning) materials programme, number of batches representing almost all linguistic group have attended workshops organised by State Resource Centre (SRC), NEHU at Shillong. In the series of workshops all the participants prepared study materials in different dialects of Nagaland through which literacy drive could be extended further among the communities.

Hopefully, Nagaland will attain total literacy before the stipulated time. For this, Education Department, Government of Nagaland should come forward with proper commitment of implementation of Adult Education and free Primary Education to all children up to 14 years of age. Attainment of total literacy in Nagaland would be more precious identity which could be able to eliminate the word 'dreaded head hunter Nagas of Nagaland'.

NOTES

1. Census of India 1991, *Final Population Tables,* Series I, Paper 2 of 1992.
2. Directorate of School Education, Kohima, Nagaland, 1993.
3. Census of India 1991, *Final Population Tables,* Series I, Paper 2 of 1992.
4. *People of India, Nagaland,* Vol. XXXIV, ed. K.S. Singh & *et al.*, Anthropological Survey of India, Seagull Books, Calcutta, 1994, p. 24.
5. Issued by the Directorate of Information and Public Relations, Nagaland, Kohima.

37

WHITHER "HABITABILITY"
A Note on Environmental Sanitation and Urbanization

A.C. MOHAPATRA

The Great Transformation

At this vantage of the twenty-first century, when there is a great deal of enthusiasm on the emergence of a "global village", within this village is a great urban transformation, silently but steadily. Of the 6 billion inhabitants of this village, 42 per cent live in urban centres. The projection (UNO) is for over 50 per cent urbanization level by the turn of the century. The impetus for this steady and fast urban transformation do not come from the developed and urbanized world of the west but from the developing world. Only in a handful of the emerging economies that the urban transformation is associated with an economic upsurge, in the rest it is ecological degradation, desertification, war, famine, a stagnant agriculture which has resulted in uprooting the people in their owned journey to towns and cities.

The ongoing HABITAT-II (The UN Conference at Istambul, Turkey) which was inaugurated recently by the Secretary General Dr. Boutous B. Ghali emphasised the global concern on the question of "habitability" of the cities, especially in the LCDs where growing urban poverty, lack of resources and urban management issues have led to cardinal decline in the quality of life in the urban areas.

In India the situation is no different. Of the 844 million

people (1991) 217 million live in urban areas. Perhaps another 200 million depend wholly on the urban areas for their daily living about which the Indian Census is silent (due to the methodology of enumeration by place of residence). This amounts to 27 per cent of the population living in urban areas (some 40001) and another 20 per cent depending directly on the urban centres without a place to live there due to either shortage of space or high cost of living. Though compared to the 1971-81 decade when the overall urban growth was 46 per cent, the 1981-91 decade has witnessed an apparent slow down (36%), the fact remains that people who are otherwise urbanized (by their activities/occupations) have found a different solution to acute space constraints in urban centres by deciding to stay back in villages of their residence but commute to the urban centres for their vocations and living. Even within the 217 million urban population nearly one third is below the officially stated poverty line. May be another one third are on the perilous margin.

The situation in the 23 million + cities and 300 class I cities can safely be said as appalling. Forty to fifty per cent of the inhabitants in large cities live in slums, roughly two third live in one room tenements, without any civic amenities like water, sanitation etc. The various urban poverty alleviation programmes of the government life EIUS, LCS, NRY, UBSP & PMUPEP (for Class II towns) have at best touched the urban question in the country on the surface only. The paradigm has been that of containment.

The Bubble

The apparent urban implosion which most of the LCDs are going through has telling effect on the urban environment itself, therefore, on the general quality of the urban habitat as well as the lives of the citizens. India is no exception. Of course, it is widely acknowledged that the global environment as a whole is under serious threat in recent times, but the process within the LCDs are even worse. There is lack of awareness, political will, outright greed and above all the sheer lack of resources to undertake remedial measures or even preventive actions. The problem in the urban areas is further accentuated due to the fact that the population densities and the nature of urban circulation systems are many times higher than the rural habitat and thus requires much careful habitat planning and civic service systems commensurate with the specific requirement. These require large resources, participation and consent of the citizens. For reasons which are well-known by now, the city governments rarely functioned in this country. The municipal acts were archaic and lost their relevance in the changing circumstances. There were umpteen interference in the functioning of the city governments and approach was that of direct administration by the concerned state governments. There was no initiative, no incentive and no effort to generate resource of the cities. Whatever little grant came from the government went towards paying salaries of the ever burgeoning municipal staff without the services. The thing has come to such a pass, it is unsustainable without a serious soul searching and creating institutional and financial arrangements keeping in view the changing reality and needs. The urban bubble has already burst in the plague outbreak in Surat and other towns and cities in the country in recent times.

The 74th Constitutional Amendments (The Nagar Palika Act, 1993), was brought as one of the responses where a statutory institutional structure and financing was for the first time introduced for the city governments. Apart, from a major philosophical shift towards emphasizing peoples participation, the reinforced agenda for the city governments also include the city environment and poverty alleviation, the latter two are intricately linked with each other.

The North-East Scenario

The North-Eastern region of the country consisting of the seven sisters (Arunachal Pradesh, Assam, Manipur, Meghalaya, Mizoram, Nagaland and Tripura) is the least urbanized region of the country with the overall level of urbanization around 14 per cent compared to the 26 per cent for the country. But the recent processes indicate a faster change in the situation, especially in some of the constituent states like Mizoram which moved from 24 per cent in 1981 to 46 per cent in 1991, Manipur with 28 per cent urbanization etc. Due to lack of any impressive industrialization process the level is still low but is likely to change quickly in the future. The current impact on urbanization comes from the process of administrative and commercial expansions in the region.

Of the 150 odd towns and cities of the region, there is no semblance of urban local bodies (with the perhaps, exception of Tripura), particularly in the Sixth Schedule areas where the 74th Constitutional Amendments have no immediate relevance. Even in other areas (e.g. Assam) the ULB elections are yet to be completed. The ULBs have no resources and have to entirely depend on the meagre government grants. The planners have no statutory powers on land use restrictions and, therefore, no possibility of remedial planning interventions, least of all taking of new projects. The report of NIUA (1988) on the urbanization and urban development in the North-Eastern Region sponsored by NEC very clearly indicates the problems associated with the urban infrastructure, urban finance and urban management in region. But there appears, no state in the region has taken up the recommendations of the report with any degree of seriousness. Under the circumstances, the situation is getting difficult day by day. With accentuation of the process of urbanization in the coming decades, the question of habitability and the quality of urban centres of the region will remain a big question and a great risk to the inhabitants. (An Example is the outbreak of cholera in Aizawl in 1994 which took 13 lives).

The Blue Print

It is to be appreciated that preventive measures are more effective and cheaper than remedial interventions. The overall level of urbanization in region is practically half of the national average and most of the towns and cities are still small and, therefore, planning interventions are possible with greater effectiveness. Many of the towns/cities in the region have a great natural advantage of being located in verdant hills with unequal scenic beauties and could, if well managed turn into great tourist attraction and a resource for the people and their economic development. But could these be achieved without the participation of people and they being at the forefront of managing their own towns/cities? If they do not participate, they have no interest in augmenting the cities resources, be it holding taxes or other levies. The question of economic liberalization. Performance incentives can act as a great catalyst to internal competition between urban centres in a state and for resource mobilization, if urban local bodies become focus of participation of the citizens. This needs great political will and courage to face the issue head on and not become complacent and allow the situation to deteriorate day by day. The 74th Amendments holds a hope, it may succeed, it may fail but it must be given a chance. In a situation when the states are chronically short of resources, it would be absurd to expect them to shell out large resources for urban development. Ultimately the cities ought to cater to their own needs. Experiences from Patna and some Tamil Nadu towns indicates that tax rationalization and compliance could greatly enhance the city's resources. But this may not be feasibly without grassroot participation. The blue print for the North-Eastern urban centres can be based on policies on the following areas:

(i) Grassroot participation.
(ii) Empowerment of the ULBs.
(iii) Close working of the administration/city managers with the citizens.
(iv) Public awareness.
(v) Demonstrating the benefits of urban planning in terms of income generation and employment to the benefits of the citizens.
(vi) Liberalization of municipal services, including private participation.
(vii) Empowering urban planners in strict enforcement of urban land use.

Time is short and is running out. Adequate and urgent political action is necessary if a beginning is to be made in direction of developing habitable cities in the region and make cities catalytic in the overall development of the region.

38

WATER POLLUTION AND ITS TREATMENT

K.K. DWIVEDI

Introduction

"Water, water everywhere and not a drop to drink." The day may not be far off when these words might be on everybody's lips. In a country like ours where the perenial rivers are continuously fed by the melting snows of the Himalayas, we should still bear this in mind that only 1 per cent of the total water available on this planet is potable water or sweet water, the rest being either saline or locked in polar ice-caps and glaciers. Keeping in view the burgeoning population, we should not be so complacent about this problem. The need of the hour is to conserve our limited resources and as far as possible to recycle the waste water for human consumption and other useful purposes.

In order to do this we first need to have a clear idea of the major pollutants that may be present in water and how they could be effectively removed. Macroscopic pollutants which can be seen with the naked eye can be easily separated, but one may worry about the microscopic and dissolved pollutants which are of great concern due to their adverse effects on health. It may be noted that a large majority of diseases are water-borne and a proper purification of water could help in providing better and healthy living to a large population.

The sketch shown in Fig. 38.1 effectively portrays the dilemma faced by the common man regarding water pollution. How safe is our drinking water? What are the types of pollutants present in it? How can they be removed? These and many other questions are at the uppermost in everybody's mind.

FIG. 38.1: "When Water is a Killer" —Think and be Aware!

The Nature of Pollutants in Water

Before we address ourselves to the task of purifying water we should know what are the major pollutants of water.

The major water pollutants can be broadly classified under the following categories:

1. Organic pollutants.
2. Inorganic pollutants.
3. Sediments.

4. Radioactive materials.
5. Thermal pollutants.

Organic Pollutants

These include oxygen-demanding wastes, disease causing agents, plant nutrients, sewage, synthetic organic compounds and oil. They also comprise insecticides and pesticides and phenolic compounds.

Inorganic Pollutants

These comprise inorganic salts, mineral acids, finely divided metals or metal compounds, trace elements and organometallic compounds. There is a very real problem regarding inorganic pollutants involves acid mine drainage especially from abandoned coal-mines. Another major inorganic pollutant is the presence of phosphate in water. Phosphate pollutants are discharged into the water mainly through detergents. A detergent or a surfactant molecule consists of two parts—a polar and a non-polar part. While the polar part attracts the charged particles the non-polar part removes the grease or oil. This solubilises dirt which can then be removed by rinsing. Though detergents facilitate washing they contain phosphates which are mainly added as 'builders' to maintain effective detergent action even in hard water. The phosphate pollution raises the pH of water and makes it caustic. Another main cause of worry is that they are so slowly bio-degradable that high concentrations build up with time.

Sediments

These represent the most extensive pollutants of surface water. As a rough estimate suspended solid loadings in natural waters are about 700 times as large as the solid loadings from sewage discharge. Sediments and suspended particles are also important repositories of trace metals like Cr, Cu, Mg etc.

Radioactive Materials

Nuclear weapons testing in air, leakage from underground

nuclear detonations give rise to a nuclear fall out. Nuclear power plants generate (a) low level radioactive liquid wastes, (b) liquid and gaseous wastes from fuel elements (c) fission products, and (4) heat. Some of the common radionuclides found in aquatic environment are ^{226}Ra, ^{210}Pb, ^{85}Kr, ^{90}Sr, ^{131}I, ^{137}Cs, ^{144}Ce, ^{60}Co, ^{65}Zn, ^{46}Sc and isotopes of Uranium.

Thermal Pollution

Coal-fired or nuclear fuel-fired steam power plants are associated with thermal pollution. The increased water temperature leads to a lesser amount of dissolved oxygen in the water which adversely affects aquatic life.

Water Purification

After this overview on the different pollutants affecting the purity of water we now turn our attention to the methods which can be used to overcome these problems.

The important stages involved in the treatment of polluted waters are as follows:

(1) Coagulation or flocculation
(2) Sedimentation
(3) Filtration
(4) Disinfection
(5) Removal of Iron and Manganese
(6) Softening of water
(7) Prevention of Corrosion
(8) Taste and odour removal
(9) Flouridation
(10) Phosphate removal
(11) Removal of Radioactive.

Coagulation

The principal coagulants used in water treatment consist of aluminium sulphate, ferric chloride, ferrous sulphate etc. The important reactions in floc formation are the following:

$$Al_2(SO_4)_3 + 3\ Ca(HCO_3)_2 \rightarrow 3CaSO_4 + 2Al(OH)_3 + 6CO_2$$

$$Al_2(SO_4)_3 + 3\ Ca(OH)_2 \rightarrow 3CaSO_4 + 2Al(OH)_2$$

The reaction with ferric chloride coagulation process is

$$2FeCl_3 + 3Ca\ (HCO_3)_2 \rightarrow 3CaCl_2 + Fe\ (OH)_3 + 6CO_2$$

$$2FeCl_3 + 3Ca\ (OH)_2 \rightarrow 3CaCl_2 + 2Fe\ (OH)_3$$

while with $FeSO_4$ the reaction is

$$FeSO_4 + Ca\ (HCO_3)_2 \rightarrow Fe\ (OH)_2 + CaSO_4 + 2CO_2$$

$$FeSO_4 + Ca\ (OH)_2 \rightarrow Fe\ (OH)_2 + CaSO_4$$

A substantial advancement has been made in the field of synthetic coagulants or polyelectrolytes as without proper coagulation sedimentation will be difficult.

Sedimentation

Though this does not involve any chemical process it is nevertheless an important aspect of water treatment. This is a physical process of the settling of floc. Sedimentation may occur within 15-60 minutes after vigorous stirring. The settling tanks have various shapes and sizes—there may be horizontal flow, circular flow or static settling tanks.

Filtration

The main role of filters is to retain the particles contained in a liquid on the surface of the filter or in depth. Surface filtration requires supporting media while indepth filtration is performed through a filter bed. The real filtration takes place in the first 3-4 cm in a total filter bed of 80 cm.

Disinfection

This involves the elimination of taste and smell and the destruction of pathogenic micro-organism and is usually done by chlorination, ozonolysis or by UV light treatment. The disinfecting gas kills virus, bacteria and germs from the water. The cheapest and most common method of disinfection is by using chlorine gas but through experience we know that it imparts some unwanted odour and taste to the water.

Removal of Iron and Manganese

These two elements need to be removed from drinking water as they cause corrosion of pipes, and impart a metallic taste to drinking water. Water containing > 2 ppm Fe causes staining of clothes and porcelain. These metals are normally removed after peptisation or oxidation which is normally done by aeration or by reaction with Cl_2, ClO_2, $KMnO_4$ etc. A dose of 2.5 mg/l ClO_2, 1.9 mg/l $KMnO_4$ and 0.87 mg/l O_3 can be used.

$$Mn^{2+} + O_3 + H_2O \rightarrow MnO_2 + O_2 + 2H^+$$

$$3Mn^{2+} + 2MnO_4^- + 2H_2O \rightarrow 5MnO_2 + 4H^+$$

If these metals are present in small quantities then they are removed by an ion exchange method using zeolites.

Softening of Water

As we all know soft water forms lather with soap easily while hard water does not. This hardness is caused due to the soluble salts of Ca and Mg. Hard water may be softened either by the Lime-Soda Ash process or by deionisation.

Prevention of Corrosion

The first step in this direction is to control the pH. An alkaline pH prevents the corrosion of pipes seams. It is also possible to prevent corrosion by reducing the oxygen content of water. Corrosion inhibitors like Na_2SiO_3 nitrites and chromates can also be added to the water.

Taste and Odour Removal

An obnoxious odour or taste renders water unfit for drinking purposes. Dissolved organic substances such as phenols, sulphides, chloroamines and chlororganics cause odour. Algal decay also produces foul smell. These can be removed in a number of ways like aeration, coagulation, chlorination and application of certain chemicals like activated carbon, ClO_2, O_3, $KMnO_4$ and others. Activated carbon is the most prefered reagent as it not only removes odour but also the colour of water, however its only drawback is that it cannot be regenerated.

Flouridation

A small quantity of fluorine (0.4-1 mg/l) in water promotes formation of dental enamel and protects against caries. However, excess of fluoride (> 1.5 mg/l) is dangerous to health as it leads to destruction of enamel and causes fluorosis-leading to dental disorder, decalification, mineralisation of tendons, digestive and nervous disorders. Excess of fluoride may be removed by treating water with $Ca_3(PO_4)_2$, $Al_2O_3SiO_3$ or $Ca(OH)_2$ or filtration through activated carbon.

Phosphate Removal

There are two approaches to phosphate removal. One method is to reduce the phosphate content of the detergents and add a non-phosphate 'builder' to the detergents. The second method is the physical removal of phosphate and this method employs simple procedure by addition lime, alum or by using iron coagulation.

$$5Ca^{2+} + 4OH^- + 3HPO_4^{2-} \rightarrow Ca_5(PO_4)_3(OH) + 3H_2O$$

$$Al_2(SO_4)_3 + 2PO_4^{3-} \rightarrow 2AlPO_4 + 3SO_4^{2-}$$

$$FeCl_3 + PO_4^{3-} \rightarrow FePO_4 + 3Cl^-$$

These methods can effectively remove about 90 per cent of the phosphate.

Removal of Radioactive Pollutants

Radioactive nuclides are removed either by sorption - desorption process or by using special filters.

Exploitation of Micro-Organisms for Treatment of Polluted Water

Micro-organisms are sometimes also used for cleaning polluted waters. This is mainly done through adsorption, intracellular uptake and chemical transformations.

Adsorption: Adsorption of metal ions takes place due to a negative charge present on the cell wall or membrane of the micro-organism. The negative charge may be due to groups like PO_4^{3-}, COO^-, HS^-, OH^-, etc. The adsorption on the cell wall is rapid, reversible and independent of temperature and energy metabolism. *Saccharomyces Cerevisiae* (common beer yeast) and *Rhizopus Arrhizus* (a fungus) adsorp Uranium from waste water through this method.

Intracellular Uptake: It is dependent on the temperature and energy. A selective uptake of Mg^{2+}, Ca^{2+}, K^+, Na^+, SO_4^{2-} takes place and there is substitution of SO_4^{2-} by CrO_4^{2-}, SeO_4^{2-}, MgO_4^{2-}, VO_4^{2-} and WO_4^{2-} etc. A typical example of intracellular uptake is the *pseudomonas aeruginosa* which is a common soil and water bacterium. It virtually commits suicide by taking up about 56 per cent of its cell dry weight of Uranium which amounts to an accumulation of 100 mg/l of U-solution in 10 seconds.

Chemical Transformation: This involves precipitation, chelation and methylation. In the presence of *desulfovibrio* bacteria sulphate is reduced to hydrogen sulphide. The sulphide ions then combine with metal ions to precipitate metals as sulphides. Another method is chelation—a case in example is the filamentous bacterium and fungus (*C. Cladosporoides*) which encases suspended clay particles and thereby removes them.

A third method is removal of toxic metals such as Hg, Se,

Te, As, Sn, Pb, and Cd by bio-methylation whereby these metals are converted into volatile substances. However, the commercial applicability of bio-methylation is questionable.

A New Method of Water Purification

A new and innovative area of research in water purification in which my research group has been actively involved, has been in the production and application of nuclear track microfilters.

The nuclear track microfilters (NTMFs), can be prepared from thin films of suitable polymers. They are first bombarded by coolimated charged particles of high energy. The irradiated materials are then chemically etched in a suitable solution (e.g. NaOH for plastics or HF for mica) for a specified period of time till the pores are etched to a desired diameter. The diameters of the pores could be varied from 10 mm to 1 mm and accordingly a wide variety of pore sizes can be obtained.

Fig. 38.2 shows some magnified pores of a microfilter. The unique feature of these microfilters is that they can

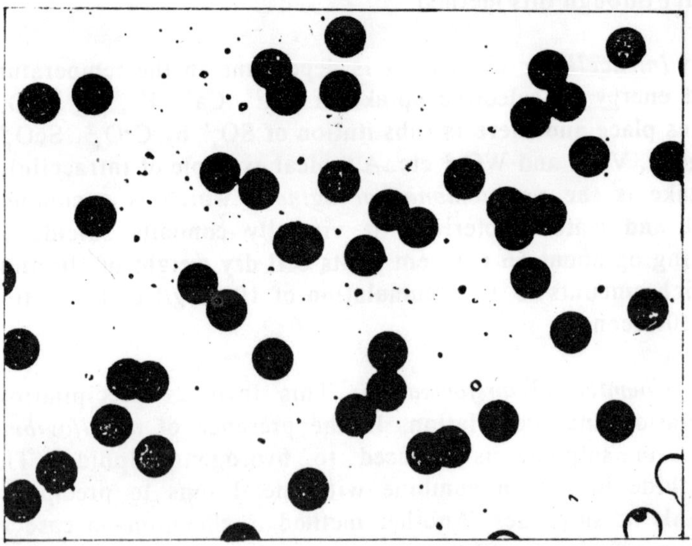

FIG. 38.2: A magnified view of a section of a nuclear track micro-filter prepared from polycarbonate (Makrofol-N) film

successfully filter out unwanted material including microscopic particles from drinking water without imparting any undesirable taste or smell. Micro-filters are very effective in selective removal of harmful bacteria from natural water to obtain pure drinking water. This also provides a cost-effective method (though the initial cost is a bit prohibitive) as each filter can be re-used a number of times for effective filtration or purification of water. This method is ideal for rural areas as no power supply is required to run it. As it can filter microscopic particles it will be effective in the desalination of water. This would provide the coastal areas with vast resources of drinking water.

Conclusion

"You never miss water till the well runs dry." This was an apt observation of Rowland Howard and so before we run out of our limited reserves of potable water we should seek methods through which this does not happen.

The conventional methods of water purification involves a number of steps and are being routinely used. The new method based on micro-filters can be employed to treat prefiltered natural wate to provide clean, odourless safe drinking water at a very minimal cost. A number of methods have now been made available through scientific advancement whereby major and trace pollutants in water can be assessed to a fair degree of accuracy.

An increased public awareness of the deleterious effects of different pollutants in water on the health of the populace and the environment would certainly pave the way to improve the quality of life. Public awareness could also tackle the problem at its root. This would go a long way in providing a better hygiene, an improved quality of life and help in preserving water—one of the most precious natural resources—which is vital for sustenance of life on this planet.

Acknowledgement

I should like to acknowledge the help of Dr. Swarnali Ghosh in the preparation of this chapter.

39

SOLID WASTE MANAGEMENT AND THE ROLE OF NON-GOVERNMENT ORGANISATIONS IN THE DISPOSAL OF CITY GARBAGE

TAPASH KUMAR BARMAN

Introduction

City wastes or garbage are the unwanted materials generally thrown out of our homes, offices, parks, shops, restaurants, hotels, hospitals and commercial establishments. In our country, it is mostly consists of rotting vegetables and food matter. Besides it also contains paper, polythene bags and materials, glass pieces, rubber, leather, porcelain, metal pieces, rags, toxic materials, (batteries, pesticides, expired medicines, hospital wastes, paints, tubelights, chemicals etc.), building materials and also soil.

Solid waste or garbage is not a menace for the urban dwellers as long as it is properly managed and it does not create any physical or mental problem for the people. But when the garbage disposal system fails, it give rise to pollution. The pollution created due to the over-burden of the solid waste can be well felt in any city of India. In Guwahati itself, when one moves around the city during the rainy days, waterlogging in the streets is a common site. But why there is waterlogging when we have sufficient number of drains all over the city. The main reason is that almost all of the drains in Guwahati are filled-up with solid wastes. In many parts of the city we find that the roads are being blocked due to excessive collection of garbage and the municipal workers are failing to clean-up the same. The garbage bins provided are not sufficient to take all the garbage. As a result, the roads have become stinky and walking on the road becomes extremely difficult.

Generation of solid waste is not a new phenomenon. In the early days, before the advent of the industrial revolution, the major constituents of the solid wastes were domestic water and agricultural residues which were bio-degradable in nature and hence manageable.

With industrialisation, not only has the quantity of the solid waste increased, but also its quality has also changed. Though, the rural wastes continue to be made-up of mainly domestic wastes and agricultural residues, wastes from the urban areas and the industries contain diverse types of materials which include toxic wastes as well.

In recent years, rapid growth of population and industrialisation resulted in the migration of rural population to the urban areas in search of employments, which in turn resulted in high population pressure in the urban areas of India. As a result, the urban support system have come under great stress and problems such as lack of cleanliness, pollution, loss of vegetation and over-crowding, to mention only a few, are beginning to spoil the beauty of towns and cities, converting them into dirty, polluted and brown dwellings.

Many citizens, may be aware of the maladies affecting the beauty and the climate of their cities. However, those issues concerning environment can be tracked down to one or more of the following deficiencies in our society:

1. Lack of civic sense among the people.
2. Lack of appreciation of the magnitude of the problem.
3. Lethargy and lack of motivation to tackle the problems.
4. Lack of infrastructural facilities.
5. Ignorance of the laws supporting cleanliness and pollution abatement.
6. Paucity of laws and regulations regarding certain issues.
7. Lack of community participation in tackling the issues.
8. Lack of coordination between different public and regulatory authorities.

9. Lack of resources generated by the community.

Methods for Solid Waste Management

There are various methods which can be best utilised for effective solid waste management in the cities. These methods are already in operation in various western and developed countries of the world.

The various method which we suggested here are:

1. Recycling of solid wastes.
2. Sanitary landfill.
3. Segregation.
4. Composting of Bio-degradable wastes.

Recycling of Solid Wastes

Recycling of material is an important aspect that will definitely go a long way in solving the garbage problem. Recycling refers to the process by which material once used is used again to substitute for virgin material. For example, paper is made from wood pulp. To make 1 tonne of paper, 17 trees need to be brought down. However, if waste paper is remade into pulp and this pulp used to substitute for part of the entire requirement of wood pulp in the making of paper, it will save trees.

Most household garbage is recyclable. Paper, plastic, metal, glass and rags can be used in various manufacturing processes. Wet organic kitchen waste can be used to generate compost rich in plant nutrients.

Most cities and towns, in our country, have retailers and wholesellers who buy recyclable material either directly from homes, shops, offices and establishments which collects these materials from the ragpickers. The ragpickers in turn collect these recyclable waste from garbage dumbs and roadside bins. These materials are then sorted and sent to various small and large industries which use them in varying proportions to substitute for virgin material in the manufacture of articles.

Recycling has several benefits. It reduces the amount of waste that reaches the roadside bin; it reduces the amount of energy needed to make new products; it reduces pollution; it reduces the requirement for virgin material and it generates employment.

Sanitary Landfill

A sanitary landfill is a place to bury waste comprising biodegradable and non-biodegradable material in a systematic and hygienic way without causing any nuisance or hazard to public health or safety. The biodegradable portion of the refuse undergoes aneorabic decomposition over a relatively long period of time and produces gases such as methane (CH_4) and Carbon-dioxide (CO_2).

The process basically consists of laying the waste material in a planned and methodical manner, than compacting the layer and finally covering it with soil. The soil cover tends to remove common landfill odour and keep away flies, rats and other vectors from thriving on the wastes.

The wastes which may be disposed off by the sanitary landfilling method are: soiled and toxic municipal wastes, demolation and construction wastes, industrial wastages, dead animals, hospital wastes, animal husbandry wastes and such other material.

Oil, solvents, volatile solids and sludges and other hazardous wastes can be used for recovering valuable material after which they can be disposed in sanitary landfills separate from other wastes.

Houses and apartments should not be constructed on landfill area because of potential problems from gas migration, corrosion, foundation bearing inadequacies and settlement besides soil and water pollution. The area may be used as car parks, bus stands etc. Light structures may be constructed on such sites.

Segregation

Segregation means separation and involves the separate collection of different materials under previously determined categories. Segregation is a very important activity that one must do before throwing out garbage. Most household garbage contains many things that can be used. We often render them totally useless by dumping them along with other waste. We could make a beginning by segregating our garbage into useful and totally useless material.

Apart from what we retain for selling to the rag-collector, there are items in the garbage, which are generally classified as 'roadwaste'. These are scraps of paper, plastic, metal, glass and rags which are retrieved by the ragpickers. By doing this they are not only helping the society, but also saving raw material and energy, in the way getting self employments. However, they are unknowingly exposing themselves and others to dirt and disease by scattering waste while looking for useful material in the garbage.

To avoid this, we can segregate even roadwaste from out garbage and hand it over to the ragpicker, thus enabling them to earn their livelihood in a safer and healthier manner while contributing to saving our environment by recycling.

Organic wastes from kitchens, gardens and dining tables are compostable and so these can be used for making organic fertilisers.

For effective segregation, separate containers can be kept in the houses for DRY, WET and TOXIC wastes.

DRY waste: Scraps of paper, plastic, metal, glass pieces, rags, rubber, leather, crockery and even some containers, which can all go into a used cardboard carton, sack or basket. This can be given to the ragpicker once or twice a week.

WET waste: Kitchen waste such as vegetable peels and remains of fruits, vegetables, bone and meat can be fed to domestic animals or along with left overs and rotton food, garden litter, hedge clippings and the like, can be collected and composted in homes, schools, gardens and parks or in the neighbourhood composting sites.

TOXIC waste: Unused medicines which have not expired can be given to free clinics and hospitals. However, unused toxic material such as expired medicines, pesticides, chemicals, used batteries, wastes from hospitals, such as used blood and saline bottles, used syringes, bandages and cotton etc. have to be disposed off in a proper manner.

Composting of Bio-degradable Wastes

Composting is one of the oldest forms of recycling. It is based on the scientific principle that nothing ever really disappears, but just changes shape and takes on new forms. Organic wastes can be burried in the soil to make compost or humus, the rich black dirt formed by the decaying of animal and vegetable wastes.

Compost is formed through the action of certain microbes that multiply when mixed with organic wastes and receive sufficient air and water Earthworms are often employed to decompose the wastes. The finished product can supply part of 16 essential elements needed by the plants, thus can act as a better fertiliser than the synthetic inorganic fertilisers. Compost can decrease the drought damage by increasing the soils ability to hold water and soil becomes easier to cultivate. It can decrease the adverse effects of excessive alkalinity, acidity or excessive application of chemical fertilisers. It helps the soils in retaining more plant nutrients over a longer period and in controlling the weed growth.

Health Hazards of Toxic Wastes

Toxic wastes are usually produced in large quantities from industries and hospitals. As long as the industries are in the outskirts of the cities, they do not affect the city population as a whole. But with the encouragement of privatisation by the government, many private hospitals and nurshing homes have sprangup in most of the Indian cities. With their only aim to make profit, they hardly care about proper disposal of the wastes produced by them, which are mostly toxic in nature and creating health hazards to the city dwellers, as most of the hospitals are situated in the highly populated area of the cities.

The wastes produced from the hospitals consist of soiled and infected cotton, drips, injection syringes and needles, diapers, sanitary napkins, dressings, used tissues, etc. can create a lot of health hazard, which may lead to an epidemic of infectious deseases. Surat is the best example, which have showed us the adversaries of mismanagement of city garbage.

These kind of toxic wastes are required to be incinerated, i.e., to be burned down completely. Because of the high cost of incinerators, small hospitals and nurshing homes cannot afford to install one, and with no interested authority to pressurise them, they resort to throwing the waste into the roadside bins, thereby creating a health hazard.

Open dumping of medical wastes has resulted in flourishing business of recycling of the medical wastes. Disposable syringes, used bandages, surgical gloves, blood bags and intravenous tubes are being cleaned, repackaged and sold at a much lower prices than they would sell for if new, putting patients at serious risk.

The new threat from clandestinely repackaged medical waste can hardly be underestimated. These may result to numerous serious infections that may spread as a result, such as AIDs, tuberculosis, hepatitis and bacterial diseases. Apart from the threat of infection, unhygienic waste disposal undermines the recent drive across the country make treatment of patients safer by introducing disposable products.

The Union Ministry of Environment and Forest shows sign of having finally woken up to the threat. It is in the final stages of formulating a guideline that will make it mandatory for every hospital with 30 beds or more to incinerate its infectious waste. The Bio-Medical Wastes (Management and Handling) Rules, 1995, will have other provisions incorporated, including those to ensure proper handling, packaging and transport of such waste. A total ban on disposal of medical waste in municipal drains is also contemplated.

Paradoxically, some ecologists have protested against the use of incinerators for burning the plastic disposables. These are known to spew toxic gases and countries such as the US have moved away from incineration to shredding, microwaving and destruction of waste at source. Since India may not be able to afford such expensive disposal techniques, most believe that incinerators are the answer. What is needed is more attention by hospital management to waste disposal and stricter monitoring of disposal systems. The Government also needs to penalise laggards and violators severely. Only then will public confidence be resorted in the nation's health services, ability to dispose of waste without infecting those they are supposed to cure.

Failure of Municipal Boards and Corporation in the Disposal of City Garbage

The primary responsibility of the Municipal Boards and Corporations is the safe removal of waste from the domestic and commercial localities of the city. But it seems that they are failing in fulfilling their basic duties. This is evident from the fact that the Delhi High Court has already served notice to the Delhi Municipal Corporation to remove the garbages from the streets of New Delhi effectively. When the condition of our prestigious capital is like this, we can well imagine what may be the conditions of other towns and cities of India. And in that respect the urban areas of the North East is not better.

The main reason for failure of the Municipalities is corruption. Since corruption is an accepted fact in the Indian governing system, we cannot go without it. The people who join in these boards and corporation are interested with their jobs only and as long as they are getting their due salaries, they are not concerned with their efficiencies.

So unless their is a pressuring body above these institutions, we cannot expect any effective serivce from them. The state or the Central Government should try to create some pressure so that these institutions can work better.

But we cannot blame the Municipal bodies for everything. Rise in population and over-crowding with the constructions of buildings have made it difficult to dispose garbage from every corner of the cities. Unplanned development of the urban areas have made it difficult for the Municipal trucks to reach the interior areas of the cities.

With the shortage of funds, it has become difficult for the Municipal bodies to employ more staff for this purpose and to acquire new trucks.

Peoples Participation and the Role of Non-Government Organisation in the Disposal of City Garbage

Peoples participation as a whole is most necessary for the

effective solid waste management of the cities. We are the main source of waste and garbage. So, we must see to it that the garbage sourced from our houses must reach their proper destination which is not the roadside bin, but the place where it should be dumped properly.

Another important aspect is that people should become more concious about the cleanliness of the environment so that the urban dwellings become more hygienic. We should realise that many of the problems are due to our lifestyles which foster wastage and over consumption. People should develop attitudes and a sense of responsibility and care for improving their environment.

We should create awareness with the family as a unit that garbage utilisation is a better method of waste management than just garbage disposal, because anything that is discarded still remains in one form or another, on our earth. Every citizen should understand that the more things we throw away, more difficult it becomes for the civic authorities like the Municipal bodies to dispose it, since the collection and disposal of garbage involves huge expenditure for infrastructure and wastage of precious fuels like diesel and petrol. With increasing population and urbanisation, the problem can become ultimately unmanageable.

People should understand that to avoid spoiling and wasting of these usable materials and instead of throwing them away with decaying garbage, it is better to separate them at home and give them away to people who can use them for making new things, just as we do with old newspapers or plastic milk packets, bottles or old clothes. Decomposable wastes such as those coming from the kitchen are best disposal off by composting in a pit or in the corner or a garden or a pot in the terrace or balcony. Compost prepared in this way in a very short period of one or two weeks forms very rich manure for the plants.

People should be aware that a lot of garbage disposed off from the houses is not thrown inside the bins or rings provided by the Municipal bodies, but strewn all around, because the person who disposes the garbage e.g., housewife, child, servant, sweepers, etc., do not take enough care to throw it into the bin and hence it becomes a breeding ground for cockroaches, mosquitoes, flies and is constantly surrounded by pie dogs, crows which litter it further. City dwellers should be aware that insanitary wastes such as blood stained cotton, baby diapers, tissues, sanitary napkins etc., are hazardous to health and should be disposed off hygeinically or burying them, but should not be mixed with other wastes which will cause rapid multiplication of disease causing germs and lead to epidemics. For these, the Municipal bodies should provide separate bins in different localities and should be carried to incinerators. Hazardous and poisonous wastes, such as empty pesticide or insecticide tins, plastic covers, tubelights, used batteries etc., should be disposed off with utmost care, so that these do no cause damage to our soil, water, air, lifeforms and particularly to the rag-pickers.

Role of Non-Government Organisations (NGOs) in the Disposal of City Garbage

Any public campaign or any work for the good of the people at large cannot be fulfilled, just by talking about it or by telling our friends. So, we need some few people from every corner of the towns and cities, who are most willing to work for the society. So, we need some leaders to take up this massive work. Thus the persons who are interested to lead the society can work to their end can form a society or Non-Government Organisations (NGOs).

NGOs can play a very important role in the disposal of city garbage. They can make the people aware of the problems created by unplanned management of the city garbage. They can educate the people regarding the issues concerning with the quality of environment and enlisting their active participation and cooperation. The NGOs can coordinate with the authorities and regulatory bodies towards establishing and maintaining necessary infrastructural facilities.

The NGOs can arrange training programme for the municipal workers for proper functioning of the public facilities. They can also conduct separate training programmes for the school students and the people of various localities regarding proper waste disposal. They can encourage the community to provide complementary support to the regulatory authorities in maintaining the services and infrastructures.

The press and the media can play a vital role for the

success of any mass movement. So, the NGOs should see to it that the press and the media cooperates with them to give free and adequate coverage and support to this movement on a sustained basis as a part of their social responsibility.

An organising committee should be constituted from among the members of various section of the society, service organisations, civic forums, companies and professional associations and other important persons concerned with cleanliness, pollution and vegetation. The organising committee will co-opt as many heads of the regulatory authorities as necessary into their committee in their ex-officio capacity so that the organising committee can have the support of the regulatory authorities in implementing the programmes.

The NGOs should form sub-committees to undertake projects in different parts of the city. The responsibilities of the Organising Committee would include:

(a) Providing direction to the whole campaign and to the projects undertaken by each of the sub-committees.
(b) Co-ordinating with the regulatory authorities.
(c) Co-ordinating with agencies willing to support the campaign.
(d) Co-ordinating the need-based training programmes.

The sub-committees thus formed will not be for short term programmes, but must be sustained till satisfactory results are achieved. The sub-committees should submit projects in the form of proposals for taking up different activities in different parts of the city, including all details regarding the proposed plans, support required and the budgetary requirements. The organising committee would take note of the support that will have to be mustered for carrying out the projects as well as scrutinising the mode of generating resources proposed by the sub-committees. After the project has been pased and resources made available, the sub-committees should launch and implement the programmes with the help of volunteers.

There should be some centralised sub-committees to function under the direct coordination of the organising committee to provide harmony, direction and centralised services to the whole campaign. Some of these would be:

(a) Sub-committee for providing directions for resources mobilisation.
(b) Sub-committee for preparing the training programmes.
(c) Sub-committee for coordination and implementation.
(d) Publicity committee from among important persons from AIR, Doordarshan, newspapers, advertising clubs, etc.

Some of the suggested campaigns, projects and problem areas which should be tackled by the various sub-committees are as follows:

(1) Personal and community hygiene.
(2) Solid waste disposal—domestic and industrial.
(3) Cleanliness problems in and around multistoreyed buildings, hotels, hospitals, clinics, markets, etc.
(4) Dumping of garbages into drains and the over-flowing of drain water into the streets.
(5) Sanitation and basic amenities to slums and pavement dwellers.

Here an innovative method can be suggested by which the various NGOs can work for the proper disposal of garbage from the urban areas of the North East. Each town and city can be divided among different sub-committees, so that whole area can be covered conveniently while the garbage disposal is done. In each unit, a garbage dumping yard should be constructed, which should be covered on all sides by sufficiently high walls, so the garbages do not spilt over. Few ricksaw-vans can be acquired for each unit. These ricksaw-vans should collect garbages from each house of the locality and dump it into the yard. The rag-pickers can be allowed to collect all the recyclible materials and all the non-degradable wastes are sorted out before the garbage is collected by the Municipal trucks from the yard. This will definitely help to keep our streets clean and also save the environment from pollution by the non-degradable wastes.

40

ECOLOGICAL DEGRADATION AND FOREST RESOURCES IN MEGHALAYA

RANGAN DUTTA

Perhaps no natural resource has undergone such wanton destruction as a result of man's profligacy as forests. These precious resources containing valuable flora and fauna are receding rapidly. Many wildlife species that once inhabited these forests are either extinct or on the verge of extinction. This issue has now become a global concern and the problems have been reflected in the deliberation of World Government representatives at the last Rio de Janerio summit.

Meghalaya has not escaped this loss. The situation of environment here is an grim as in other parts of India and the world. The state which has been blessed with the rarest and most exotic ecological wealth is in the throes of a major environmental imbalance unless reversed through massive human intervention.

We do not have to look at satellite imageries to know the gravity of the situation. A journey to the interior will reveal even to the causal observer the scene of whole mountain ranges bereft of vegetation. In rainy seasons water flows unchecked down these barren slopes causing flash floods in the plains below. The top soil that sustains vegetation is being washed away leaving these lands unfit for vegetation. Environmental degradation has become an inescapable reality.

The question that arises is—was this mammoth loss inevitable? Sadly enough, the answer is 'no'. It was possible for man to derive all the benefits he had secured without creating an environmental mess of the magnitude by adopting an approach to development without destruction. He could have met his basic needs of food, clothing and shelter without destroying the environment. This loss has occurred not because man had too many needs but because he was too greedy and careless. It may well be said that man's need has been converted into greed. The exploitation of the environment has been done in the most careless manner. This is most obvious in the practice of *jhuming* or shifting cultivation. This totally unscientific technique involves clearing a certain tract of forest and using it for cultivation. When the fertility of the land diminishes, it is abondoned and a fresh forest area cleared. This single factor is most responsible for loss of vegetal cover in vast areas of Meghalaya. It is alarming to note that annually about 579 sq. km. of the degraded forests in the State are shaved off and put under this harmful system of *jhuming*.

Forest and wildlife have also come under stress because of unsystematic removal of tree cover. Most of the forests in the State are supposed to be under the control of respective District Councils. But in reality, the control vests with the individual in case of private forest, the clan in case of clan forest, the village *durbar* in case of village forest and the community in case of community forests.

In the absence of proper management scheme, these forests have been exploited without any corresponding scheme for compensatory afforestation. Today most of these forests are barren and contains only isolated bamboo cover. The management by District Councils has been clearly unsuccessful.

It must be understood that it takes several years to recover the environmental losses. It requires only one day to destroy a forest but a hundred years to raise another mature crop. Every inch of top soil washed away in floods will take hundreds of years to be formed again. Once the plants and animals are extinct they are lost for ever. Another reason of forest loss in the state is the reckless commercial exploitation of the forest resources by unscrupulous timber merchants, mostly from outside the state.

Normally, the climate in the form of precipitation is no

benevolent that the natural regeneration takes place by itself, but the biotic interference by way of annual crown fire and browsing by cattle used to destroy most of the tender seedlings that come out as an aftermath of felling. Hence, intensive human action is required if the area is to be greened again.

Nevertheless, steps are in full swing to halt and reverse the process. The most immediate step is to contain the wanton practice of shifting cultivation. In this context, the system is to be regulated by localising the *jhuming* area in particular pockets only and regrouping of the villages accordingly. People may be induced to take up permanent cultivation by availing government incentives of subsidised fertilisers, quality seeds etc.

Alternatively, people must be enthused to take up cultivation of minor forest product with short gestation period. The experiences of the forest department in this regard must be shared by others, in which *phuljharu* plantation has been able to wean away quite a number of *jhumias* from their age-old habit of *jhuming*. It is worthwhile mentioning that a hectare of *phuljharu* plantation could yield an income of about 5500-6000 per year.

Regarding the degraded areas can be through pure artificial plantation or through aided natural regeneration by using quality planting materials and adoption of relevant technique. Government have adopted a multi-disciplinary approach to the problem by involving different landuse organisations in taking up these works. But the effort cannot be successful if it remains only a government programme. People's involvement and participation are to be obtained at every step of the programme through various extension processes.

According to the satellite imagery, about 8000 and odd square kilometers of barren areas exist in the state and these are invariably to be greened as quickly as possible. It is a gigantic task, no doubt, but with people's co-operation and involvement nothing is impossible. It is gratifying to note that another satellite imagery reveals about the gradual increase of forest areas in Meghalaya and Karnataka due to human intervention. It is imperative that the organisations should be so restructured as to tackle the problems on a war footing. Areas that contain large numbers of important fauna should be constituted as national parks and sanctuaries and proper protection measures initiated.

The steps outlined above will constitute a small beginning of a massive task ahead. It will need concerted effort to make this successfull or also the ecological catastrophe is impending. The vast deserts of the world and the events in North-East Africa remind us of that danger.

41

THE CYBORG ENVIRONMENT AND THE END OF ETHICS
A Capitalist Predicament

B.S. BUTOLA

Every year June the 5th is observed as the World Environment Day. But, the question is which environment? The environment it was, the environment it is or the environment it will be? To answer these and other similar questions it is important to differentiate various notions of time particularly in relation to environment particularly the natural environment. For, as far as physical environment is concern its past, present and future does not constitute a continuum in its historical continuity. On the contrary these stand for at least three different environments with equal number of discrete ontologies, i.e. beings. In the past environment was regarded as God Created (Theogenic) or Self Created (Autogenic) entity. The Modernist conception of environment based on the Enlightenment Rationality views it as Human Created (Anthropogenic) entity. The Post-modernists, the Deconstructionists and also the Philosophies of the future view it as Technogenic (Cybernetic). Whereby, the Tool Making Animal of Benjamin instead of being the architect of his environment has become a tool in the hands of machine thus, giving technology not only access to humanity but also the meaning and essence of both i.e. human beings and the environment (physical) has become a function of technology. Therefore, the choice of Environment in general or any one in particular is possible either by incorporating a conceptual fallacy in ones construct about the Environment or positioning oneself ideologically for or against the instrumental/emancipatory reasons. Meaning thereby, though the past has inevitable as well as indispensable links with the present yet, to talk of the past and interpret the present in the light of the past experiences and blame or celebrate the same for most of the present ills and wells does not only bring back the nostalgia of the paradise lost/paradise regained but it also places one in the conservative mode with total blindness towards the present and also the future. Since, the present is always encountered and faced on the bases of past experiences, so the ability to cope with it largely depends upon ones ability to assimilate the past to its optimum level in order to face the very transient present. Otherwise, precious little remains possible to be done for facing the present with certain amount of authority other than the past experiences and the preparations based on it. Therefore, for all practical purposes the present greatly belongs to the past. Moreover, the present is also the mapping of the experiences and hopes of the past and any significant change in the contour of this map is possible only in future. It is also pragmatic to concentrate and prepare for the future. In this chapter apart from mapping of the future environment its ethical and philosophical repercussions will be the main focus of discussion.

The future environment will be different from all the preceding ones including the present one both in its form and content. It will be an environment which will be constituted neither by Human nor by Nature. On the contrary it will belong to the hybrid of both, i.e. the 'Cyborg'. A 'Cyborg' is a hybrid of machine and organism a creature of social reality as well as a creation of fiction.[1] It is a creature simultaneously organic and inorganic, or theogenic/autogenic and technogenic, anthropogenic and instrumentogenic. It is a genetic organism or an exogenously extends organisational complex functioning as an integrated homeostatic system unconsciously.[2] It is a joining of a living thing with non-living device or devices[3] which once populate the space will convert the environment into ambiguously natural and crafted[4] such that every substance of it will be chimeras, theorised and fabricated hybrid of machine and organism.[5] The process of hybridisation of the organic and the inorganic has become so all pervasive that

Cyborg has become the ontology of the new environment as much as the various constituents of it live and work continously as refabricated hybrids of machine and organism.[6]

It is not for the first time that living things have been joined with non-living devices. Such combination have existed for millennia. The entire concept of 'Homo Faber' and the narratives build around it amply exhibit the existence of Cyborg ontology. But, it is only under the enlightenment rationality and its associated modernity paradigm that one observes some kind of resurge in episteme and economy centred upon constructing particular fusion of non-living devices and living things like plants, animals, humans etc. with the non-living Technogenic entities in the elaboration of global networks of exchange.[7] This new creature is a hybrid simultaneously within the natural and human environment and also outside it. Its organic links with the living environment subjects it to the laws of organism and its crafted and mechanical part subjects it to the mechanical processes. Such that its remedy and cure lies in Cyborg medicines and controlled by CCCI (Command-Control-Communication Intelligence). The tool making animal of Franklin[8] has become a tool in the hands of machine giving technology an access to humanity. The ontology of the Cyborg lies neither in humans and their culture, value, customs, sacred, and profane, nor does it lie in the nature and its regenerativity, diversity and self regulatory ability. On the contrary the ontology of the Cyborg lies in a technologically induced intelligent agents who is genetically engineered, bionically supplemented, pharmaceutically enhanced, artificially inseminated, Cybernetically guided with a combination of living/non-living devices. This new technologically induced inelligent agent will be equipped with speech synthesisers, voice cards, electric eyes, artificial life, robot historians, programming demons, software societies, gobotic packages, groupware formations, terminal identities, POST (power on self testing) recollections, boot responses, pace.makers, hearing devices, dialysis filter and ultimately will become a digital being. Thus, in case of human beings the beauty of the world and the paragon of the animal (human being) endowed with infinite facilities[9] will thus be interconnected with others through on line affinities and off line interests and will be intercommunicated with others through telecommuting, telebanking, telelearning, telehealing, telemarketing, teleplaying, telebuying qualities of multimedia techno-humanities.[10] In the process of universal and generalised hybridisation (living/non-living or organism-machine) the new environment will have nothing except commercialised artifacts, mediating the metabolism of immense mega-machines of production and consumption thriving in technogenic habits of elaborate artificially built ecologies.[11] Human beings will become the Cyborganised products/producers of those mechanic products that produced the environments like supermarket foods, mall fashion, suburban housing, automotive transport, electronic communication, petro-chemical energy and corporate entertainment such as the "Disney Land".[12] The life of such an environment will exclusively depend upon the functioning of mega-machines and once these channels are disrupted due to any reason including war and sanction their survival itself will be imperiled and Sarajevo, Goma, Grozney, Beirut, Karachi etc. will be witnessed everywhere.[13]

Cyborg Ontology or Capitalist Hauntology

The emergence of such a hybrid creature instead of affirming the norms of existing ontologies has come more like their hauntology independent of the laws of all lives and existence. it is neither aware nor capable of involving transcendence and immanence. It can neither expand towards future nor can it integrate the past. While intercommunicating with others it neither finds itself in self-affirmation nor expansion on temporal as well as extra-temporal dimensions. The mechanised organism once inhabit the space will transform it into Cyber Space and the so-called modernisation process once complete the Nature is gone for good.[14] This will be the *End of Nature*[15] because, the instrumentalist logic of late capitalism has caused the *Death of Nature*.[16] This tragic end has come after over two and a half centuries of techno-cratisation under the enlightenment rationalising mission which has unscathingly and brutally attacked the past theogenic (God-created), autogenic (self created) notions of the environment by the anthropogenic (human created) and ultimately technogenic (technological created) nature. Thus, ethics in general, life and environmental ethics in particular have banished along with *Practical Reason* and have been replaced by *Instrumental Reason* surviving on its ability to technical control life and nature.[17] According to Habermas "our civilization has become increasingly scientific, the dimension within which theory was once directed towards praxis has become correspondingly constructed. In this phase of capitalist development the laws of self reproduction demand of an industrially advanced society that it looks after its survival on the escalating scale of a continually expanded technical control over nature and continually refined administration of human being.... In this system science, technology, industry and administration interlock in a circular process."[18]

The natural habitat, that virgin lands of the Romantics have been replaced by "build environment", "planned habitat", "concrete jungle", and "ecological disaster". There is (de) naturisation of nature and (de) humanisation of humanity. Both co-evolving and co-inhabitating. Individual compassion, sympathy and concern etc. have been replaced by response behaviour and culture, value and enjoyment are annexed by corporate entertainments and standardised codes of public conducts. There is standardisation of identities and diversity into *Digital Beings*. Thus, all socio-cultural and political links by interconnection of an integrated circuit which can neither live nor die but only became obsolete and redundant measured in *full-life* and *half-life* bases.

The Cyborg Episteme

The absence of any specific "being" the ontology of the cyborg degenerates into hauntology of a "being of non-being" and "non-being of being". A text in search of its context and context devoid of its own text. This poses a serious epistemic problem. The existing epistemies of understanding, reasoning and emancipation in the polymorphous society of Cyborg creativity stands and replaced by *Game* and *work* or *labour* by *Play*. A deadly Game with its deadly rules of domination by informatics without any material, cultural, ideological and political retrieve and reproduction but only retrieve, storage, stacking and redundance. A unique combination of material and ideological, organic and inorganic. Thus, the discourses and conceptions of the past epistemies stands transformed into the new codes of the polymorphic system such as:

Post episteme	Epistemies of Polymorphous System
Consciousness	Memory Space RAM/ROM
Mind	Motherboard, CPU
Representation	Simulation (false image)
Bourgeois novel	Scientific fiction
Realism	Post-Modernism
Organism	Biotic Component
Depth, Integrity	Surface, Boundary
Heat	Noise
Biology as clinical practice	Biology as Inscription
Physiology	Communications Engineering
Small Groups	Subsystems
Perfection	Optimisation
Eugenics	Population Control
Decadence	Obsolescence
Hygiene	Stress Management
Microbiology	Immunology
Tuberculosis	AIDS
Organic Division of Labour	Ergonomics/Cybernetics of labour
Functional Specialisation	Modular Construction
Reproduction	Replication, Cloning
Organic Sex Role Specialisation	Optimal Genetic Strategies
Biological Determinism	Evolutionary Inertia, Constraints
Community Ecology	Ecosystem
Racial Chains of Being	Neo-Imperialism, United Nations, Humanism
Scientific Management in Home/Factory	Global Factory, Electronic Cottage
Family/Market/Factory	Human in the Integrated Circuit
Family Wage	Comparable Worth
Public/Private	Cyborg Citizenship
Nature/Culture	Field of Difference
Cooperation	Communication Enhancement
Freud	Lacan
Sex	Genetic Engineering
Labour	Robotics
Reasoning	Artificial Intelligence
World War III	Star Wars
White Capitalist Patriarchy	Information of Domination

The Cyborg and Political Economy of its Genesis

'Cyborgs' have their origin in the Homo Faber (The tool making, tool using Animal). But, its march from the realm of exception to rule and from rarity to universality owes greatly to the rise and growth of capitalism. It is an accepted fact that capitalism as a system of economic, social, political and environmental relationship is incomprehensible without colonies. Colonies form the dialectical unity with capitalism. These are also the mother of capitalism. Similarly, it is also accepted that capitalism and colonisation have a cause and effect interrelationship. But surprisingly what is a little know and therefore less accepted is that all the narratives about capitalism and colonialism suffer from an all pervasive ocular centricism. In fact, the interrelationship between capitalism-colonialism have shifted from explicit exploitation and domination by the coloniser out side the colony to an invisible yet more potent and insidious relationship. A new kind of *Capillary Power* relationship. Meaning thereby systematic, ubiquitous, diffused relations of power and exploitation mechanism such as to circulate and percolate through progressively finer channels, thus gaining access to individuals themselves, to their bodies, gestures, symbols, signs and all their daily action and value system. Today, these new finer capillary channels have replaced the outdated colonial relationships. Colonisation of the mind and self, commercialisation and tarrification of the being and ultimately its estrangement and imprisonment through an all pervasive, impersonal system of surveillance and correction and ultimately production of regimented, isolated yet self policing individual in a *Panoptic Society* have increasingly become the norm of our social existence. Tarrification of being and self have accentuated the competition, stress, strain and ultimately a rate race among the individuals in the society which in its turn demands much more from everyone than what one can afford or is capable of giving. Ruthless competition, large scale wear and tear of both environment and human beings have become inevitable aspects of capitalist development. But, the process of wear and tear is never total. According to Sartre, while formulating a critique of capitalism and also *Dialectical Reason* he says, through capitalism is a retrogressive and dehumanising system yet it has its own limitations. For example it is not only incapable of creating condition for releasing and therefore full realisation of human creativity but it is also incapable of appropriating them totally. Thus, the simulacra of the whole it claims without totality exposes the inherent limitations of capitalism. However, to over come these deficiencies, the missing and incomplete parts of the totality in the simulacra it tries to compensated by creating its own archetypes. The organic losses are hypothetically gained by their technological and mechanical substitution. Hybridisation of organic and inorganic material and ideological are some such archetypes. This is what has formed the genesis of the *Cyborgs*. The discourses carried and build around such entities are mechanistic theoretical infraphysics which recast nature as a vast machine driven by mechanical cycle, force and structure. Man as a machine and market as economic mechanism and society operating as complex mechanical structure.[19]

The modern nature of Cyborg was first popularised by J.D. Bernal in 1929. In the aftermath of First World War with total denigration of human beings under the imperialist capitalism he imagined a *Mechanised Man* destined to succeed a *Natural Man* in terrestrial evolution.[20] It was further elaborated by Manfred Clynes and Nathan S. Kline in 1960.[21] According to these scholars a "Cybernetic Organism" or an "exogenously extended organisational complex functioning as an integrated homostatic system unconsciously"[22] populating the future environment is the inevitable outcome of present path of development. According to Halacy "a Cyborg is a joining of a living thing with a non-living device or devices".[23] Arthur C. Clarke while depicting the *Profiles of the Future* too conceived the existence of such an entity in 1963.[24] Thereafter, the *Cyborg Beings* have become indispensable themes in various fields of Cybernetics, cognitive sciences, medicine, social theory, genetic engineering, biotechnology, forestry, natural and environmental sciences, architecture, agriculture, politics, culture, economics, psychology, and literature. Finally

Donna Haraway formulated *A manifesto for Cyborgs.*[25] According to her "world ambiguously natural and crafted such that we are all Chimeras, theorised and fabricated hybrid of machine and organism... The Cyborg is our ontology".[26] This new creature once populate a new space including the living space it becomes a *living machine* where the fusion of man and machine evolves into *machine living* and ultimately, the new environment of *Dehumans* and *De-nature*.

End of Environmental Ethics—A Capitalist Predicament

Ethics as a concept which deals with the aspects like, general pattern or ways of life, a set of rules or conduct or moral code and inquiry about ways of life and rule of conduct etc. does seem to have little significance in the new i.e., "Cyborg" environment. The good old principles of moral guidance which would guide our treatment of wild nature thus, becoming the theme of environmental ethics have become things of the past. But the end of the environmental ethics under capitalism had taken place in different phases first by replacing *Deontology* by *Teleology*[27] and ultimately *Practical Reason* by *Technological Reason.*[28]

In the changed environment and along with its attributes the age old concept of environmental ethics have only but little relevance. Environmental ethics have so far been guided mainly by our concern for both human and the nature, its flora and fauna; its rocks and micro organism and human concern and treatment for all these. But, of late there have been an upsurge of a variety of environmental ethics in circulation. Some of the important ones are:

Human Centred Environmental Ethics

Baxter[29] and Norton[30] are of the view that environmental policies must be evaluated on the basis of their influence and affect on human beings. The sole purpose of all position lies in maximising human happiness over human sufferings. All talk of ecological imbalance, loss of recreational and aesthetic enjoyment, decline in bio-diversity, loss of species, climatic changes, increased environmental hazards like floods, drought, etc. are if environmentally bad then they should have adverse effects on human happiness. Therefore a human centred environmental ethics is substantive to environmental policies and ethics. This branch of environmental ethics treat only human beings as morally considerable and no other species is morally considerable.

Animal Centred Ethics

As opposed to human centre ethical view there are some who believe that not only human beings but also non-humans particularly the animals are morally considerable. But, definitely they rank animal equal to human beings. Most of the human action do adversely affect the non-human animals. However, they talk and fight for the rights of animals.[31] According to Regan "Only being with inherent value have right... only subject of a life have inherent value, only self conscious being capable of having beliefs and desires, only deliberate actors who can conceive of the future and entertain goals, are subjects of a life. He believe that basically all mentally normal mammals of a year or more are *subjects-of-a-life* and then have inherent value which allows them to have rights. Thus, they are worth moral consideration.

Life Centred Ethics

Living things do not include human beings and animals only but also all the other living organisms like plants, algae, single called organisms, viruses and their micro organisms including the biosphere itself. That makes a self regulatory system which strives not necessarily consciously towards certain goals. These all living things making the biosphere is decidedly morally considerable though with varying degree of moral significance. A life centred ethics views the impact of human action on the entire living system and aspire to achieve *biotic Egalitarianism.* Human being necessarily do not acquire special significance as the preservation of the biosphere and of larger eco-systems might be more significant than the preservation of large number of humans.

Rights of the Rocks

The above mentioned ethics are nothing more than the subset of the succeeding ones. Therefore all agree that all living things are the only one those are morally considerably. But, such an approach too is an arbitrary one because it is difficult to distinguish and separate living from non-living things. Therefore, both living and non-living things are morally considerable. This view point is known as *Everything Ethic*. It argues that destruction of rocks, disturbing its geological structure will disturb the geomorphological processes which will ultimately damage life and eco-system. This view of ethics recognises the *Right of Rocks* as the fundamental basis of ethics particularly the ongoing chemical poisoning, radio-active charging of rocks and non-biodegradable waste dumping on the rocks.

Ecological Holism

Environmental ethic is one that guides our treatment of the natural environment. Fritjof Capra particularly viewed environmental ethics in its ecological wholeness. A proper balance betwen *Yin* and *Yang*.[32] Ecological holism considers two kinds of things as morally considerable the *biosphere* as a whole and the large *eco-system* which constitute it. Thus all other ethics are part of this and thus could be considered the universal principle of environmental ethics.

The Predicament

It is evident from the forgoing discussion that environmental ethics is intrinsically based on and focuses on the living and organic system in which eco-system, biosphere and soil etc. are part of the overall living system. But, with the emergence of a hybrid mechanical organism and technological accessibility to the being of an organism we have created an environment sustaining on proliferation and replication by hybridisation of machine and organism which continues even though it cannot be measured against any clear goals. It is an excrescential environment whose development is uncontrollable, occurring without regards for self definition, where the accumulation of effects goes hand in hand with the disappearance of causes.[33] On the name of modernisation the latest fads of capitalism pluralism has become synonymous to it. But, proliferation of various competing mechanistic systems over environment through the use of capillary power and capillary sub-assembles of mechanic enhancement of bio-power species, gene banks, germ plasma etc. are nothing but essentially component of Cyborg environment. Modernisation brings in more of such cyborg in this environment. New inventions brings in new machines and these produces new hybrids rejoicing the illegitimate fusion of organism and machine. No organism particularly human being ever chooses to be a cyborg but unfortunately this is the predicament of a human being under capitalism. To be modernised mean to be prone to stresses and strains and be subjected to enhanced wear and tear and then try to repair the losses by fusion with technology: *Dehumanised Denaturalised* to be a Cyborg in a Cyborg environment.

NOTES

1. Donna Haraway, "A Manifesto for Cyborgs : Science, Technology and Socialist Feminism" in 1980s, *Socialist Review*, Vol. 15, No. 2, March-April, 1985, p. 65.
2. Clynes and Kline as cited in Halacy D.S. (Jr.), *Cybor—Evolution of the Superman*, Harper and Row, New York, 1965, p. 12.
3. Halacy, D.S. (Jr.), *Cybor—Evolution of the Superman*, Harper and Row, New York, 1965, pp. 12-13.
4. Donna Haraway, *Simians, Cyborgs and Women: The Reinvention of Nature*, Routledge, New York, 1911, p. 149.
5. *Ibid.*, pp. 149-50.
6. Timothy W. Luke, "Liberal Society and Cyborg Subjectivity". The Politics of Environments, Bodies and Nature, *Alternatives*, 21, 1996, p. 3.
7. *Ibid.*, p. 3.
8. K. Marx, *Capital: A Critique of Political Economy*, Vol. I, Progress Publishers, Moscow, 1978, p. 175.
9. William Shakespeare, *Hamlet, Prince of Denmark*, Complete Works, Collin Clear, Type Press, London, 1923, p. 1141.
10. T.W. Luke, *Op. cit.*, pp. 9-10.
11. Donald Miller Lev, *The Levis Numfold Reader*, Pantheon, New York, 1986, pp. 299-347.

12. Timothy W. Luke, *Op. cit.*, p. 11.
13. *Ibid.*, p. 11.
14. Fredric Jameson, *Postmodernism or the Cultural Logic of Late Capitalism*, Duke University Press, Durham, 1991. p. ix.
15. Bill McKibben, *The End of Nature*, Double Day, New York, 1989, as cited in Luke, *Op.cit.*, p. 6.
16. Carolyn Merchant, *The Death of Nature: Women, Ecology and Scientific Revolution*, Harper and Row, San Francisco, 1980, as cited in Luke, *Op.cit.*, p. 6.
17. Paul Connerton (ed.), *Critical Sociology*, Penguin Books, Harmondsworth, 1976, p. 27.
18. J. Habermass, *Theory and Practice*, Heinemann, 1974.
19. Timothy W. Luke, *Op.cit.*, p. 2.
20. J.D. Bernard, *The World, the Flesh and the Deil*, Indiana University Press, Bloomington, 1969.
21. Manfred Clynes and Nathan Kline, "Drugs, Space and Cybernetics Evolution to Cyborgs", *Proceedings of the Psycho Physiological Aspects to Space Flight Symposium*, Columbia University Press, New York, 1961, as cited in Luke *Ibid.*, p. 29.
22. Manfred Clynes and Nathan Kline, *Ibid.*, as cited in D.S. Halacy Jr., *Cyborg—Evolution of the Superman*, Harper and Row, New York, 1965, p, 12.
23. Halacy, *Ibid.*, pp. 12-13.
24. Arthur C. Clarke, *Profiles of the Future*, Holt, Rinehart and Winston, New York, 1963.
25. Donna Haraway, "Cyborg Manifesto for Cyborgs: Science, Technology and Socialist Feminism in the 1980's", *Socialist Review*, Vol. 15, No. 2, March-April, 1985, pp. 65-107.
26. *Ibid.*, p. 67.
27. *Deontologgs*, Philosophies which recognise something moral and human beings will not do no matter what. For example, lying and murder are wrong and just not bad. These are the things one must not do no matter what. The Deontologist believes that something could be good for individual and other for the society but there are something those are good and also bad in themselves. Such acts are unacceptable mean to persue any end even then the end may be morally admirable or morally obligatory.

    Teleology: As opposed to Deontologist the teleologist believe that right or wrongness of ones act is determined by a comparative assessment of their consequences. No acts are good or bad in themselves. It is only the end that can make them so. John Rawhs an eminent liberal political thinker also believes in two different theories. "The main concept of ethics are those of right and good... Thus, the structure of an ethical theory is then largely determined by how it defines and connects these two basic notions... The simple way of relating them is taken by *Teleological Theories*. The good is defined as that which maximises good" John Rawh, *A Theory of Justice*, Cambridge Mass Harvard

University Press. 1971, p. 24. A deontological theory is defined by contrast with teleological theory as "One that either does not specify the good independently from the right or does not interpret the right as maximising the good", p 30. For C. Fried, "The goodness of the ultimate consequences does not guarantee the rightness of the action which produce them. The two realm are not only distinct for the Deontologist but the right in prior to the good", C. Fried, *Sight and Injury*, Cambridge Mass Harvard University Press. 1978, p. 9.

28. Practical reason found in the liberalism from externally imposed compulsion and it implies good life both private and collective of individual as well as citizens. Instrumental reason is found in the technical control of nature, Paul Connecton, *Op.cit.*, p. 27.
29. W.F. Baxter, *People of Penguins: The Case for Optimal Pollution*, Columbia University Press, New York. 1974.
30. B. Norton, *Why Preserve Natural Variety*, Princeton University Press, Princeton, 1988.
31. Tom Regan, *The Case for Animal Rights*, University of California Press, Berkeley, 1983 also Tom Regan and P. Singer (ed.) *Animal Rights and Human Obligation*, Prentice Hall, Englewood Cliff, 1989.
32. Fritz of Capra, *The Turning Point*, Flamingo Fontana Paperbacks, London, also *The Tao of Physics*, Flamingo Fontana Paperback, London, 1983.
33. Jean Baudrilland, *The Transparency of Evil*, Verso NLB, London, 1993, pp. 45-46.

42

AIR POLLUTION
A Global Environmental Problem

B.P. DEY

Introduction

Pollution is an undesirable change in the physical, chemical and biological characteristics of our air, water and soil that may or will harmfully affect human life, industrial progress, living conditions and cultural assets (National Academy of Science, USA, 1966).

In the process of domination and controlling nature, man has interfered with nature, he has disrupted and altered his biotic and abiotic environment discarding the basic principles governing the ecosystems of biosphere. The consequences of this unprecedented interference of nature by man during the last two decades have been to disastrous to him that he has started realising the great danger ahead of him—the problem of environmental pollution—a global problem. In the past, environmental problems used to be local and minor in nature because of the earth's own ability to absorb and purify minor quantities of pollutants.

Sources of Air Pollution

The principal sources of air pollution are: industries like steel plants, petroleum refineries, fertilizer factories, rubber manufacturing plants, automobiles, refuse disposal etc. From these sources, large amount of pollutants like dust, smog, toxic gases like sulphurioxide, carbonmonoxide and varieties of corrosive vapours are emitted. Similarly, large amounts of carbondioxide fumes are emitted into the atmosphere by internal combustion from millions of automobiles in urban areas with oxides of nitrogen, sulphurioxide and pollutants from refuse disposals even gradually covering the capitals of North-Eastern states including Shillong known for its healthy environment.

Air Pollution Causing Health Problems

Air pollution from industry and use of petrol as fuel in about 630 million automobiles worldwide is causing a number of diseases like lung cancer, asthma and bronchities. Delhi is ranked fourth among the 41 cities of the world for air pollution. The pollution is caused mainy by automobiles numbering over 2.2 million in Delhi at the top of lung diseases with 30 per cent of its population suffering. Other badly affected Indian cities are Bombay, Calcutta, Kanpur and Ahmedabad. The role of automobiles which is the biggest culprit threatening the city life of Meghalaya where almost every ten persons own a vehicle—a positive clue for many diseases due to emission of carbonmonoxide (CO) and lead content of petrol. Automobile and diesel engine exhausts contain lead which is carcinogenic. Every kilogram of dust on city roads has been found to contain two grams of lead. On inhalation organic lead emitted from automobiles gets easily absorbed in the brain, liver, kidney and blood which over the time could lead to brain damage, muscular paralysis, convulsions and even death. Lead-petrol has been banned in many developed countries and India too has now introduced unleaded petrol in its four metropolitan cities. According to a study, lead emission in Delhi has doubled in the last eight years alone, about 844 kg of lead was released into the atmosphere by 2.2 million vehicles in Delhi. India has permitted 0.15 gm lead per litre of blood which is 30 times more than the amount allowed in the most developed countries.

Cigarette is another source of carbonmonoxide. Smoke is also produced from fertilizer plants. When taken in during respiration, it combines with haemoglobin of human blood to form carboxy-haemoglobin which reduces the oxygen carrying capacity of blood. Presence of 2 to 5 per cent of carboxy-haemoglobin in blood affect the normal functioning of nervous system. It has been established that there is a correlation between high concentration CO in blood and coronery heart attacks.

Sulphuroxides or oxides of sulphur in the form of SO_2, SO_3, H_2SO_4, H_2S and SO_4 are serious air pollutants produced during: combustion of coal, petroleum, refining of petroleum, smelting of ores, manufacturing of SO_2 and burning of refuse. SO_2 undergoes further reaction in sunlight to form SO_3 as follows:

$$2SO_2 + O_2 \xrightarrow[\text{Sunlight}]{} 2SO_3$$

SO_3 in turn reacts with moisture to form sulphuric acid (H_2SO_4) which produce and promote respiratory illness in man. SO_2 are highly injurious to plant, animal and human life. Similarly oxides of nitrogen in the form of NO, NO_2, N_2O_3, N_2O_4 and N_2O_5 emitted through domestic burning, thermal power plants, diesel engines of automobiles come in contact with fog droplets, the atmospheric conversion of NO_2 into NO_3 and finally producing nitric acid (HNO_3).

Acid Rain

Acid rain is caused by severe air pollution from power stations, factories and cars. When fossil fuels like coal or oil are burnt they give off a mixture of chemicals chiefly sulphurdioxide and nitrogen oxides. When these chemicals are discharged into the air in sufficiently large quantities, they may combine to form a dangerous pollution cocktail which will sooner or later return to earth. Acid rain is ever present in the air around us in many guises. It is in the air we breath and in the soil beneath us. It is affecting our health, endangering our forests, lakes and wildlife causing millions of pounds worth of damage to buildings. The arrival of black snow in Britain and Norway have been due to industrial pollutants. During the early 1990s the fish population of Norway's lakes began noticeably to decline. The toll of acidified 5,000 lakes in Norway (1982) suffering from acidification and about 1750 lakes had lost all their fish. In Europe and North America, thousands of lake fishes have either died or failed to breed though acidity itself is not often the direct causes. All soils contain large amounts of aluminium normally insoluble. But acid rain mobiles and wash the metal into rivers and lakes where it interferes with fish's breathing. The combustion of acid and aluminium has a profound effect on fresh water ecosystem. As wildlife species are sensitive to acidity die out, then those species reliant on them for food also disappear.

In Sweden, acid rain turned fair hair green. This strange phenomenon was caused by high level of acidity in well water having serious effects on health including diarrhoea in infants. Acid rain has been also linked with abnormally high levels of aluminium in drinking water having serious effects on health including diarrhoea in infants. Acid rain has been also linked with abnormally high levels of drinking water with frequent incidence of Alzheimer's disease—a form of senile and pre-senile dementia associated with high levels of aluminium in the brain.

Forest Damage

Forest decline caused by acid rain was first identified in Silverfir in Germany in 1970 and other tree species such as spruce, beach, oak and mountain ash began to show the same symptoms. In 1983, survey was carried out on a national basis and found that 34 per cent of trees were affected and in subsequent year (1984), the survey revealed that half the trees were affected. The rate at which forests were declining had outstripped the rate at which the process could be maintained.

Photochemical Smog

It is formed of fog and smoke. It is produced by a complex series of chemical reactions, when hydrocarbons and oxides of nitrogen of the exhaust gases from engines of automobiles are exposed to ultra-violet rays of sunlight. Photochemical smog is a major health hazard cause asthma and bronchities in man though not produced on large scale in India.

Exhaust Gases

Exhaust gases are emitted from chimneys of factories and from smoke of automobiles contain partially oxidised hydrocarbons, particles of heavy metals like lead, zinc, copper, cadmium, carbonmonoxide, carbondioxide, oxides of nitrogen and hydrogen fluorides. Heavy metals are toxic to plant, animal and human life.

Nuclear Explosion

As a result of nuclear explosion, radioactive elements in the form of dust called 'radioactive fallout' are often emitted which pollutes the air and is highly dangerous to human life and animal life.

If large scale pollution threatening people's health are not met by various world bodies with imposition of taxes and levies on industrial units causing pollution, it would be difficult to achieve the goal of 'Health for All' by 2000 AD in India.

INDEX